Public School Emergency Preparedness and Crisis Management Plan

Edited by
Don Philpott and Paul Serluco

GOVERNMENT INSTITUTES
An imprint of
The Scarecrow Press, Inc.
Lanham • Toronto • Plymouth, UK
2010

Government Institutes

Published by Government Institutes
An imprint of The Scarecrow Press, Inc.
A wholly owned subsidary of The Rowman & Littlefield Publishing Group, Inc.
4501 Forbes Boulevard, Suite 200, Lanham, Maryland 20706
http://www.govinstpress.com

Estover Road, Plymouth PL6 7PY, United Kingdom

British Library Cataloguing in Publication Information Available

Library of Congress Cataloging-in-Publication Data

Philpott, Don, 1946–
  Public school emergency preparedness and crisis management plan / Don Philpott and Paul Serluco.
       p. cm.
  Includes bibliographical references and index.
  ISBN 978-1-60590-652-2 (cloth : alk. paper) — ISBN 978-1-60590-670-6 (pbk. : alk. paper) — ISBN 978-1-60590-653-9 (electronic)
  1. School crisis management—United States. 2. Public schools—Security measures—United States. 3. Public schools—Safety measures—United States. 4. Emergency management—United States. I. Serluco, Paul. II. Title.
  LB2866.5.P55 2010
  371.7068—dc22
                                                                    2009026337

♾™ The paper used in this publication meets the minimum requirements of American National Standard for Information Sciences—Permanence of Paper for Printed Library Materials, ANSI/NISO Z39.48-1992.
Printed in the United States of America

Contents

APPENDIXES

Figures and Tables

Figures

Tables

Key Definitions

The following are notable terms and definitions associated with emergency response functions operating under the National Incident Management System framework.

Command Staff. In an incident management organization, the Command Staff consists of the incident commander, public information officer, safety officer, and other positions as required.

emergency operations center (EOC). The physical location at which the coordination of information and resources to support incident management activities normally takes place. An EOC may be a temporary facility or may be located in a more central or permanently established facility, perhaps at a higher level of organization within a jurisdiction.

Finance Section chief. Operating within an Incident Command System framework, is responsible for financial tracking, procurement, and cost analysis related to the disaster or emergency. This person maintains financial records and tracks and records staff hours.

first responder. Local and nongovernmental police, fire, and emergency personnel who in the early phases of an incident are responsible for the protection and preservation of life, property, evidence, and the environment.

incident commander (IC). Operating within an Incident Command System framework, is solely responsible for emergency/disaster operations and remains at the on-scene Command Post to observe and direct all operations.

Incident Command System (ICS). A standardized, on-scene emergency management construct specifically designed to provide for the adoption of an integrated organizational structure that reflects the complexity and demands of single or multiple incidents, without being hindered by jurisdictional boundaries. ICS is the combination of facilities, equipment, personnel, procedures, and communications operating within a common organizational structure, designed to aid in the management of resources during incidents. ICS is used for all kinds of emergencies and is applicable to small as well as large and complex incidents. ICS is used by various jurisdictions and functional agencies, both public and private, or organized field-level incident management operations.

liaison officer. Operating within an Incident Command System framework, serves as the point of contact for agency representatives from assisting organizations and agencies outside the school district and assists in coordinating the efforts of these outside agencies by ensuring the proper flow of information.

Logistics Section chief. Operating within an Incident Command System framework, is responsible for providing facilities, services, personnel, equipment, and materials in support of the incident.

National Incident Management System (NIMS). A system mandated by Homeland Security Presidential Directive-5 that provides a consistent, nationwide approach for federal, state, and local governments; the private sector; and nongovernmental organizations to work effectively and efficiently together to prepare for, respond to, and recover from domestic incidents, regardless of cause, size, or complexity. To provide for interoperability and compatibility among federal, state, and local capabilities, the NIMS includes a core set of concepts, principles, and terminology.

National Response Center. A national communications center for activities related to oil and hazardous substance response actions. The National Response Center, located at the Department of Homeland Security/U.S. Coast Guard Headquarters in Washington, D.C., receives and relays notices of oil and hazardous substances releases to the appropriate federal agency.

Operations Section chief. Operating within an Incident Command System framework, manages the direct response to the disaster, which can include a site facility check/security, search and rescue, medical, student care, and student release.

Planning Section chief. Operating within an Incident Command System framework, is responsible for the collection, evaluation, documentation, and use of information about the development of the incident and the status of resources. This position maintains accurate records and site maps and provides ongoing analysis of situation and resource status.

public information officer (PIO). Operating within an Incident Command System framework, acts as the official spokesperson for the school site in an emergency situation. If a school district PIO is available, he or she will be the official spokesperson. A school site-based PIO should be used only if the media is on campus and the district PIO is not available.

safety officer. Operating within an Incident Command System framework, ensures that all activities are conducted in as safe a manner as possible under the existing circumstances.

unified command. An application of ICS used when there is more than one agency with incident jurisdiction or when incidents cross political jurisdictions. Agencies work together through the designated members of the unified command to establish their designated incident commanders at a single Incident Command Post and to establish a common set of objectives and strategies and a single Incident Action Plan.

Foreword

Virginia Tech Shooting

On April 16, 2007, Seung Hui Cho, an angry and disturbed student, shot to death thirty-two students and faculty members of Virginia Tech, wounded seventeen more, and then killed himself. The incident horrified not only Virginians but also people across the United States and throughout the world.

Tim Kaine, governor of the Commonwealth of Virginia, immediately appointed the Virginia Tech Review Panel to review the events leading up to this tragedy; the handling of the incidents by public safety officials, emergency services providers, and the university; and the services subsequently provided to families, survivors, caregivers, and the community.

MAIN FINDINGS

1. Cho exhibited signs of mental health problems during his childhood. His middle and high schools responded well to these signs and, with his parents' involvement, provided services to address his issues. He also received private psychiatric treatment and counseling for selective mutism and depression.

   In 1999, after the Columbine shootings, Cho's middle school teachers observed suicidal and homicidal ideations in his writings and recommended psychiatric counseling, which he received. It was at this point that he received medication for a short time. Although Cho's parents were aware that he was troubled at this time, they state they did not specifically know that he thought about homicide shortly after the 1999 Columbine school shootings.

2. During Cho's junior year at Virginia Tech, numerous incidents occurred that were clear warnings of mental instability. Although various individuals and departments within the university knew about each of these incidents, the university did not intervene effectively. No one knew all the information and no one connected all the dots.

3. University officials in the Office of Judicial Affairs, Cook Counseling Center, campus police, the dean of students, and others explained their failures to communicate with one another or with Cho's parents by noting their belief that such communications are prohibited by the federal laws governing the privacy of health and education records. In reality, federal laws and their state counterparts afford ample leeway to share information in potentially dangerous situations.

4. The Cook Counseling Center and the university's Care Team failed to provide needed support and services to Cho during a period in late 2005 and early 2006. The system failed for lack of resources,

incorrect interpretation of privacy laws, and passivity. Records of Cho's minimal treatment at Virginia Tech's Cook Counseling Center are missing.

5. Virginia's mental health laws are flawed, and services for mental health users are inadequate. Lack of sufficient resources results in gaps in the mental health system including short-term crisis stabilization and comprehensive outpatient services. The involuntary commitment process is challenged by unrealistic time constraints, lack of critical psychiatric data and collateral information, and barriers (perceived or real) to open communications among key professionals.

6. There is widespread confusion about what federal and state privacy laws allow. Also, the federal laws governing records of health care provided in educational settings are not entirely compatible with those governing other health records.

7. Cho purchased two guns in violation of federal law. The fact that in 2005 Cho had been judged to be a danger to himself and ordered to outpatient treatment made him ineligible to purchase a gun under federal law.

8. Virginia is one of only twenty-two states that report any information about mental health to a federal database used to conduct background checks on would-be gun purchasers. But Virginia law did not clearly require that persons such as Cho—who had been ordered into outpatient treatment but not committed to an institution—be reported to the database.

    Governor Kaine's executive order to report all persons involuntarily committed for outpatient treatment has temporarily addressed this ambiguity in state law. But a change is needed in the Code of Virginia as well.

9. Some Virginia colleges and universities are uncertain about what they are permitted to do regarding the possession of firearms on campus.

10. On April 16, 2007, the Virginia Tech and Blacksburg police departments responded quickly to the report of shootings at West Ambler Johnston (WAJ) residence hall, as did the Virginia Tech and Blacksburg rescue squads. Their responses were well coordinated.

11. The Virginia Tech police may have erred in prematurely concluding that their initial lead in the double homicide was a good one, or at least in conveying that impression to university officials while continuing their investigation. They did not take sufficient action to deal with what might happen if the initial lead proved erroneous. The police were no longer on campus.

12. The Virginia Tech police department erred in not requesting that the Policy Group issue a campus-wide notification that two persons had been killed and that all students and staff members should be cautious and alert.

13. Senior university administrators, acting as the emergency Policy Group, failed to issue an all-campus notification about the WAJ killings until almost two hours had elapsed. University practice may have conflicted with written policies.

14. The presence of large numbers of police at WAJ led to a rapid response to the first 911 call that shooting had begun at Norris Hall.

15. Cho's motives for the WAJ or Norris Hall shootings are unknown to the police or the panel. Cho's writings and videotaped pronouncements do not explain why he struck when and where he did.

16. The police response at Norris Hall was prompt and effective, as was triage and evacuation of the wounded. Evacuation of others in the building could have been implemented with more care.

17. Emergency medical care immediately following the shootings was provided very effectively and timely both on-site and at the hospitals, although providers from different agencies had some difficulty communicating with one another. Communication of accurate information to hospitals standing by to receive the wounded and injured was somewhat deficient early on. An emergency operations center at Virginia Tech could have improved communications.

18. The Office of the Chief Medical Examiner (OCME) properly discharged the technical aspects of its responsibility (primarily autopsies and identification of the deceased). Communication with families was poorly handled.
19. State systems for rapidly deploying trained professional staff members to help families get information, crisis intervention, and referrals to a wide range of resources did not work.
20. The university established a family assistance center at The Inn at Virginia Tech, but it fell short in helping families and others for two reasons: lack of leadership and lack of coordination among service providers. University volunteers stepped in but were not trained or able to answer many questions and guide families to the resources they needed.
21. In order to advance public safety and meet public needs, Virginia's colleges and universities need to work together as a coordinated system of state-supported institutions.

The panel made more than seventy recommendations directed to colleges, universities, mental health providers, law enforcement officials, emergency service providers, lawmakers, and other public officials in Virginia and elsewhere.

RECOMMENDATIONS

Emergency Planning

1. Universities should do a risk analysis (threat assessment) and then choose a level of security appropriate for their campus. How far to go in safeguarding campuses, and from which threats, needs to be considered by each institution. Security requirements vary across universities, and each must do its own threat assessment to determine what security measures are appropriate.
2. Virginia Tech should update and enhance its emergency response plan and bring it into compliance with federal and state guidelines.
3. Virginia Tech and other institutions of higher learning should have a threat assessment team that includes representatives from law enforcement, Human Resources, student and academic affairs, legal counsel, and mental health functions.

   The team should be empowered to take actions such as pursuing an additional investigation, gathering background information, identifying additional dangerous warning signs, establishing a threat potential risk level (1 to 10) for a case, preparing a case for hearings (for instance, commitment hearings), and disseminating warning information.
4. Students, faculty members, and staff members should be trained annually about responding to various emergencies and about the notification systems that will be used. An annual reminder provided as part of registration should be considered.
5. Universities and colleges must comply with the Clery Act, which requires timely public warnings of imminent danger. "Timely" should be defined clearly in the federal law.

Campus Alerting

6. Campus emergency communications systems must have multiple means of sharing information.
7. In an emergency, immediate messages must be sent to the campus community that provide clear information on the nature of the emergency and actions to be taken. The initial messages should be followed by updated messages as more information becomes known.
8. Campus police as well as administration officials should have the authority and capability to send an emergency message. Schools without a police department or senior security official must designate someone able to make a quick decision without convening a committee.

Police Role and Training

9. The head of campus police should be a member of a threat assessment team as well as the emergency response team for the university. In some cases where there is a security department but not a police department, the security head may be appropriate.
10. Campus police must report directly to the senior operations officer responsible for emergency decision making. They should be part of the policy team deciding on emergency planning.
11. Campus police must train for active shooters (as did the Virginia Tech police department). Experience has shown that waiting for a SWAT team often takes too long. The best chance to save lives is often an immediate assault by first responders.
12. The mission statement of campus police should give primacy to their law enforcement and crime prevention role. They must also be designated as having a function in education in order to review records of students brought to the attention of the university as potential threats. The lack of emphasis on safety as the first responsibility of the police department may create the wrong mindset, with the police yielding to academic considerations when it comes time to make decisions on, say, whether to send out an alert to the students that may disrupt classes. On the other hand, it is useful to identify the police as being involved in the education role in order for them to gain access to records under educational privacy act provisions.

Mental Health

1. Universities should recognize their responsibility to a young, vulnerable population and promote the sharing of information internally, and with parents, when significant circumstances pertaining to health and safety arise.
2. Institutions of higher learning should review and revise their current policies related to

   a. recognizing and assisting students in distress;
   b. the student code of conduct, including enforcement;
   c. judiciary proceedings for students, including enforcement; and
   d. university authority to appropriately intervene when it is believed a distressed student poses a danger to himself or others.

3. Universities must have a system that links troubled students to appropriate medical and counseling services either on or off campus, and to balance the individual's rights with the rights of all others for safety.
4. Incidents of aberrant, dangerous, or threatening behavior must be documented and reported immediately to a college's threat assessment group, and must be acted upon in a prompt and effective manner to protect the safety of the campus community.
5. Culturally competent mental health services were provided to Cho at his school and in his community. Adequate resources must be allocated for systems of care in schools and communities that provide culturally competent services for children and adolescents to reduce mental illness–related risk as occurred within this community.
6. Policies and procedures should be implemented to require professors encountering aberrant, dangerous, or threatening behavior from a student to report them to the dean. Guidelines should be established to address when such reports should be communicated by the dean to a threat assessment group and to the school's counseling center.
7. Reporting requirements for aberrant, dangerous, or threatening behavior and incidents for resident hall staff members must be clearly established and reviewed during annual training.

8. Repeated incidents of aberrant, dangerous, or threatening behavior must be reported by Judicial Affairs to the threat assessment group. The group must formulate a plan to address the behavior that will both protect other students and provide the needed support for the troubled student.

9. Repeated incidents of aberrant, dangerous, or threatening behavior should be reported to the counseling center and reported to parents. The troubled student should be required to participate in counseling as a condition of continued residence in campus housing and enrollment in classes.

10. The law enforcement agency at colleges should report all incidents of an issuance of temporary detention orders for students (and staff members) to Judicial Affairs, the threat assessment team, the counseling center, and parents. All parties should be educated about the public safety exceptions to the privacy laws that permit such reporting.

11. The college counseling center should report all students who are in treatment pursuant to a court order to the threat assessment team. A policy should be implemented to address what information can be shared with family and roommates pursuant to the public safety exceptions to the privacy laws.

12. The state should study what level of community outpatient service capacity will be required to meet the needs of the commonwealth and the related costs in order to adequately and appropriately respond to both involuntary court-ordered and voluntary referrals for those services. Once this information is available, it is recommended that outpatient treatment services be expanded statewide.

13. Virginia Code 37.2-808 (H) and (I) and 37.2-814 (A) should be amended to extend the time periods for temporary detention to permit more thorough mental health evaluations.

14. Virginia Code 37.2-809 should be amended to authorize magistrates to issue temporary detention orders based upon evaluations conducted by emergency physicians trained to perform emergency psychiatric evaluations.

15. The criteria for involuntary commitment in Virginia Code 37.2-817 (B) should be modified in order to promote more consistent application of the standard and to allow involuntary treatment in a broader range of cases involving severe mental illness.

16. The number and capacity of secure crisis stabilization units should be expanded where needed in Virginia to ensure that individuals who are subject to a temporary detention order do not need to wait for an available bed. An increase in capacity will also address the use of inpatient beds for moderately to severely ill patients that need longer periods of stabilization.

17. The role and responsibilities of the independent evaluator in the commitment process should be clarified and steps taken to ensure that the necessary reports and collateral information are assembled before the independent evaluator conducts the evaluation.

18. The following documents should be presented at the commitment hearing:

    - the complete evaluation of the treating physician, including collateral information;
    - reports of any lab and toxicology tests conducted;
    - reports of prior psychiatric history; and
    - all admission forms and nurse's notes.

19. The Virginia Code should be amended to require the presence of the prescreener or other Community Services Board (CSB) representative at all commitment hearings and to provide adequate resources to facilitate CSB compliance.

20. The independent evaluator, if not present in person, and treating physician should be available where possible if needed for questioning during the hearing.

21. The Virginia Health Records Privacy statute should be amended to provide a safe harbor provision that would protect health entities and providers from liability or loss of funding when they disclose information in connection with evaluations and commitment hearings conducted under Virginia Code 37.2-814 et seq.

22. Virginia Health Records Privacy and Virginia Code 37.2-814 et seq. should be amended to ensure that all entities involved with treatment have full authority to share records with each other and all persons involved in the involuntary commitment process while providing the legal safeguards needed to prevent unwarranted breaches of confidentiality.

23. Virginia Code 37.2-817 (C) should be amended to clarify

- the need for specificity in involuntary outpatient orders;
- the appropriate recipients of certified copies of orders;
- the party responsible for certifying copies of orders;
- the party responsible for reporting noncompliance with outpatient orders and to whom noncompliance is reported;
- the mechanism for returning the noncompliant person to court;
- the sanction(s) to be imposed on the noncompliant person who does not pose an imminent danger to himself or others; and
- the respective responsibilities of the detaining facility, the CSB, and the outpatient treatment provider in ensuring effective implementation of involuntary outpatient treatment orders.

24. The Virginia Health Records Privacy statute should be clarified to expressly authorize treatment providers to report noncompliance with involuntary outpatient orders.

25. Virginia Code 37.2-819 should be amended to clarify that the clerk shall immediately upon completion of a commitment hearing complete and certify to the Central Criminal Records Exchange a copy of any order for involuntary admission or involuntary outpatient treatment.

26. A comprehensive review of the Virginia Code should be undertaken to determine whether there exist additional situations where court orders containing mental health findings should be certified to the Central Criminal Records Exchange.

Information Privacy Laws

1. Accurate guidance should be developed by the attorney general of Virginia regarding the application of information privacy laws to the behavior of troubled students. The lack of understanding of the laws is probably the most significant problem about information privacy. Accurate guidance from the state attorney general's office can alleviate this problem. It may also help clarify which differences in practices among schools are based on a lack of understanding and which are based on institutional policy. For example, a representative of Virginia Tech told the panel that the Family Educational Rights and Privacy Act (FERPA) prohibits the university's administrators from sharing disciplinary records with the campus police department.

   The panel also learned that the University of Virginia has a policy of sharing such records because it classifies its chief of police as an official with an educational interest in such records. The development of accurate guidance that signifies that law enforcement officials may have an educational interest in disciplinary records could help eliminate discrepancies in the application of the law between two state institutions. The guidance should clearly explain what information can be shared by concerned organizations and individuals about troubled students. The guidance should be prepared and widely distributed as quickly as possible and written in plain English.

2. Privacy laws should be revised to include "safe harbor" provisions. The provisions should insulate a person or organization from liability (or loss of funding) for making a disclosure with a good-faith belief that the disclosure was necessary to protect the health, safety, or welfare of the person involved or members of the general public. Laws protecting good-faith disclosure for health, safety, and welfare can help combat any bias toward nondisclosure.

3. The following amendments to FERPA should be considered:

FERPA should explicitly explain how it applies to medical records held for treatment purposes. Although the Department of Education interprets FERPA as applying to all such records, that interpretation has not been universally accepted. Also, FERPA does not address the differences between medical records and ordinary educational records such as grade transcripts. It is not clear whether FERPA preempts state law regarding medical records and confidentiality of medical information or merely adds another requirement on top of these records.

FERPA should make explicit an exception regarding treatment records. Disclosure of treatment records from university clinics should be available to any health-care provider without the student's consent when the records are needed for medical treatment, as they would be if covered under the Health Insurance Portability and Accountability Act (HIPAA). As currently drafted, it is not clear whether off-campus providers may access the records or whether students must consent. Without clarification, medical providers treating the same student may not have access to health information. For example, Cho had been triaged twice by Cook Counseling Center before being seen by a provider at Carilion St. Albans in connection with his commitment hearing. Later that day, he was again triaged by Cook. Carilion St. Albans's records were governed by HIPAA. Under HIPAA's treatment exception, Carilion St. Albans was authorized to share records with Cook. Cook's records were governed by FERPA. Because FERPA's rules regarding sharing records for treatment are unclear about outside entities or whether consent is necessary, Carilion St. Albans could not be assured that Cook would share its records. This situation makes little sense.

4. The Department of Education should allow more flexibility in FERPA's "emergency" exception. As currently drafted, FERPA contains an exception that allows for release of records in an emergency, when disclosure is necessary to protect the health or safety of either the student or other people. At first, this appears to be an exception well-suited to sharing information about seriously troubled students. However, FERPA regulations also state that this exception is to be strictly construed.

   The "strict construction" requirement is unnecessary and unhelpful. The existing limitations require that an emergency exists and that disclosure is necessary for health or safety. Further narrowing of the definition does not help clarify when an emergency exists. It merely feeds the perception that nondisclosure is always a safer choice.

5. Schools should ensure that law enforcement and medical staff members (and others as necessary) are designated as school officials with an educational interest in school records. This FERPA-related change does not require amendment to law or regulation.

   Education requires effective intervention in the lives of troubled students. Intervention ensures that schools remain safe and students healthy. University policy should recognize that law enforcement, medical providers, and others who assist troubled students have an educational interest in sharing records. When confirmed by policy, FERPA should not present a barrier to these entities sharing information with each other.

6. The Commonwealth of Virginia Commission on Mental Health Reform should study whether the result of a commitment hearing (whether the subject was voluntarily committed, involuntarily committed, committed to outpatient therapy, or released) should also be publicly available despite an individual's request for confidentiality. Although this information would be helpful in tracking people going through the system, it may infringe too much on their privacy.

7. The national higher education associations should develop best practice protocols and associated training for information sharing. Among the associations that should provide guidance to the member institutions are the following:

   - American Council on Education (ACE)
   - American Association of State Colleges and Universities (AASCU)
   - American Association of Community Colleges (AACC)

- National Association of State and Land Grant Universities and Colleges (NASLGUC)
- National Association of Independent Colleges and Universities (NAICU)
- Association of American Universities (AAU)
- Association of Jesuit Colleges and Universities

Guns and Campus Policies

1. All states should report information necessary to conduct federal background checks on gun purchases. There should be federal incentives to ensure compliance. This should apply to states whose requirements are different from federal law. States should become fully compliant with federal law that disqualifies persons from purchasing or possessing firearms who have been found by a court or other lawful authority to be a danger to themselves or others as a result of mental illness. Reporting of such information should include not just those who are disqualified because they have been found to be dangerous but all other categories of disqualification as well. In a society divided on many gun control issues, laws that specify who is prohibited from owning a firearm stand as examples of broad agreement and should be enforced.

2. Virginia should require background checks for all firearms sales, including those at gun shows. In an age of widespread information technology, it should not be too difficult for anyone, including private sellers, to contact the Virginia Firearms Transaction Program for a background check that usually only takes minutes before transferring a firearm. The program already processes transactions made by registered dealers at gun shows. The practice should be expanded to all sales. Virginia should also provide an enhanced penalty for guns sold without a background check and later used in a crime.

3. Anyone found to be a danger to themselves or others by a court-ordered review should be entered in the Central Criminal Records Exchange database regardless of whether they voluntarily agreed to treatment. Some people examined for a mental illness and found to be a potential threat to themselves or others are given the choice of agreeing to mental treatment voluntarily to avoid being ordered by the courts to be treated involuntarily. That does not appear on their records, and they are free to purchase guns. Some highly respected people knowledgeable about the interaction of mentally ill people with the mental health system are strongly opposed to requiring voluntary treatment to be entered on the record and be sent to a state database. Their concern is that it might reduce the incentive to seek treatment voluntarily, which has many advantages to the individuals (e.g., less time in hospital, less stigma, and less cost) and to the legal and medical personnel involved (e.g., less time, less paperwork, and less cost). However, there still are powerful incentives to take the voluntary path, such as a shorter stay in a hospital and not having a record of mandatory treatment. It does not seem logical to the panel to allow someone found to be dangerous to be able to purchase a firearm.

4. The existing attorney general's opinion regarding the authority of universities and colleges to ban guns on campus should be clarified immediately. The universities in Virginia have received or developed various interpretations of the law. The commonwealth's attorney general has provided some guidance to universities, but additional clarity is needed from the attorney general or from state legislation regarding guns at universities and colleges.

5. The Virginia General Assembly should adopt legislation in the 2008 session clearly establishing the right of every institution of higher education in the commonwealth to regulate the possession of firearms on campus if it so desires. The panel recommends that guns be banned on campus grounds and in buildings unless mandated by law.

6. Universities and colleges should make clear in their literature what their policy is regarding weapons on campus. Prospective students and their parents, as well as university staff, should know the policy related to concealed weapons so they can decide whether they prefer an armed or arms-free learning environment.

Response

1. In the preliminary stages of an investigation, the police should resist focusing on a single theory and communicating that to decision makers.
2. All key facts should be included in an alerting message, and it should be disseminated as quickly as possible, with explicit information.
3. Recipients of emergency messages should be urged to inform others.
4. Universities should have multiple communication systems, including some not dependent on high technology. Do not assume that twenty-first-century communications may survive an attack or natural disaster or power failure.
5. Plans for canceling classes or closing the campus should be included in the university's emergency operations plan. It is not certain that canceling classes and stopping work would have decreased the number of casualties at Virginia Tech on April 16, but those actions may have done so. Lockdowns or cancellation of classes should be considered on campuses where it is feasible to do so rapidly.

Training

1. Campus police everywhere should train with local police departments on response to active shooters and other emergencies.
2. Dispatchers should be cautious when giving advice or instructions by phone to people in a shooting or facing other threats without knowing the situation.
3. Police should escort survivors out of buildings, where circumstances and manpower permit.
4. Schools should check the hardware on exterior doors to ensure that they are not subject to being chained shut.
5. Take bomb threats seriously. Students and staff members should report them immediately, even if most do turn out to be false alarms.

Emergency Medical Services Response

1. Montgomery County, Virginia, should develop a countywide emergency medical services, fire, and law enforcement communications center to address the issues of interoperability and economies of scale.
2. A unified Command Post should be established and operated based on the National Incident Management System Incident Command System model. For this incident, law enforcement would have been the lead agency.
3. Emergency personnel should use the National Incident Management System procedures for nomenclature, resource typing and utilization, communications, interoperability, and unified command.
4. An emergency operations center must be activated early during a mass casualty incident.
5. Regional disaster drills should be held on an annual basis. The drills should include hospitals, the Regional Hospital Coordinating Center, all appropriate public safety and state agencies, and the medical examiner's office. They should be followed by a formal postincident evaluation.
6. To improve multicasualty incident management, the Western Virginia Emergency Medical Services Council should review/revise the Multi-Casualty Incident Medical Control and the Regional Hospital Coordinating Center functions.
7. Triage tags, patient care reports, or standardized Incident Command System forms must be completed accurately and retained after a multicasualty incident. They are instrumental in evaluating each component of a multicasualty incident.
8. Hospitalists, when available, should assist with emergency department patient dispositions in preparing for a multicasualty incident patient surge.

9. Under no circumstances should the deceased be transported under emergency conditions. It benefits no one and increases the likelihood of hurting others.
10. Critical incident stress management and psychological services should continue to be available to emergency medical service providers as needed.

Chief Medical Examiner

1. The chief medical examiner should not be one of the staff members performing the postmortem exams in mass casualty events; the chief medical examiner should be managing the overall response.
2. The OCME should work along with law enforcement, the Virginia Department of Criminal Justice Services (DCJS), chaplains, the Department of Homeland Security, and other authorized entities in developing protocols and training to create a more responsive family assistance center (FAC).
3. The OCME and Virginia State Police in concert with FAC personnel should ensure that family members of the deceased are afforded prompt and sensitive notification of the death of a family member when possible and provide briefings regarding any delays.
4. Training should be developed for FAC, law enforcement, OCME, medical and mental health professionals, and others regarding the impact of crime and appropriate intervention for victim survivors.
5. OCME and FAC personnel should ensure that a media expert is available to manage media requests effectively and that victims are not inundated with intrusions that may increase their stress.
6. The Virginia DCJS should mandate training for law enforcement officers on death notifications.
7. The OCME should participate in disaster or national security drills and exercises to plan and train for effects of a mass fatality situation on medical examiner operations.
8. The Virginia Department of Health should continuously recruit board-certified forensic pathologists and other specialty positions to fill vacancies within the OCME. Being understaffed is a liability for any agency and reduces its surge capability.
9. The Virginia Department of Health should have several public information officers trained and well versed in OCME operations and in victims services. When needed, they should be made available to the OCME for the duration of the event.
10. Funding to train and credential volunteer staff members, such as the group from the Virginia Funeral Director's Association, should be made available in order to utilize their talents. Had this team been available, the FAC could have been more effectively organized.
11. The commonwealth should amend its emergency operations plan to include an emergency support function for mass fatality operations and family assistance.

Recovery

1. Emergency management plans should include a section on victim services that addresses the significant impact of homicide and other disaster-caused deaths on survivors and the role of victim service providers in the overall plan. Victim service professionals should be included in the planning, training, and execution of crisis response plans. Better guidelines need to be developed for federal and state response and support to local governments during mass fatality events.
2. Universities and colleges should ensure that they have adequate plans to produce a Joint Information Center with a public information officer and an adequate staff during major incidents on campus. The outside resources that are available (including those from the state) and the means for obtaining their assistance quickly should be listed in the plan. Management of the media and of self-directed volunteers should be included.
3. When an FAC is created after a criminal mass casualty event, victim advocates should be called immediately to assist the victims and their families. Ideally, a trained victim service provider should be

assigned to serve as a liaison to each victim or victim's family as soon as practical. The victim service should help victims navigate the agencies at the FAC.

4. Regularly scheduled briefings should be provided to victims' families as to the status of the investigation, the identification process, and the procedures for retrieving the deceased. Local or state victim advocates should be present with the families or on behalf of out-of-state families who are not present so that those families are provided the same up-to-date information.

5. Because of the extensive physical and emotional impact of this incident, both short- and long-term counseling should be made available to first responders, students, staff members, faculty members, university leaders, and the staff of The Inn at Virginia Tech. Federal funding is available from the Office for Victims of Crime for this purpose.

6. Training in crisis management is needed at universities and colleges. Such training should involve university and areawide disaster response agencies training together under a unified command structure.

7. Law enforcement agencies should ensure that they have a victim services section or identified individual trained and skilled to respond directly and immediately to the needs of victims of crime from within the department. Victims of crime are best served when they receive immediate support for their needs. Law enforcement and victim services form a strong support system for provision of direct and early support.

8. It is important that the state's Victims Services Section work to ensure that the injured victims are linked with local victim assistance professionals for ongoing help related to their possible needs.

9. Since all crime is local, the response to emergencies caused by crime should start with a local plan that is linked to the wider community. Universities and colleges should work with their local government partners to improve plans for mutual aid in all areas of crisis response, including that of victim services.

10. Universities and colleges should create a victim assistance capability either in-house or through linkages to county-based professional victim assistance providers for victims of all crime categories. A victim assistance office or designated campus victim advocate will ensure that victims of crime are made aware of their rights as victims and have access to services.

11. In order to advance public safety and meet public needs, Virginia's colleges and universities need to work together as a coordinated system of state-supported institutions.

Preface

On February 28, 2003, the President of the United States issued the Homeland Security Presidential Directive (HSPD)-5, which directs the Secretary of Homeland Security to develop and administer a National Incident Management System (NIMS). The U.S. school system, already committed to the safety and welfare of its students, teachers, support staff members, visitors, and any others involved in its mission to provide a safe learning environment and high-quality education, was directly affected by this directive.

In response, in part, to HSPD-5, a number of school systems have already embarked on a program to enhance their capabilities in the areas of emergency preparedness in accordance with procedures outlined by the individual school system's State Homeland Security Plan, the National Response Plan, and guidelines within "Practical Information on Crisis Planning: A Guide for Schools and Communities" by the Office of Safe and Drug-Free Schools, U.S. Department of Education, Washington, D.C., May 2003. For those schools and institutions that have not developed a plan responsive to HSPD-5, Homeland Defense Journal Publications has produced this comprehensive planning document to assist in developing the plan. This planning document

- outlines programs and procedures that can be applied to any U.S. school system to address hazard mitigation and prevention, emergency preparedness and response, and recovery and restoration of school functions to an effective learning environment;
- predetermines to the extent possible operational procedures across any U.S. school system and cooperating governmental, private, and volunteer agencies for responding to and recovering from any and all types of natural, human, or technology-based emergencies that may occur directly within school system operations, or that may occur outside the jurisdiction of the school system but nonetheless causes/could cause collateral impact to school system operations;
- describes specific actions and assigns responsibilities and response roles to district and individual school staff emergency teams, cooperating agencies, and community response partners that have agreed to share responsibilities and resources as defined in this plan;
- outlines, in the event of an emergency involving response by fire and/or law enforcement, the district/school site personnel who should establish an Incident Command System–based response organization in accordance with procedures outlined in NIMS.

The authors would like to thank the Akron Public School System for permitting us to replicate their Safety Plan as the template for this publication. The Akron Public School System Safety Plan was led by Robert Boxler, manager of Health and Safety, and Dave Nunley, grant coordinator. In addition, the Ohio Red Cross, the Ensafe Corporation, and the University of Akron Emergency Management Program contributed to the Akron Plan. The Akron Police and Akron Fire/EMT were also major contributors and partners in the planning process.

For the purpose of providing examples, the titles and names specific to the Akron Public School System Safety Plan have often been retained. The actual names of offices and organizations may differ for each individual region and school system.

CHAPTER ONE

Introduction

1.1. Plan Overview and Purpose

The U.S. school system is committed to the safety and welfare of its students, teachers, support staff members, visitors, and any others involved in its mission to provide a safe learning environment and high-quality education within the community. To fulfill its mission, a number of school systems have embarked on a program to enhance capabilities in the areas of emergency preparedness in accordance with procedures outlined by the individual school system's State Homeland Security Plan, the National Response Plan, and guidelines within the "Practical Information on Crisis Planning: A Guide for Schools and Communities" by the Office of Safe and Drug-Free Schools, U.S. Department of Education, Washington, D.C., May 2003.

This plan outlines programs and procedures that can be applied to any U.S. school system to address hazard mitigation and prevention, emergency preparedness and response, and recovery and restoration of school functions to an effective learning environment.

This plan predetermines to the extent possible operational procedures across the school system and cooperating governmental, private, and volunteer agencies for responding to and recovering from any and all types of natural, human, or technology-based emergencies that may occur directly within school system operations, or that may occur outside the jurisdiction of the school system but nonetheless causes/could cause collateral impact to school system operations.

This plan describes specific actions and assigns responsibilities and response roles to district and individual school staff emergency teams and cooperating agencies and community response partners that have agreed to share responsibilities and resources as defined in this plan.

In the event of an emergency involving response by fire and/or law enforcement, the district/school site personnel will establish an Incident Command System–based response organization in accordance with procedures outlined in the National Incidental Management System.

At individual schools, principals will serve as the school system's incident commanders during the initial response initiation and, if required, will transfer command to the appropriate responding agency(ies) when they arrive.

Depending upon the type, magnitude, scope, and expected duration of response efforts, the superintendent may assume the role of incident commander and participate in joint response direction with responding agencies under the unified command, employing an expanded Incident Command System organization.

Individual schools will maintain site emergency response teams employing staff members familiar and trained in procedures included within this plan.

1

The school system will maintain a Crisis Response Team that will provide response support and/or will assume authority for response management, depending upon the nature of the incident. The Crisis Management Team will function within the district emergency operations center.

1.2. Crisis Management Policy

The school system policy for emergency preparedness and crisis management should be simply stated as follows: "We will develop and maintain crisis management programs to ensure we are prepared to deal with incidents and crises that could affect our students, teachers, staff members, visitors, and other persons involved in school-related operations."

This approach includes proactive involvement and cooperation of the district-level administrative and support staff, the local school administrative and support staff, the student body, and external local, state, and federal agency and community response partners. Response plans, procedures, and information networks will be shared with parochial and charter schools to assist their efforts in response preparedness.

As a foundation for this policy, the school system will maintain capabilities in the form of plans, procedures, skilled and trained staff members, resources, external relationships, management presence, and advocacy in the following core areas:

- Mitigation and Prevention—Programs to identify and address actual and potential hazards, threats, and emerging problems in order to reduce or eliminate risk to people and school system operations.
- Preparedness and Response—Programs and procedures to address emergency preparedness and response capabilities.
- Recovery—Programs devoted to restoring school system operations to a learning and teaching environment after an incident.

The school system will advocate a proactive stance in the following manners:

- The school system will remain vigilant and be proactive in its assessment of the worst-case potential of an incident. First discoverers will report incidents per established notification procedures. School and district-level personnel with designated response roles will collaborate in the assessment and initiation of response actions. When in doubt, appropriate response actions should be initiated to protect the safety and welfare of people, and notification procedures should immediately follow.
- The school system will maintain a districtwide Crisis Management Plan that includes comprehensive provisions for preparation and planning, intervention and response, and postemergency activities.
- Individual schools will maintain site-specific emergency response plans including Quick Reference "Emergency Procedures Flip Charts" defining specific response actions for various incidents. These plans include provisions for interacting with safety first responders and the school system district Crisis Response Team.
- The school system will maintain a training and exercise program to ensure that all aspects of the district Crisis Management Plan, school emergency response plans and procedures, and appropriate staffing are available for emergency preparedness and response readiness. Training and exercise programs will be in conformance with the National Incident Management System guidance established within Homeland Security Presidential Directive-5 as utilized by safety response agencies.
- The school system will maintain a proactive relationship with safety and community emergency response professionals in the maintenance of prevention, mitigation, emergency preparedness, training, and crisis exercise programs.
- The school system will keep this Crisis Management Plan evergreen through routine updates and timely incorporation of lessons learned.

1.3. Operations Covered

This plan addresses crisis management policy, emergency preparedness and response procedures, and related staff roles and responsibilities in effect within the school system. The plan defines a crisis management organizational structure at the district level and defines Crisis Response Teams in place at each individual school. This plan outlines how these teams will coordinate with each other and with external response entities during an incident to work effectively toward a common and successful outcome. This plan further identifies key contacts and mutual aid considerations in place between the school system and parochial and charter schools.

Copies of this plan will be maintained at the school system administration building and at each individual school within the school system. Copies of this plan should be furnished to each parochial and charter school within the boundaries of the school system. These schools should maintain and update their plans individually.

1.4. Plan Maintenance and Annual Start-Up Procedures

It is the responsibility of the school system's Energy, Environmental, Health, and Safety Department program managers to ensure this plan is updated at least annually or more frequently, such as when a significant change in personnel or operations occurs, when new key information becomes available, or to incorporate "lessons learned" when the plan has been utilized in an incident and, thus, maintain the plan as a living document. This person is also responsible for maintaining the distribution of the plan as requested and for coordinating annual start-up review procedures.

Ideally, annual review of the overall plan should be timed to coincide with the start of each new school year (August time frame). The following items should be considered during annual review and start-up sessions.

- Confirm membership of the crisis team; fill vacancies that have occurred.
- Review assigned roles and responsibilities of team members and revise, as needed.
- Review incident notification procedures with administration and other staff members.
- Update notification lists.
- Review incident management procedures and scenarios and update in light of changes in conditions and resources within the school system and in light of lessons learned during actual incidents.
- Advise the staff of any changes in Crisis/Response Management Team membership and procedures including identification/intervention, crisis/incident response, and postincident recovery.
- Include review of Crisis Management Plan and related procedures in new staff orientation.
- Review equipment, crisis kits, and other emergency preparedness/response resources.
- Schedule mitigation, prevention, response, and recovery orientation and training program sessions to be conducted throughout the upcoming school year.
- Conduct interim review meetings as deemed appropriate.

A master copy of this plan and copies of all other school system emergency plans will be kept with the program manager, Energy, Environmental, Health, and Safety Department.

CHAPTER TWO

Emergency Notification and Immediate Actions

It is the policy of the school system (SS) to be proactive in assessing all incidents and in responding as appropriate to ensure the safety and welfare of its students, staff members, and others associated with SS operations.

The designated district staff and individual school staff will confer to confirm the following:

- Incident type
- Status of initial response actions
- Additional required follow-up response actions
- Need to activate the district Crisis Management Team

This chapter addresses notification procedures to be followed for all incidents within the SS. This includes but is not limited to accidents, injuries, deaths, fires, property damage events, security-related incidents, school-related disruption threats and/or actual incidents, or other incidents or threats to students, staff members, the property, or other SS interests.

Figure 2.1 provides a listing of emergency contact phone numbers. Figure 2.2 provides a flow chart that illustrates initial notification and incident assessment procedures intended to guide effective response actions and decision making.

Table 2.1 provides an assessment tool to assist the key initial response team decision makers (the principal, security, and Business Affairs representatives) in determining appropriate initial response actions.

Table 2.2 includes an Incident Discussion Checklist to assist the key initial response team decision makers in completing an incident and potential SS impact assessment and in deciding other critical response actions.

Section 2.1 provides criteria governing activation of the Crisis Management Team (CMT).

Section 2.2 contains emergency contact information for CMT and School Crisis Team members, school administration, principals, the staff, and other key SS emergency response support functions as well as contact information for other key external, community, and emergency services.

2.1. Crisis Triggers

The executive director of SS Department of Business Affairs will consult with the superintendent and Crisis Management Team representatives to assess the incident and its worst-case implications. Initial response actions will be determined accordingly.

The affected school should only contact Student Services and Security (xxx) xxx-xxxx
Notifications will expand as each office notifies the next.
Call 911 and Student Services and Security at (xxx) xxx-xxxx for emergencies occurring outside school hours.

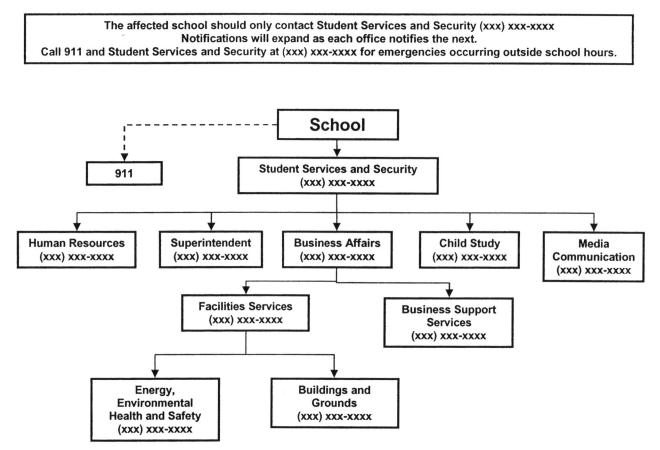

Figure 2.1   Crisis Contacts

As a rule, the Crisis Management Team will be activated when an incident has the potential to escalate and/or the following has occurred or is likely to occur:

- Fatality(ies) and/or serious personal injury(ies)
- Incidents requiring partial and/or full evacuation
- Major threat to school/school system, for example, terrorism alert, direct threat to school/district, threat to adjacent institutions that could result in school/district impact, severe weather threat, information technology systems disruption/threat, power outage, transportation system impact, and other natural disasters
- Adverse/media attention that could affect district image and reputation
- Significant or catastrophic incident occurring at a school, facility, or school function
- Hostage/kidnap/shooting/criminal act/violence-based incident, and so forth
- Adverse government or political scrutiny

2.2. Emergency Contact Information

This section contains emergency contact information for the following SS teams, groups, and other internal and external support functions:

Contact:	Table
Initial Call Assessment	2.1
Incident Discussion Checklist	2.2

Additional contact lists for the following resources are found in chapter 5:

- Staff Members with Skills in Medical Care
- Bi/Multilingual Staff Members
- Staff Members with Sign Language Skills
- Staff Members with Mobile/Cellular Phones
- Students Needing Special Assistance in an Emergency
- SS Staff Members Needing Special Assistance in an Emergency
- Evacuation Partners School Facility
- Contact List for Charter and Parochial Schools

Note: In a nonemergency situation, various city and county agencies may be contacted for assistance or information on various problems. If outside assistance is needed, contact SS Student Services and SS security for information.

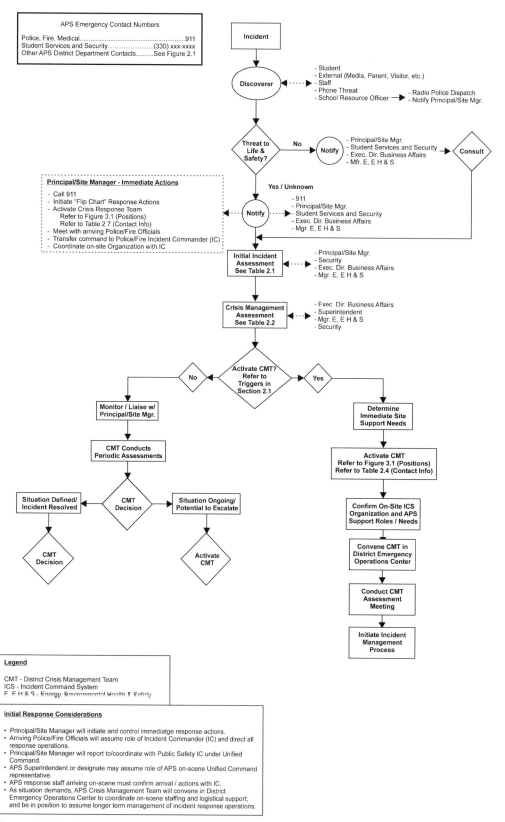

APS Emergency Contact Numbers

Police, Fire, Medical...911
Student Services and Security.....................(330) xxx-xxxx
Other APS District Department Contacts..........See Figure 2.1

Incident

Discoverer
- Student
- External (Media, Parent, Visitor, etc.)
- Staff
- Phone Threat
- School Resource Officer → - Radio Police Dispatch
                             - Notify Principal/Site Mgr.

Threat to Life & Safety?

No → **Notify**
- Principal/Site Mgr.
- Student Services and Security
- Exec. Dir. Business Affairs
- Mfr. E, E H & S

→ **Consult**

Yes / Unknown

Principal/Site Manager - Immediate Actions

- Call 911
- Initiate "Flip Chart" Response Actions
- Activate Crisis Response Team
    Refer to Figure 3.1 (Positions)
    Refer to Table 2.7 (Contact Info)
- Meet with arriving Police/Fire Officials
- Transfer command to Police/Fire Incident Commander (IC)
- Coordinate on-site Organization with IC

Notify
- 911
- Principal/Site Mgr.
- Student Services and Security
- Exec. Dir. Business Affairs
- Mgr. E, E H & S

Initial Incident Assessment See Table 2.1
- Principal/Site Mgr.
- Security
- Exec. Dir. Business Affairs
- Mgr. E, E H & S

Crisis Management Assessment See Table 2.2
- Exec. Dir. Business Affairs
- Superintendent
- Mgr. E, E H & S
- Security

Activate CMT? Refer to Triggers in Section 2.1

No ← | → Yes

Monitor / Liaise w/ Principal/Site Mgr.

Determine Immediate Site Support Needs

CMT Conducts Periodic Assessments

Activate CMT Refer to Figure 3.1 (Positions) Refer to Table 2.4 (Contact Info)

CMT Decision

Situation Defined/ Incident Resolved ← | → **Situation Ongoing/ Potential to Escalate**

Confirm On-Site ICS Organization and APS Support Roles / Needs

CMT Decision

Activate CMT

Convene CMT in District Emergency Operations Center

Conduct CMT Assessment Meeting

Initiate Incident Management Process

Legend

CMT - District Crisis Management Team
ICS - Incident Command System
E, E H & S - Energy, Environmental Health & Safety

Initial Response Considerations

- Principal/Site Manager will initiate and control immediatge response actions.
- Arriving Police/Fire Officials will assume role of Incident Commander (IC) and direct all response operations.
- Principal/Site Manager will report to/coordinate with Public Safety IC under Unified Command.
- APS Superintendent or designate may assume role of APS on-scene Unified Command representative.
- APS response staff arriving on-scene must confirm arrival / actions with IC.
- As situation demands, APS Crisis Management Team will convene in District Emergency Operations Center to coordinate on-scene staffing and logistical support; and be in position to assume longer term management of incident response operations.

Figure 2.2   Incident Notification and Crisis Management Activation Procedure Flow Chart

Table 2.1.   Initial Call Assessment

Used initially by SS incident commander (principal/delegated representative) and district Crisis Management Team representative (security, executive director of Business Affairs) to decide initial response actions

Incident description
- What has happened?
- Where has it happened?
- When did it happen?
- Is everybody accounted for? Casualties?
- How did we find out about it?
- Who is at risk?
- How did it happen?

Incident status
- Contained or escalating? Potential to escalate—what/who is potentially at risk?
- What safety and security measures are being implemented?
- Has a 911 call been made?
- Is the on-site SS officer involved?
- What are your/our response objectives? (What are you trying to make happen/prevent from happening)?
- Have fire/police departments provided any orders or recommendations?
- What actions are being taken? Is area secured from unauthorized access?
- Who is taking these actions? Who is responding? What resources (equipment/manpower) are being used?
- Are exterior evacuation routes or staging areas accessible?
- Are the effects of wind direction and slope of the grounds on the spread of smoke, fire, toxic gases, or liquids being considered in response/evacuation planning?

Incident assessment
- What are the health and safety issues?
- Do we need to evacuate?
- Is a lockdown required?
- Do we need to shelter-in-place?
- What immediate messaging do we want to provide to the staff?
- Do we need to isolate building ventilation systems?
- What community impact?
- What contacts have been made with community, government, and media?
- What advice has been received from safety officials?
- What is the operational impact—short, medium, and long term?

Immediate response decisions
- Evacuation, shelter-in-place?
- Lockdown?
- Staff notification?
- CMT activation and staffing (emergency operations center and on-site)?
- Emergency operations center activation?
- Crisis Management Plan activation?
- Support school site/facility?
- Interact with the Safety/Incident Command Organization? Where? How?

Table 2.2. Incident Discussion Checklist

For executive director of Business Affairs, superintendent *(and Crisis Management Team members)*

Situation status:
- What is status of safety and security of students, staff members, and others?
- What happened, when, and what do we know about how and why?
- What is the current status of the incident/site?
- What is the magnitude and probable duration of the incident? (one day—local coverage, or multiple days—national coverage)
- What has been or potentially can be the human impact on employees, community, contractors—casualties, evacuations?
- Has there been any media interest? Have we issued any press releases?
- Should the Crisis Management Team come to the remote scene? Who? When? Is there a plan to get them in/out?
- What other organizations are involved? Law enforcement, fire department, government/political entities, and so forth.
- What is the impact on the school/facility? And on other SS interests? Are there secondary impacts on other areas that need consideration?
- Are there national implications to this incident?
- Have all necessary notifications been made?
- Has the emergency operations center been notified?
- Who is the incident commander? Crisis manager? Relations leader?
- What role is the superintendent going to assume and where will he/she be located?

Strategy for handling incident:
- What are the current objectives, priorities, and plans to deal with the situation?
- What message(s) are we giving/proposing to give to our employees/students/families?
- Who should make the contacts with government—federal /state/local? Messages?
- What community/special interest groups are being contacted? By whom? Messages?
- Have we sent any messages updating employees?
- What should we be telling the community?
- What community contacts should be made? By whom? Messages?
- Who is going to be the SS spokesperson(s)?
- What resources are needed? What help is needed?
- Who is staffing the key positions at the site and at the emergency operations center?

Communications:
- Let's agree on schedule of when next to talk, how often to talk, and where each of us will be.
- How are we going to deal with off-hours coverage?

Special agreed actions:

Table 2.3. Contacts: Police, Fire, Medical, Health, and Security

Police	911
Fire	911
Emergency Medical Service	911
Health Department	911
State Highway Patrol	911
County sheriff	911

Table 2.4. Emergency Contacts: School System Crisis Management Team

Crisis Management Team Position	Name	CMT Position	Work	Pager
Superintendent				
Executive director of Business Affairs				
Coordinator, Facility Services				
Coordinator, Business Support Services				
Director, Information Services				
Assistant superintendent, Curriculum and Instruction				
Manager, Energy, Environmental, Health, and Safety				
General Counsel				
Executive director, Communications				
Executive director, Human Resources				
Student Services and Security				
Director, Community Partnership and Customer Services				
Treasurer				

Table 2.5. Contacts: School System Crisis Team(s)

This Table Can Be Used to Identify Team Members during an Actual Incident/Mobilization						
Crisis Management Team Position	**Contact/Location**	**Work**	**Home**	**Mobile**	**Fax**	**E-mail**
Incident commander						
Safety officer						
Information officer						
Liaison officer						
Operations Section						
• Chief						
• Student Care						
• Search and Rescue						
• Student Release						
• Site Facility/Security						
Planning Section						
• Chief						
• Documentation						
• Situation Analysis						
Logistics Section						
• Chief						
• Supplies/facilities						
• Staffing						
• Communications						
Finance/Administration Section						
• Chief						
• Timekeeping						
• Purchasing						

Table 2.6. Contacts: Utilities

Utility Type	Company Name	Daytime #	24-Hour #
Electric Power			
Natural Gas			
Water/Sewer			
Telephone			
Steam			

Table 2.7.   Other Key Contacts

Entity	Contact
Federal Regulatory Agencies • State Environmental Protection Agency • Food and Drug Agency • State Division of Labor and Worker Safety	
City of • Mayor's Office • Safety Director • Fire Marshall • Police Chief • Regional Transit Authority	
Hospitals • City Hospital • General Medical Center • Children's Hospital	
American Red Cross (/Summit County)	
Child Abuse Hotline	
Local TV • Channel 3 • Channel 5 • Channel 8 • Channel 10 • Channel SS 12	
Local Radio • WXYZ - • WXYZ - • WXYZ -	
Newspapers •	

CHAPTER THREE

Concept of Operations

The school system (SS) should have a comprehensive, two-tier, fully integrated Incident Command System (ICS)–based organization capable of responding to all incident and crisis situations that may arise and affect its operations. The organization should consist of the following:

- Tier 1: School Crisis Response Teams (CRTs)—composed of designated principals, teachers, and other trained staff members located at individual schools who can respond safely and rapidly to an incident at their respective school/site and mount and sustain initial tactical response operations. The on-scene SS initial incident commander (IC, principal/delegate) will assume initial command and control of the incident response until arrival of a safety official (fire/police), whereupon command and control will transition to fire/police officials.
- Tier 2: District Crisis Management Team (CMT)—composed of district-based administrative staff and other personnel. The CMT provides strategic and on-site tactical assistance to the CRTs. The CMT interfaces with government agencies, the media, and the public; analyzes the implications of an incident and response operations on the SS's viability, operability, and credibility; and assists CRTs in establishing postincident recovery programs and operations.

3.1. Chain of Command

The ICS provides a unified command in a multi-responder emergency in which all agencies that have jurisdictional responsibility for multi-jurisdictional incidents contribute to the process of

- determining the overall objectives to gain control of the incident;
- selecting strategies to achieve those objectives;
- planning jointly for tactical activities;
- integrating appropriate tactical operations; and
- making maximum use of all assigned resources

Generally, if a crime is involved, the police department will initially take control of the scene. However, under individual state law, for most incidents, the senior fire official on scene will assume the role of IC until the exact nature of the incident has been determined. In certain crime-related incidents, the Federal Bureau of Investigation may assume control. Other noncriminal events (e.g., fire, evacuations, injuries, accidents, infrastructure failures, etc.) will be controlled by the fire department and/or emergency medical service. Law enforcement, emergency personnel of the fire department, paramedics, and other regulatory agencies adhere to a clear ICS-based chain of command, as defined within the National Incident Management System (NIMS). The SS response organization will be expected to conform and readily integrate into the Unified ICS to ensure an efficient and effective ramp-up of response efforts.

TIER 1: SCHOOL CRISIS RESPONSE TEAMS

Tier 1 involves the maintenance of school CRTs at each school and major operating facility. The role of the CRT is to immediately assess and respond to incidents and emergencies at their respective locations. Each CRT will be led initially by a senior school/site representative with delegated authority to direct initial response actions, interface with safety emergency first responders, and interact with school district administration. CRT leaders are referred to as ICs. The SS IC may be relieved by arriving police and/or fire officials who assume command of the incident response from the SS initial IC. Command can formally transition back to the SS at an appropriate time once life safety and other agency jurisdictional issues have been resolved. The initial SS IC will interact with the district as noted below.

CRTs are predominately composed of local site staff members but are supported by other school/facility as well as district-level staff members. Table 3.1 provides a matrix that identifies specific staff positions that can be mobilized to assume various response roles and positions within the CRT. The nature and extent of actual team mobilization and staffing will greatly depend on the type, severity, and magnitude of the incident. Site-specific staffing will be supplemented with additional personnel activated by the CMT from other SS and facility sites. The CRT organization is illustrated in figure 3.2. CRT membership rosters are included in table 2.4. CRT position description and action checklists are included in chapter 4. Certain CRT functions, included within Planning, Logistics, and Finance, may be staffed at the district CMT level and be housed within the district emergency operations center (EOC). In these cases, delegates will be deployed to the scene to assist in on-site support coordination between the site and the CMT.

TIER 2: DISTRICT CRISIS MANAGEMENT TEAM

Tier 2 involves the maintenance of a district-level CMT. The CMT will be activated in situations where the CRT requests support; the incident involves serious injury or death, or serious crime; the incident exceeds resource capabilities of a single facility; the incident has disrupted or has the potential to disrupt school/school district operations; and the incident has resulted in or has the potential to result in significant attention and/or involvement of parents, community officials, media, and/or other special interest groups. The CMT will operate within the district EOC and be composed of the district administrative and support staff. The CMT will support initial efforts of the CRT and assume responsibility for sustaining response and restoration operations upon completion of initial emergency response actions. The CMT organization is illustrated in figure 3.1. CMT membership rosters are included in table 2.4.

3.2. Key First Actions

Initial response actions and decision making will depend upon many factors including the following:

- Nature of the incident or threat
- Magnitude of the impact or perceived potential impact on people and property
- Particular school, facility, or other related affected site
- Whether the incident occurs during or outside of normal school hours
- Extent of external involvement by governmental agencies, the community, and the media

Table 3.1. School Crisis Team

Function / Staff Position	Command	Communications	Information	Search and Rescue	Safety and Security	First Aid	Mental health	Hazmat	Utilities	Logistics	Family Reunion
Primary and Support Roles											
Principal	P	P	P						S1		
Assistant principal	S1	S2	S1						S2		P
Resource officer	S2			P	P						
Nurse						P	S1			S2	
Counselor			S2				P				S2
Custodian								P	P	P	
Cafeteria manager						S1				S1	
Secretary		S1			S2	S2					
Teacher											S1

P—Primary   S1—Support 1 (First alternate)   S2—Support 2 (Second alternate)

Refer to figure 3.2 for School Crisis Team organization chart
Refer to section 3.5 for School Crisis Team member response action checklists

When the primary designee is not able to perform the assigned functional leadership role, the first alternate (S1) assumes that responsibility. Likewise, if both the primary and first alternate are unable to perform the leadership responsibility, then the second alternate (S2) assumes the role.

Terminology of the Incident Command System will be utilized to make clear the role and relationships of various school personnel and safety emergency responders.

As soon as the principal or alternate is ready (on-scene and informed of the situation) she/he assumes incident command. The incident commander should appoint a safety coordinator and liaisons (to district office and emergency services as required) to serve the command group. For most emergency operations, the principal will turn over incident command to the safety emergency response professional arriving on the scene.

The district Crisis Management Team will arrange to staff all unfilled positions that may be required in a particular emergency event.

Critical and immediate actions and considerations by staff members and administrators must focus on the safety and welfare of people.

It is imperative that designated on-scene staff members (principal/delegate/facility manager), the SS executive director of Business Affairs (SS CMT manager), and SS security consult with each other to confirm the following critical first actions:

- Confirm actual or potential emergency situation. An emergency is considered to be any sudden event that endangers or threatens to endanger the safety or the health of any person or that destroys or threatens to destroy or damage property or the environment. Examples are listed in table 3.2.
- Conduct initial incident assessment.
- Ensure appropriate notifications are completed (refer to figure 2.1).
- Determine on-site support needs. Assist on-scene SS IC in deploying and staffing the on-scene School Crisis Team as appropriate.

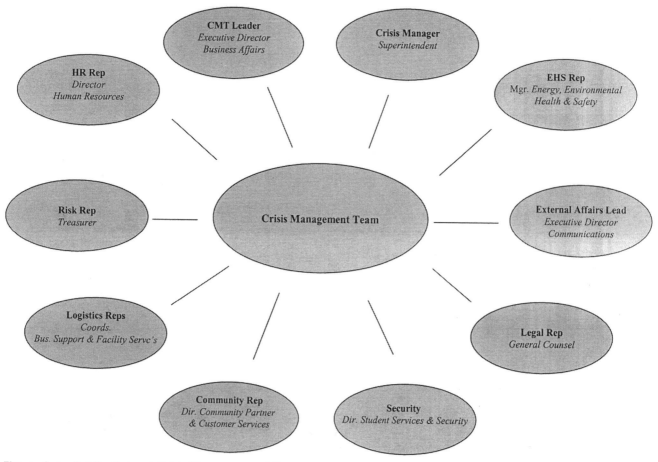

Figure 3.1   Public School Crisis Management Team

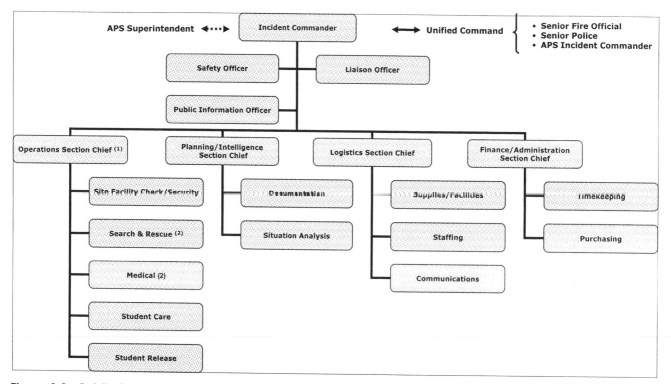

Figure 3.2   Public School Crisis Management Team Organization Chart

- Ensure immediate life/safety decisions are addressed:
  - Notification of authorities
  - Evacuation/shelter-in-place/lockdown
  - Communication/messaging to staff members and students
  - Activation of immediate emergency response actions
  - Student/staff member/visitor status accounting
  - Aid to injured/missing persons
- Determine extent of involvement of safety first responders.
- Employ Initial Incident Assessment Checklist (by security and the executive director of Business Affairs or delegate) (refer to table 2.1).
- Hold incident assessment consultation between the executive director of Business Affairs and the district superintendent.
- Agreement/modification of initial actions.
- Initial impact assessment.
  - Need for consultation/conference calls with SS CMT and the school/facility staff to discuss school district impact issues (refer to table 2.2).
  - Determine whether and to what extent the SS CMT should be activated to the EOC. If CMT is activated,
    —establish communication protocol and schedule;
    —activate the EOC (located in SS Distribution Center); and
    —convene CMT at designated EOC at earliest practicable time to direct response operations.
  - Determine and implement most appropriate means to interact with on-site safety first responder organizations using the Unified ICS.
  - Agree to staff and student messaging and communication protocols.
  - Engage in incident management planning by the CMT to support initial response operations.
  - Position the CMT to assume direct control and longer term management of response operations.

Table 3.2. Incidents and Emergencies That Could Result in Activation of the SS Crisis Management Team

An emergency is considered to be any sudden event that endangers or threatens to endanger the safety or the health of any person or that destroys or threatens to destroy or damage property or the environment. Examples include but are not limited to the following:	
❖ Fatality	❖ Impact by equipment/machinery/aircraft
❖ Serious injury/serious assault/sexual assault	❖ Earthquake or other natural event
❖ Siege/hostage/firearms	❖ Fire in school/on grounds
❖ Disappearance or removal of student/other	❖ Fumes/spill/leak contamination by hazardous material on-site
❖ Bomb threat	❖ Fumes/spill/leak contamination caused by off-site non-school-related incident
❖ Collapse/major damage to building or equipment	❖ Outbreak of disease
❖ Motor vehicle impact with school	❖ Flood/windstorm/ice/other inclement weather
❖ Suicide/attempted suicide	❖ Violent crime
❖ Gang violence/threats	❖ Perceived threats/rumors
❖ Accidents/incidents associated with school activities and excursions occurring before/after hours; on-site/off-site, and while traveling to and from school.	
When in Doubt—Report it!	

3.3. School Crisis Response Team

Minor and other day-to-day incidents will be managed by local schools and facilities employing appropriate members of their respective school CRTs. These incidents will be reported to the district via routine, written reporting protocols and verbal briefings during staff meetings.

More significant incidents, accidents, injuries, disruptions to school functions, threats, perceived threats, and/or other related concerns will be immediately reported to the district per notification procedures highlighted in figure 2.1.

The executive director of Business Affairs, serving as the district CMT manager, will engage in an incident assessment process and, if appropriate, will confirm that the incident should be handled locally. He or she may also assign staff members or other resources to assist the local team in resolving the incident.

Depending on the magnitude and severity of the incident, the executive director of Business Affairs may activate the district CMT to either support or assume control of response efforts, as appropriate.

In situations involving fire and/or law enforcement response, the SS local school/facility will activate its school CRT and assimilate team members into the safety agency ICS organization, as required.

The SS CRT IC (principal or facility manager) will cooperate with the safety IC(s) (police and fire) to coordinate on-scene response actions.

3.4. Partnering with Community Agencies Using Incident Command System

Homeland Security Presidential Directive-5 establishes a comprehensive NIMS to enhance the abilities of federal, state, and local agencies and response entities to manage domestic incidents effectively. The SS will collaborate with community safety agencies to establish an on-scene organization and incident management procedures in conformance with the NIMS. NIMS is the nationally recognized emergency operations system that is adapted for incidents where multi-agency response is required.

NIMS facilitates priority setting, interagency cooperation, and the efficient flow of resources and information. NIMS establishes common standards of organization, procedures, communications, and terminology among agencies. This unified command structure functions under the direction of the ICS. All agencies and organizations work together under this system to respond more effectively to any major incident.

The basic principle behind the Unified ICS is that all agencies and jurisdictions involved in an incident will work together toward a common set of goals and objectives, with centralized management of operations and resources. It is a team effort and process. All agencies continue with their own authority, responsibility, and accountability, but they all work together and share information.

There are several advantages to using the Unified Incident Command concept:

- One set of objectives is developed for the entire incident.
- A collective approach is made for developing strategies to achieve incident goals.
- Information flow and coordination is improved between all jurisdictions and agencies involved in the incident.
- All agencies with responsibility for the incident have an understanding of one another's priorities and restrictions.
- No agency's authority or legal requirements will be compromised or neglected.
- Each agency is fully aware of the plans, actions, and constraints of all others.
- The combined efforts of all agencies are optimized as they perform their respective assignments under a single Incident Action Plan. A coordinated effort equals a safe response.

- Duplicate efforts are reduced or eliminated, thus reducing costs and chances for frustration and conflict.

By adopting and utilizing this system, the SS will be able to respond to any incident with better communication and coordination with other responding agencies and organizations.

The SS CRT organization is based on the ICS and is illustrated in figure 3.2. It consists of five functions:

- Management
- Planning/Intelligence
- Operations
- Logistics
- Finance/Administration

CRT members are listed in table 2.7. A brief description of each functional area follows. Position-specific roles, accountabilities, and action checklists are found in chapter 4.

- Management—Provides overall policy and operational direction.
  - Incident commander: This position assumes sole responsibility for directing emergency response operations. Until the arrival of the safety (police/fire) Incident Command officer, the site administrator is in charge. The site administrator is most often the principal or building/site manager, unless circumstances dictate otherwise.
  - Safety officer: This position ensures that all activities are conducted in as safe a manner as possible under existing circumstances.
  - Information officer: This position acts as the official spokesperson for the school/district in an emergency situation.
  - Liaison officer: This position serves as the point of contact for agency representatives from assisting organizations and agencies outside the school district, and assists in coordinating the efforts of these outside agencies by ensuring proper flow of information.
- Planning/Intelligence—Collects, evaluates, documents, and uses information about the development of the incident and the status of resources. Maintains accurate records and site map. Provides ongoing analysis of situation and resource status.
  - Documentation: This position is responsible for collection, evaluation, documentation, and use of information about the development of the incident and status of resources.
  - Situation Analysis: This position is responsible for collection, evaluation, documentation, and use of information about the development of the incident and status of resources. Maintains accurate site map. Provides ongoing analysis of situation and resources.
- Operations—Implements priorities established by the IC, which can include site facility check/security, search and rescue, medical response, student care, and student release.
  - Student Care: Ensures the care and safety of all students and staff members except those in the medical treatment area. This position knows where all first aid supplies are located, oversees first aid prior to paramedics' arrival, and coordinates with paramedics.
  - Search and Rescue: Accounts for everyone on-site as quickly as possible. Position must have access to attendance records, visitor sign-in sheets, emergency data cards of students, and any other information that will assist in accounting for the school population. This position works closely with the student assembly Shelter and Release coordinator.
  - Student Release: Assures the reunification of students with their parents or authorized adult using preestablished protocols and documentation procedures.

- Site Facility Check/Security: Provides site safety and security support. Knows layout of building and grounds, knows location of shutoff valves and utility lines, and is familiar with school blueprints.
- Medical Response: Provides emergency medical response, first aid, and counseling. Notifies IC when the situation requires health or medical services that staff members cannot provide and ensures that appropriate actions are taken in the event of deaths.
- Logistics—Provides facilities, services, personnel, equipment, and materials in support of the incident.
  - Supplies/Facilities: Provides facilities, equipment, supplies, and materials in support of the incident.
  - Staffing: Coordinates assignment of personnel (staff members, students, and disaster volunteers) in support of the incident.
  - Communications: Establishes, coordinates, and directs verbal and written communications within the school disaster site and with the school district. If the school district cannot be contacted, communications may be made with outside agencies when necessary.
- Finance/Administration—Performs financial tracking, procurement, and cost analysis related to the incident. Maintains financial records and tracks and records staff hours.
  - Timekeeping: Maintains accurate and complete records of staff hours.
  - Purchasing: Maintains accurate and complete records of purchases.

3.5. Crisis Management Team

The CMT determines what, if anything, must be done to support CRT response efforts, and to identify, evaluate, and proactively address the implications of the incident and incident response operations on the SS in its entirety.

When activated, the CMT is responsible for strategic planning and control of incident-related activities. The group consists of district and school administrators and support staff members with authority to determine short- and long-term strategies and objectives, order evacuation or shutdown of the facilities, commit SS resources, and interface with outside organizations and media.

The SS superintendent serves as the chief district spokesperson to the outside world, supported by relations and communications. Table 3.3 summarizes the specific roles of the CMT. The CMT comprises the following individuals:

- Superintendent
- Executive director, Business Affairs
- Executive director, Communications
- General Counsel
- Executive director, Human Resources
- Director, Community Partnerships and Customer Services
- Coordinator, Business Support Services
- Coordinator, Facility Services
- Manager, Energy, Environmental, Health, and Safety
- Director, Student Services and security
- Treasurer

CMT members are listed in table 2.4. CMT position responsibilities and specific action checklists are provided in chapter 4.

Table 3.3. Overview of Crisis Management Team Roles

• Ensure response is consistent with SS policy and meets or exceeds stakeholder expectations.
• Consider worst-case scenarios for all situations and issues and identify triggers to assist in proactive recognition of escalation toward a worst-case scenario. Develop an action contingency strategy, as appropriate.
• Ensure all key emergency response and statutory notifications have been made.
• Develop response strategy based on priorities.
• Protect people/environment; implement response and recovery measures.
• Locate and mobilize additional resources requested by CRT members.
• Identify all stakeholders and associated issues and develop a communications strategy to keep all informed.
• Draft and coordinate release of information to media, staff members, and relevant third parties to ensure a common and consistent messaging.
• Consider how the SS makes the best of the situation, and identify the positives for the company.
• Maintain an auditable trail including Events and Issues and Actions Logs.
• Initiate and support the incident investigation.
• Identify strategic issues and response strategies as they might affect other SS interests and/or the community at large; coordinate actions with external response partners.
• Draft and coordinate the release of information to the media liaising with relevant third-party organizations to ensure a common and consistent message is transmitted.
• Notify and liaise with insurers. Track the cost of response to maximize insurance returns.
• Liaise with emergency services at a senior level.
• Forecast costs and provide data for use in discussions with stakeholders.
• Provide finances as necessary.

3.6. Emergency Operations Center Activation

CMT members will consult with each other via telephones, mobile phones, radios, and/or text messaging pagers.

If so decided, the CMT will convene in the EOC to undertake a more thorough incident assessment and to initiate and coordinate sustained response operations.

EOC Locations:

• Primary: _____

• Alternate: _____

The CMT administrator will be responsible for setting up the EOC facilities to support the CMT. The critical first actions include the following.

• Advise security that the EOC has been activated.
• Set up communications equipment.
• Set up incident information center status boards.
• Distribute office supplies as needed.
• Distribute copies of Crisis Management Plan, other relevant emergency plans, responder checklists, and contact lists.

Table 3.4 provides a detailed EOC activation checklist. Figure 3.3 provides a layout of EOC information center status boards. Copies of the displays are included in appendix F. Full-size copies are maintained in the EOC.

Table 3.4. Emergency Operations Center Activation Checklist

_____ **Communications Setup**
Remove all telephones from telephone cabinet and place on tables.

_____ **Group Page**
Notify the CMT via group phone/page/text message that the EOC has been activated.

_____ **Security**
Notify security that the center has been activated. Determine if center needs to be secure. If so, request a security guard be stationed at the center.
Instruct security to forward all calls that they take to the EOC.

_____ **Computers**
Notify director of Information Services that the center has been activated. Determine need for additional computers, printers, network connections, and peripheral equipment. Request activation of agreed-to equipment and support personnel.

_____ **Facsimile Machines**
Ensure that machines are on and properly loaded with paper. Two machines are immediately available.

_____ **Contact Lists**
Distribute latest updated listing of emergency contact listings and SS phone directory.

STATUS BOARDS
_____ **Contact Board**
Place all pertinent contact names and numbers on lined contact board in the center.

_____ **Incident Board**
Set up board to maintain log of factual information known, and update as facts are received.

_____ **Communications Board**
All facsimile numbers should be written on the communications board. Include confirmation name and numbers as well. Place an incoming and outgoing facsimile log form on the board and maintain.

_____ **Message Board**
Located at the entrance to the center, assign personnel to a block on the board, and inform responder of where to locate messages.

_____ **Response Team Support**
Make available to all responders the following support items: in-/out-box, pen, pencil, paper, blank responder log books, phone instruction handbooks, SS telephone book, and so on.

_____ **Organization Chart**
Use poster-size form and slot responder positions held in the center. _Organization chart and phone numbers should be developed for other locations as well._

_____ **Reference Items**
Depending on school/facility involved, pull emergency plans relating to the incident. Question what other reference items you can supply.

_____ **Secretarial Support**
Secretarial support personnel should be activated.

_____ **Digital Camera**
Plug in and recharge batteries. Shoot pictures for permanent records of wall charts and other key information written on white boards.

Time Clocks
Set incident time clocks.

Forms
Refer to the form cabinet in the support area and pull any appropriate forms.

Copy Machine
Contact **General Services** and request relocation of copy machine to EOC.

Telephone Forwarding
Forward individual office phones to EOC.

Television/VCR
Turn TV on to CNN (picture only, no volume). Turn on VCR and make machine ready for taping. Blank videocassette tapes are located in the TV cabinet in the center.

Repdials
Determine any and all pertinent telephone numbers (site telephone number, etc.), and set up repdials on all phones in the center. Key numbers would also be on the contact board.

Marker Boards
Erasers and markers should be in both marker board trays as well as the tray. Check supply cabinet in main support area.

Easel Board
Check pad of paper for easel board and place markers in trays. Additional easels and pads can be obtained from Facility Services.

Food
Contact Facility Services to notify them of possible rush food requests. Order refreshments (coffee, pop, tea, etc.), and have them replenish food on an ongoing basis until they are further notified. Determine what the needs are for breakfast, lunch, and dinner.

Cash Advance
Contact Finance for Emergency Cash Procedures. Key contact numbers are located in the SS Crisis Management Plan, sections 2 and 5.

SHUTDOWN PROCEDURES
Return center to original nonactivation status. Refer to this list.
The two most critical items are as follows.
- Deactivate the phone system.
- Notify security that center is no longer in emergency mode.

Collect all incident documentation and consult with legal to determine disposition.

| Incident Facts | CMT Issues/Impacts | | CMT Action Plan | Action Items from CMT Meetings |

| | | Maps & Charts | | |

| Help Requested | | | | Stakeholder Management Plan |

| Schedule CMT Meetings | CMT Sign-In | | | |

Figure 3.3 Information Center Layout

3.7. Initial Briefing

This is the recommended format for initial briefing of the CMT. CMT leader and coordinator should ensure briefing is kept short and effective.

- CMT leader:

  Introduce self to establish team leadership.
  Conduct roll call.
  Brief the CMT on the incident using the checklist below.
- CMT coordinator: Capture key information on display boards.
- Documentation leader:

  Record time of briefing.
  Capture key issues/actions on display boards.

The CMT should brainstorm on the following issues (see also checklist in tables 3.5a and 3.5b):

- Identify additional resources/support required.
- Identify major stakeholders/issues.
- Identify strategies for dealing with stakeholders and issues.
- Identify triggers to assist in proactive recognition of escalation toward worst-case scenario.
- Consider how to make the best of the situation and determine positives for SS.

The CMT leader should

summarize issues identified, set priorities, and initial objectives;
assign actions for each CMT member; and
set time of next meeting.

Table 3.5a.   Initial Incident Briefing Checklist

Incident description:
- **What** has happened?
- **Where** has it happened?
- **When** did it happen?
- Are all **personnel** accounted for? Casualties?
- **Potential to escalate**   what is potentially at risk?
- What is the **impact on the facility**/SS?
- **Who** is supplying information?
- How **accurate** is the information?
- What are the **timing issues**—security mandates, weather, daylight, and so forth?

Incident Status:
- What are the CMT objectives? (What are we trying to make happen/prevent from happening?)
- What actions are being taken and who is taking them? Responding?
- What resources (equipment/manpower) are being used?
- How effective is the response?

Table 3.5b.   Initial Incident Briefing Checklist—Supplemental

Incident Status:
- Are there additional facilities at risk?
  - — Administration Building
  - — Other building/facility
  - — Neighboring properties
  - — Third parties
- What is the impact on the facility/district?
  - — Open/lockdown/shelter-in-place/evacuate
  - — Late open/early dismissal
  - — Continuing
- Is the area secured from unauthorized access?

Personnel Issues:
- Safe and accounted for
  - — Employees, visitors, contractors, others
- Casualties
  - — Injured
  - — Dead
  - — Missing/unaccounted for
- Interaction with Employers/Affiliations, and so on
  - — Contractors/subcontractors
  - — Neighbors
  - — Visitors
  - — General

Administration Building Status:
- Evacuation plans activated?
  - — What floor(s)?
  - — Status/location of people?
  - — Any injuries?
  - — Persons with disabilities taken care of?
- Status of involvement of safety within building? (fire/police/medical)
- What messaging to the staff regarding building status?
  - — Certain floors OK?
  - — Building safe/all clear?
  - — Building closed?
  - — Other message?

(continued)

Table 3.5b. *(continued)*

Incident/Threat Assessment Update:

Real incident or hoax:

- Does the safety incident commander agree with initial evacuation or shelter-in-place decision?
- Has a search of the building been conducted and the incident commander advised of results?
- Has there been an actual detonation, fire, shooting, or other incident?
- Has anything unusual been discovered?
- If anything has been found, will fire, police, and so on, conduct a further search?
- Has the area, office, or floor with the suspicious item been closed off; all employees, visitors, and contractors evacuated; and items of obvious evidentiary value left untouched?
- Are there any suspicious unidentified persons in the building? If yes, has another search been ordered? By whom?
- Does the Incident Command safety officer agree with another search?
- Is the CMT prepared for media interest or arrival at the scene?
- Have the cable news, television, and radio monitors discovered any new information regarding the extent of the incident?
- If electrical power is out in the building, is it also out in the surrounding area?
- Have any additional local or federal safety/law enforcement responders arrived on the scene?
- If safety and CMT incident commanders agree that the incident is a hoax or under control, have employees been formally dismissed or encouraged to reenter the building?
- Has a formal "All Clear" order been issued by safety?
- If the incident is a bomb threat and a search was conducted, do CMT and safety incident commander agree that nothing was found and that it is safe to reenter?
- Is the log keeper keeping the log updated and current?

Incident classified as actual:

- Is the incident a natural disaster or a man-made event? By whom?
- If it is a man-made event, has it been classified as a crime or a terrorism incident? By whom?
- Since a terrorism incident is a federal crime and the affected area has been designated as a crime scene, has a decision been made to close the building?
- Has any SS property deemed essential been damaged, contaminated, or removed as evidence?
- Has the CMT communicated with safety incident commander regarding building or area reentry?
- Has a decision been made concerning a joint press release/conference?
- Do the CMT/CRT and the safety incident commander agree on the media statement?
- Has a formal, complete "hands off" of the incident to the incident commander taken place and been so logged by the log keeper?

Stakeholders:

- Which stakeholders do, or potentially will, have interest?

Media:

- What is the SS media strategy?
- What media coverage has there been so far (radio, TV, print—local, national, international)?
- Has it been accurate?
- Is it negative toward SS?
- Has a statement/release been given to the media so far?
- What is the potential for additional media coverage?
- Who is the most appropriate SS spokesperson?
- Has the safety incident commander designated an information officer?
- Have we liaised with him/her?
- Has a press conference been called/is one necessary? Does the safety incident commander concur?
- Who else is making press releases?

Incident Management Capability:

- What cannot be done that should be done? Why?
- Has the county Emergency Management Agency (EMA) been notified?
- What human/material resources are required?
  - SS internal/facility/county EMA/other governmental
  - Specialty consultants and contractors, other specialists?

Incident Assessment:

- What are the health, security, and safety issues?
- What is the likely environmental impact?
- What are the community, government, media, and/or reputation issues?
- What are the legal implications?
- What is the operational impact—short, medium, and long term?

Set Objectives and Priorities? Objectives must be

- Appropriate
- Clear
- Measurable
- Achievable

3.8. Incident Management

Once the CMT is fully engaged, the CMT leader should advise the on-site IC (principal) at the incident facility that the CMT is fully functional and is in a position to perform required duties. A communications protocol should be established. At a minimum, the protocol should cover the following topics.

- Names and contact numbers of the CMT and contact number for the EOC
- CMT and CRT participation in briefing and assessments
- Mutual expectations regarding information reporting and document sharing and timing

The purpose of the protocol is twofold. First, it is designed to ensure that appropriate communications occur in a timely and intelligible fashion. Second, it reinforces the chain of command within the CMT and remote team(s) relationship(s) by ensuring clear guidance and consistency in objectives, priorities, strategies, messaging, and actions.

3.9. Emergency Operations Center: Information Center

As information is gathered from the incident site(s) and generated in the EOC, it should be prominently displayed for use by all CMT members at the information center.

The information center should be viewed as the one place in the EOC where anyone can go, at any time, to learn about the nature and status of an incident and incident response operations, and the nature and status of CMT response efforts.

One of the primary purposes of the information center is to assist the CMT in its efforts to establish and maintain command and control, and to assist in forward action planning.

The EOC information center should include status boards addressing the following issues.

- Incident Facts
- CMT Sign-In Status Board
- CMT Issues/Impacts Status Board
- Help Requested by Affected Asset Status Board
- CMT Action Plan Status Board
- Schedule of CMT Meetings Status Board
- Action Items from CMT Meetings
- Stakeholder Management Plan

Examples of these status boards are provided in appendix F.

The information center should be established and maintained by the CMT coordinator and log keeper. It is the obligation of all CMT members to ensure that information pertaining to their respective activities is accurately posted and up to date.

3.10. CMT Assessment and Issue Identification Meetings

The duration that the CMT resides within the EOC will be incident specific and depend upon many variables. If the CMT elects to staff the EOC intermittently versus continually, then additional CMT meetings should be held at a frequency determined by the CMT leader and the CMT members.

The objectives of the subsequent Assessment and Issue Identification Meetings are the identification of issues and concerns, and the development of actions to address the issues and concerns. The topics to be discussed include the following.

- Progress being made on work under way
- Problems being encountered that are restraining progress
- Action items to address prior to the next meeting
- Agreed action items for CMT members

To the maximum extent possible, CMT meetings should be scheduled to follow assessment/incident status updates received from the incident site from either the SS or safety IC. This would allow the CMT to benefit from having access to the latest information available on the incident and tactical response operations. The CMT leader may elect to participate in the incident site briefings via conference call. Likewise, the CMT leader may elect to invite remote response team management to participate in select portions of CMT meetings to foster information transfer.

3.11. CMT Action Plan

The product of the CMT's work and deliberations should be a written CMT Action Plan. This document should list the issues and concerns raised by CMT members, the agreed-upon actions to be taken to address the issues and concerns, and the name(s) of the CMT member(s) responsible for ensuring that the actions are carried out in a timely fashion. The plan itself should be a stand-alone document that is constantly updated as new issues/actions are identified and work progresses on the actions. In addition, the EOC information center contains a status board that can be used to summarize the action plan.

To the extent that the actions listed in the plan involve, or have an impact upon, the remote response team staff, the plan should be forwarded to the remote response team manager.

CHAPTER FOUR

Crisis Management Team Action Checklists

4.1. Crisis Management Team

This chapter contains response checklists and job aids that define key actions to be undertaken by members of the Crisis Management Team (CMT). These procedures identify recommended school system (SS) officials that should staff various CMT positions and address individual key roles, actions, strategy, and action plan considerations appropriate to supporting on-scene response operations needs and near/longer term strategic needs and actions.

Actions listed are considered minimum and should be supplemented with additional steps and considerations deemed appropriate to the incident at hand.

These checklists should be updated periodically based on new information and lessons learned.

4.2. Crisis Response Team

This section contains response checklists and job aids for use by SS Crisis Response Team (CRT) personnel involved in on-site incident/emergency response operations (see tables 4.1 through 4.18). These procedures adopt National Incident Management System protocols and are intended to conform to Incident Command System procedures that will be implemented by safety emergency responders during significant emergency events.

These procedures address on-scene response team member position-specific responsibilities, operational duties, and recommended equipment and supplies, as well as reporting relationships across the entire incident command structure.

Table 4.1. Action Checklist: Crisis Manager (Superintendent/Delegated Authority)

Key roles:
1. Represent SS to external world 2. Delegate authority to CMT decision makers/team 3. Communicate/negotiate with stakeholders who have an interest in the event 4. Provide policy or position guidance to CMT
Actions
Seek briefing from CMT leaders/decision makers and discuss initial assessment: • What has happened? • Why has it happened? • What is the potential for escalation? Is incident contained? • How has it happened? • Is anyone injured? • When did it happen? • Where has it happened?
Confirm the need to activate the CMT: • Overreaction better than under-reaction • Play it safe in case of escalation
Discuss management strategy with CMT leaders. Monitor response; be updated by CMT leaders and liaise with other SS facilities and Mayor's Office, as required: • Agree upon follow-up schedule
If CMT activated, then inform Mayor's Office as the situation warrants.

If possible, attend initial briefing with CMT:
• Brainstorm—identify issues, assign and track actions. Determine SS responsibility for incident and posture that district should adopt.
• Remember role and focus of CMT:
  — PROTECT WELFARE AND SAFETY OF PEOPLE FIRST—THIS IS PARAMOUNT
  — District response
  — Support joint venture partners/government/media strategy/local response team

Review media strategy with External Affairs and advise CMT leaders. Consider the following:
• Prime district spokesperson
• Timely and appropriate press statements
• Media reaction to date
• Is incident on TV/news?
• Is a press conference likely to be required?
  — When, where?
  — Have Q&As been developed?

Ensure initial media statement drafted (and released as soon as possible as appropriate).
Confirm statutory notifications have been made and updates are being provided:
Confirm SS internal communications are effective and timely.

Identify and conduct executive liaison with all relevant stakeholders:
- Partners with vested interest
- Government entities
- Parents
- Local community
- Political entities

Attend regular CMT updates as appropriate.

Make strategic decisions to minimize impact on SS image, operability, and liability.

Monitor the effectiveness and morale of the CMT.

Ensure that SS decisions are implemented.

If city/county CMT(s) are(is) in place, ensure CMT coordinator liaises with them:

- Is it supporting or micromanaging?

Any signs of stress within the CMT?
- SS employee assistance program (EAP)
- Consider member substitutions or relief

Is composition of CMT appropriate?
- Too many/too few?
- Does CMT need to remain in place all the time?

Ensure student/employee support programs activated?
- What programs are being initiated to take care of students/employees?
- Support to family/significant others?
- Financial

Is normal business able to continue?
- If not, confirm strategy for continuity of operations
- What actions are being taken to advise parents/community of potential disruption?
- How long before business operations resume and in what capacity?

Sample strategic issues:
- What are the district's real liabilities?
- Who is responsible for this incident?
- What posture should asset/district take?
- What are the impacts and effects?
- What other strategic issues?

Table 4.2. Action Checklist: Crisis Management Team Leader (Executive Director, Business Affairs/Delegated Authority)

Key roles:
1. Evaluate overall execution of CMT 2. Communicate activities to superintendent, and remote locations, as applicable 3. Provide additional input and guidance as requested 4. Keep superintendent informed

Action
Make initial assessment (in consultation with security and manager of Energy, Environmental, Health, and Safety): • What has happened? • Why has it happened? • What is the potential for escalation? Is incident contained? • How has it happened? • Is anyone injured? • When did it happen? • Where has it happened?
Determine the need to activate the CMT. Consider the following: • Full or partial activation required • Other potential emergency support groups
Assess the incident using the Crisis Triggers (section 2.1); initiate the CMT activation if required.
Contact the superintendent and provide an update. Confirm intentions for management of incident: • Monitor only • Monitor and liaise with CMT as required • Mobilize, lead, and liaise with CMT
Contact on-scene SS incident commander and get an update. Ensure response is appropriate and fully resourced. • What does the site need? • Determine call schedule with site
Set and agree on priorities with CMT: • Take care of people • Protect environment • Protect assets • Business continuity as efficiently and safely as possible
Determine support required by CMT: • Additional response staff • Employee assistance programs • Liaise with safety officials • Support staff/administrative staff • Other resource specialists

Attend initial briefing with CMT:
- Brainstorm—identify issues, assign and track actions
- Determine SS responsibility for incident and posture that district should adopt
- Agree on objectives developed by CMT
- Remember role and focus of CMT:
  - — Protect welfare and safety of people
  - — District response
  - — Government/media strategy/local response team
- No shortcuts of emergency management structure

Agree on media strategy with External Affairs and superintendent. Consider the following:
- Prime district spokesperson
- Timely and appropriate press statements
- Media reaction to date
- Is incident on TV/News?
- Is a press conference likely to be required?
  - — When, where?
  - — Q&As

Ensure initial media statement drafted (and released as soon as possible, if appropriate).

Ensure a Stakeholder Management Plan is developed and implemented:
- Prioritize
- Ensure statutory notifications are made and updates provided

Ensure Planning takes into account escalation and worst-case scenarios.

Ensure SS internal communications are effective and timely.

Is Telephone Response Team in place, briefed, and ready to take calls?
- Ensure switchboard operators are briefed on how to handle calls

Identify and conduct executive liaison with all affected constituencies:
- Partners with vested interest
- Government agencies
- Parents
- Local community
- Political entities
- Other stakeholders

Ensure that External Affairs keeps Telephone Response Team fully briefed and that the Telephone Response Team has the latest press releases.

Hold regular CMT updates:
- Time-out phones off hook

Make strategic decisions to minimize impact on SS image, operability, and liability.

Monitor the effectiveness and morale of the CMT.

Determine the need for alternates and the rotation of team members.

Ensure that arrangements are made to continue normal business operations, if appropriate:

(continued)

Table 4.2. *(continued)*

•   Confirm need/implementation of business continuity plans as appropriate
If city/county CMT is in place, coordinate and confirm mutual information and support needs and expectations.
Are Information Boards being kept up to date?
Is there an auditable trail of information?
Are personnel matters being sympathetically handled? •   Are student/employee/family support programs being implemented, as appropriate?
Are you getting good feedback from External Affairs over what questions are being asked by callers?
Any signs of stress in CMT, or other responding SS units? •   Brief Employee Assistance/Counseling Program(s) and ensure teams are aware of the numbers to call
Is composition of CMT appropriate? •   Too many/too few? •   Does CMT need to remain in place all the time?
Is normal business able to continue? If not, what actions are being undertaken to address?
Ask yourself—How am I holding up?
Continually review all of the above.
Strategic issues for consideration: •   Is SS effectively positioning itself for a successful outcome? •   Will there be an inability to meet commitments/delivery? •   Impact on student body/staffing (long, medium, and short term) •   Impact on suppliers or other service providers? •   Other direct business interruptions? •   Any indirect constraints on business? •   Risk/need to shut down similar operations? •   Other threat to operations •   How long for repair/replacement •   Any regulatory impacts? •   Additional load on management? Managing the incident/recovery

Table 4.3. Action Checklist: Crisis Management Team Coordinator (Manager, Energy, Environmental, Health, and Safety/Delegated Authority)

Key roles:
1. Manage Crisis Center facilities
2. Facilitate meetings
3. Ensure all actions are documented and tracked
4. Provide resources to CMT
5. Keep CMT up to date on objectives and focused on appropriate issues
6. Liaise with other coordinators and teams

Action
Set up Crisis Center facilities (see table 3.2 activation checklist).

Evaluate status of emergency and emergency response system needs.
• Understand priorities
• Mobilize recorder if appropriate
• Brief log keeper and recorder
• Ensure faxes, telephones, photocopiers are all in working order, with a plentiful supply of paper, and so on
• Set up PCs, log on, and open e-mail account (send test messages to CRT/CMT, as appropriate)
• Hang information displays on wall
• Produce issues/actions tracking sheet and hang on wall for meetings and/or use PC projectors
• Issues/actions/responsibility/target completion
• Track status throughout and follow up as required
• Ensure action/event log is displayed on main screen and data entered by log keeper
• Ensure all office supply requirements are available
• Distribute incident checklists and office supplies
• Ensure white boards have been set up correctly and that markers are available
• Check that clock time is correct and working properly
• Ensure CMT has mobilized the Telephone Response Team (TRT)—minimum of two members for all incidents. Review incident and increase numbers of TRT if appropriate.
• When TRT is manned, direct switchboard to transfer all incident-related calls to TRT
• Arrange for copies of Crisis Management Plan for each team member
• Check miscellaneous documentation for relevant supplementary information
• Ensure auditable trail of information is maintained
   — CMT members to use bound notebooks for all notes
   — Enter name, date, and time when coming on shift
• Contact and liaise with Logistics.
   — Organize staff relief
   — Food/water/drinks, and so forth
   — Accommodation
   — Taxis, and so on
• Contact security for any advice and/or for additional support/assistance

(continued)

Table 4.3. (continued)

Brief switchboard operator and the security staff:
• Outline of incident
• Press/media inquiries
• Use of TRT as filter for CMT (no calls to be transferred directly to the CMT)
• Ensure switchboard operator and security know the transfer numbers for the TRT
• Ensure security is sufficient and consider restricting staff access to the Crisis Center
Facilitate initial CMT briefings:
• Review setup checklist and ensure team is fully briefed
• See initial briefing checklist
• Ensure the school/facility is represented/aware
• Brainstorm issues and help identify actions
Initiate and maintain contact as required with other team coordinator(s):
• Ensure CMT remains focused on business response—no micromanaging
• Share issues and plans for next period
• Ensure call schedule is appropriate
• Ensure auditable trail of information is being maintained
• Encourage use of e-mail to pass updates
Ensure that the CMT and support staff are regularly briefed and kept up to date:
• Ensure initial briefing follows checklist
• Ensure personnel members review checklists and understand roles and responsibilities
• Issue press statements to Telephone Support Team
If mobilized, initiate and maintain contact with city/county CMT coordinator:
• Share issues and plans for next period
• Ensure call schedule is appropriate
• Determine CMT issues/concerns/themes
Monitor the level of resources required to support the CMT:
• Ensure all personnel members involved in the Emergency Management have everything they require
• Ensure that the CMT is operating as designed
• Coordinate the collection, display, and dissemination of relevant information
• Maintain a display of the CMT workload, actions, and priorities
• Identify and mobilize additional technical support/expertise required
Ongoing checks:
• Individual team efficiency checks: are they working effectively?
• Team interaction or communication issues, breakdowns
• Is communication logging and recording being maintained?
• Are call logging sheets being used by TRT, and are actions being closed out?
• Are communication processes working? Potential bottlenecks or overload?
• Are teams maintaining their focus?
• Does CMT need to be completely manned full time?
• Can CMT achieve aims by meeting at regular intervals (determine frequency)?

Coordinating ongoing health checks:
- Stress monitoring, support, and management
- Provision of a quiet room or area with facilities to unwind
- Consider the need for specialist counseling or support agencies
- Additional Human Resource specialist support

Resource drawings, plans, charts, and photographs:
- Ensure copies of emergency plans are available
- Are approved actions being undertaken?
- Identify outstanding issues, hurdles, and challenges, and bring to CMT's attention for evaluation

CMT staffing review forward planning:
- Establish or estimate anticipated incident duration, hours, and days
- Conduct a staffing review with the CMT leader
- Coordinate a strategy for mobilizing the staff to the incident site
- Request shift rotations for extended periods of operation
- Notify off-duty coordinator for logistics planning

Consider the need or potential for school function relocation and resource movements:
- Review business continuity and alternate relocation plans and procedures
- Identify resource and logistics support needs
- What and where is it required?
- How to achieve it
- Prompt CMT leader

Incident termination:
- Consider when it is appropriate to declare the incident over and return to normal business
- Full stand-down
- Partial stand-down
- Ensure that all teams are informed of the stand-down irrespective of the level
- Create a master file of all data and pass to legal for retention
  - Ensure all log sheets are collected before the team leaves the room
  - Arrange for copies of all e-mail traffic and incident files to be transferred to a CD Rom and stored
  - All notebooks to be copied and/or originals to be retained
- Lead team debrief on stand-down or soon after. Capture lessons learned/actions.
- If there is deemed to be any value in photographing the room layout and key display boards, ensure this is done before the room is tidied
- Ensure that a clear action is initiated to have CMT room reset/restocked immediately after stand-down

Table 4.4. Action Checklist: External Affairs Leader (Executive Director, Communications/Delegated Authority)

Key roles:
1. Protect district reputation and development of External Affairs Strategy for response
2. Maintain oversight and provide advice for External Affairs issues
3. Liaise with third-party External Affairs representatives to ensure common and consistent messages are transmitted to stakeholders
4. Identify all stakeholders and development of stakeholder management strategy
5. Liaise with city/county counterparts

Action
Register arrival at Crisis Center.
Work with CMT leader and evaluate status of emergency: • Agree to priorities • Agree to the media strategy • Assist with the preparation of press releases using confirmed information only • Ensure that the Media Response Team is properly briefed on handling media inquiries
Relocate to External Affairs Room between CMT update meetings: • Draft press statements • Liaise with government, partners, media teams, and so forth, as required by CMT leader • Brief switchboard operator on transfer of calls to Consumer Affairs • Brief Telephone Response Team (TRT) • Activate TRT direct-dial numbers once TRT is established and fully manned • Monitor/manage TRT (under TRT supervisor) • Liaise with Logistics and Human Resources • Monitor/record all media broadcasts
Ensure that CMT are kept up to date and are fully informed about incident: • Prompt CMT leader for update meetings as required • Ensure a rapid flow of the latest factual and releasable information • Advise on media and government relations • Brief on current media tone and themes • Advise on the current or likely effects of the emergency on SS's image or reputation
Ensure appropriate resources are available. Consider need for the following: • Mobilization of the External Affairs Group • External Affairs support at scene • Call out of the External Affairs Team • Liaise with Human Resources Team
Confirm with Human Resources Team leader what information on casualties can be given to media.

Ensure assistance to CMT:
- In the development of Q&As for news conferences
- In the consistency of the messages being prepared by SS
- In the production and documentation of all statements made to the media
- In preparation of SS management who may be speaking
- In recorded playback of news broadcasts about the incident

Ensure that copies of press releases are as follows:
- Consistent
- Scrutinized by legal counsel prior to release
- Being given wide, internal distribution
- Being given external distribution as per list of companies/authorities/agents/stakeholders, and so on
- Agreed to coordinate/coordinated with safety/law enforcement/vested business partners/contractors

Ensure that the district is established as the single authoritative source of information:
- Press conferences arranged
- Media requests for additional information discussed with CMT leader
- Are you up to date on facts?
- Is another press release due now?
- Next steps?

Provide update of number and nature of calls received at regular intervals.

Table 4.5. Action Checklist: Legal Representative (General Counsel/Delegated Authority)

Key roles: 1. Assess legal liabilities, criminal and civil actions 2. Provide legal advice to CMT leadership 3. Review press releases
Action
Register arrival with Crisis Center.
Contact other disciplines and seek advice/mobilize them if required: • Risk • Legal • Finance
Work with CMT leader and evaluate status of emergency relating to the following: • Communication of operational incident details within SS • Students, employees, and families • Partners • Government agencies • Safety and law enforcement agencies • Neighbors • Special interest groups • Suppliers • General • Unions
Determine and advise CMT: • Potential criminal actions • Legal liabilities • Preparation of testimony and counseling of SS representatives at government and legal hearings • Legal advice on communication with the media • Where actions could be interpreted as admission of guilt • Giving clarity to affected parties' legal responsibilities within contractual context • Provide input to situation reports
Ensure CMT responses are recorded for use during postincident investigations: • Recording tapes for emergency lines • Copy of all notes/records/e-mails • CMT notebooks • Message sheets • TRT records
Brief CMT: • On decisions taken • Actions and concerns of the CMT • On legal/finance skills and resources required
Provide input/recommendations for the form and scope of the postincident investigation.

Strategic issues for consideration:

- What insurance coverage is applicable?
- Cost of repair/replacement
- Cost of response to emergency
- Cost of clearance/recovery/cleanup/own resources/other resources
- Cost of liabilities, claims, fines, and compensation. Significant claims to be expected?
- Penalties/fines/damages to be expected? Are actions likely?
- Legal situation on continuing operations. Any injunctions possible?
- Legal costs
- Compensation payment necessary?
- SS professional liability? Partner costs?
- Casualties/medical costs/legal liabilities
- Cash flow implications
- Impact on SS?
- Any other financial impacts
- How will legislators react?

Table 4.6. Action Checklist: Security Officer (Director Student Services and Security/Delegated Authority)

Key roles: 1. Initial incident assessment and notification   2. Prime interface with safety incident commander   3. Security control and support to response operations   4. Security guidance to CMT   5. Take charge of security delegation
Action
Make initial assessment (in consultation with CMT leader and on-scene SS incident commander):   • What has happened?   • Why has it happened?   • What is the potential for escalation? Is incident contained?   • How has it happened?   • Who is injured?   • When did it happen?   • Where has it happened?
Liaise with safety (police, fire, and emergency medical) and building security: • Threat assessment: real, false alarm, hoax, or uncertain   • Determine/agree appropriate immediate response action   • Appoint security representative that will interact with safety incident commander   • Agree to communications protocol and schedule
Notify/activate security staff, as appropriate: • SS   • Contract services
Provide access control and enhanced physical security as deemed necessary: • Buildings   • Areas   • Surrounding areas   • Emergency operations center   • Staging areas   • Medical care receiving areas (hospitals and clinics)   • Remote sites
Coordinate and communicate security buildup with CMT, building security, and with safety organizations.
Liaise with on-site safety incident commander (fire, police, and FBI):   • Conduct threat assessment   • Review, agree, and modify response actions under way as directed   • Advise incident commander of SS response organization and location(s)
Confirm extent of safety and law enforcement involvement:

- Determine/confirm command and control relationships between SS and federal and state law enforcement agencies

Advise CMT of safety incident commander directives.

Attend initial briefing with CMT:
- Brainstorm—identify issues, assign and track actions
- Advise CMT on security-related directives, issues, concerns, and actions
- Establish/agree on objectives developed by CMT

Agree on media strategy with External Affairs:
- Confirm prime district spokesperson
- Determine whether/when safety desires to issue press releases, make press statement, conduct media interviews, or establish a Joint Information Center
- Facilitate/liaise between External Affairs and safety spokespersons(s)

Keep CMT informed and current on security-related matters.

Ensure a Stakeholder Management Plan addresses all relevant law enforcement and security-related constituencies:
- Ensure statutory notifications are made and updates provided

Ensure security arrangements are made to support execution of school function relocation plans, as appropriate:
- Headquarters building
- Schools
- Personnel/operations in transit
- Receiving sites
- Other locations

Maintain records to ensure an auditable trail of information.

Ask yourself—How am I holding up?

Continually review all of the above.

Strategic Issues for consideration:
- Is SS effectively positioning itself for a successful outcome?
- New/changing threats?
- Need to expand/modify liaisons with external safety and law enforcement agencies
- Maintaining effective and current information flow to CMT to support decision making

Table 4.7. Action Checklist: Environmental, Health, and Safety Representative (Manager, Energy, Environmental, Health, and Safety/Delegated Authority)

Key roles:
1.   Responsible for management of environmental-, health-, and safety-related issues

Action
Determine the following: • Nature of incident   • Personnel status (injured/missing/deaths, and so forth)   • Response operations status   • Environmental, health, and safety (EHS) concerns

Work with the CMT leader and evaluate status of emergency:
 • Agree on priorities
     — Take care of people
     — Protect environment
     — Protect assets
     — Ensure business continuity

Ensure that CMT has appropriate systems and resources in place for managing EHS issues: • Contribute to the CMT tactical and general deliberations   • Advise the CMT on the EHS issues arising from the emergency   • Ensure that systems and resources are in place for managing issues related to EHS matters
Ensure that appropriate resources are available: • Consider need for on-site EHS support
Coordinate EHS advice between CMT and the site.
Advise the CMT on whether actual or potential EHS hazards exist and on options to minimize their effect: • Take action, where appropriate, to implement decisions made by the CMT on EHS issues   • Keep the CMT leader advised of any pressing safety issues   • Ensure safety-related information is accurate and up to date
Consider need for, propose, and initiate appropriate investigations into and reports on the incident.
Provide advice to the CMT on the availability of additional technical advice.
Ensure written situation reports are provided by the CRT, and draft situation reports for the CMT: • Use e-mail if practicable
Brief CMT: • On decisions taken   • On actions and concerns of the CRT
Provide EHS input into recommendations for the form and scope of postincident investigation.
Other strategic issues for consideration: • What district assets are affected?   • What are likely to be the effects on the EHS?   • Short term—implement short-term response   • Longer term—decide on longer term responses   • How will regulatory agencies react?   • How will pressure groups react?   • What do our employees need?   • What EHS considerations are immediate?

Table 4.8.   Action Checklist: Risk Representative (Treasurer/Delegated Authority)

Key roles: 1. Liaise with insurance providers   2. Provide general risk-related advice on the response   3. Record and manage all claims
Action
Register arrival with Crisis Center.
Contact other disciplines and seek advice; mobilize them if required: • Risk   • Legal   • Finance
Work with CMT leader and evaluate status of emergency relating to the following: • Communication of operational incident details within SS   • Students, employees, and families   • Other SS facilities/sites   • Partners   • Government   • Site neighbors   • Special interest groups   • Suppliers   • General   • Unions
Liaise with insurance providers: • Keep insurers informed   • Liaise with Finance and develop the optimum cost-recording mechanism to capture insurance-related costs to maximize recovery   • Provide risk- and insurance-related advice on the response strategies   • Record of all claims (set up a claims hotline)   • Strategy for managing claims   • Provide advice on recoverable/nonrecoverable costs
Ensure appropriate controls, systems, and audit procedures are implemented with respect to emergency expenditure: • Make arrangements for cash and currency when necessary   • Set up a claims hotline as soon as possible, if required   • Estimate potential cost of response operations/impacts as requested   • Advise the CMT on financial liabilities concerning the incident and ways to minimize them
Ensure CMT responses are recorded for use at any postincident investigation: • Recording tapes for emergency lines from emergency operations center   • Copy of all notes/records/e-mails   • CMT notebooks   • Message sheets   • TRT records
Provide input/recommendations for the form and scope of the postincident investigation.
Strategic issues for consideration: • What insurance coverage is applicable?   • Cost of repair/replacement

(continued)

- Cost of response to emergency
- Cost of clearance/recovery/damage restoration/cleanup/own resources/other resources
- Cost of liabilities, claims, fines, compensation. Significant claims to be expected?
- Penalties/fines/damages to be expected? Are actions likely?
- Legal situation on continuing operations. Any injunctions possible?
- Legal costs
- Compensation payment necessary?
- SS professional liability? Partner costs?
- Casualties/medical costs/legal liabilities
- Cash flow implications
- Impact on SS?
- Any other financial impacts
- How will legislators react?

Table 4.9. Action Checklist: Planning Representative (Director Strategic Planning/Grants/Delegated Authority)

Key roles:
1. Look ahead, identify issues, consider worst-case scenarios, and develop contingency plans to ensure continuity of response and to minimize impacts
2. Draft emergency response objectives; recommend strategies and priorities for the CMT leader and to assist with stakeholder management
3. Work closely with CMT staff to coordinate production of incident briefing documentation, situation reports, and so forth

Action
Register arrival with the Crisis Center.
Establish the facts, evaluate status of emergency: • Review immediate priorities — Take care of people — Protect environment — Protect assets — Ensure business continuity as efficiently and safely as possible
Support the CMT coordinator in managing the response room and information displays: • Manage the operation and recorder • Identify key issues and ensure that they are tracked on the issues/actions board
Assess the incident using the Crisis Triggers and Assessment checklists: • Agree on the assessment with the CMT leader and present to the CMT at the next update meeting (consider whether the CMT needs to sit full time/part time/partially manned/fully manned/not at all) • Ensure the assessment board is marked up by the log keeper • Ensure that the incident facts are marked on the incident status board • Reassess at regular intervals and update boards
Maintain a high-level view of the incident and make recommendations to the CMT leader as appropriate.
Help External Affairs to develop the Stakeholder Management Plan: • Ensure appropriate internal and external notifications are made
Identify worst-case/best-case/most-likely case scenarios: • Think "outside the box" • Liaise with external organizations as appropriate • Chair planning meetings • Brief CMT • Recommend the creation of project teams as appropriate
Produce an Incident Briefing Document for transmission to senior management as appropriate: • Update regularly
Ensure that CMT has appropriate systems and resources in place for managing EHS and community issues: • Review Environment, Security, and Community Representative Checklists • Mobilize personnel as required

(continued)

Table 4.9. (*continued*)

Develop plans for maintaining the response throughout future operational periods.
• Focus on the business issues
• Liaise with CMT members to ensure that operational issues have been covered. Support as required.
• Develop plans for CMT Operations to execute tomorrow/the next day/next week/and so on. For lengthy incidents, consider the use of Incident Action Plans and turning the emergency into a project.
Strategic issues for consideration:
• Has SS management been briefed and kept up to date?
• Have all stakeholders been identified, prioritized, and engaged? Is there a Stakeholder Management Plan?
• Is the CMT planning for the worst-case scenario?
• Is the chosen strategy working?
• What SS assets are affected?
• What is the impact on the SS/local community?
• Short term—implement short-term response
• Longer term—decide on longer term response
• How will regulatory/oversight agencies react?
• How will law enforcement agencies and other government/political entities react?
• How will parents/community react?
• How will special interest groups react?

Table 4.10. Action Checklist: Community Representative (Executive Director, Communications/Delegated Authority)

Key roles:
1. Support Planning representative by identifying community issues arising from incident
2. Develop community response strategy that reflects the district's core values
3. Assist External Affairs in development of Stakeholder Management Plan

Action
Register arrival with the Crisis Center.
Start and maintain an Incident Log: • Provide regular updates to the log keeper so that relevant information can be captured in the action/event log
Work with Planning and evaluate the status of the emergency: • Review priorities • Review media strategy • Provide input for press holding statements/press releases • Provide input for the creation of incident objectives
Confirm relevant authorities have been informed: • Identify immediate issues
Assess the impact of the incident on the community: • Type and scope of impact • Magnitude and duration of impact • Areas of community affected • Casualties • Local involvement of safety, government entities, media, and so forth • Other
Seek specialist advice as appropriate: • Internal • External
Consider implications of escalation and need for SS representation on the ground to liaise with community leaders: • Who should represent the district? • What level of management? • Consider safety and security issues
Assist the local response team in providing immediate support: • Confirm the initial response is in accordance with SS core values
Identify status of current district-sponsored community projects and resources.

(continued)

Table 4.10. (*continued*)

Work with External Affairs and identify the community stakeholders and the best way of communicating with the community:

- Assist in the development of the Stakeholder Management Plan
    — Media
    — Authorities
    — Third party
    — "Town Hall" Meetings
    — Flyers
    — Door to door
    — Hotlines
    — Spokesperson(s)
    — Other

Capture feedback from the community and identify key issues:

- Share key issues with CMT, especially External Affairs and security. Sources include the following:
    — Claims lines
    — Counseling support
    — Personal contact
    — Meetings
    — Feedback from responders/authorities, and so on

Develop a sustainable strategy for supporting the community:

- Ensure strategy is achievable
- Try to include some "quick wins" at the start
- Don't make promises that can't be kept

Provide regular updates to Planning for input for the Assessment Meeting and/or attend if required.

Provide input to Planning for the Incident Briefing Document.

Assist Finance to estimate costs.

Table 4.11.   Action Checklist: Log Keeper Representative (District Secretary/Delegated Authority)

Key roles: 1. To keep the incident display boards up to date 2. Assist the Planning representative and recorder in their tasks
Action
Ensure that equipment and boards are properly set up in the Crisis Center: • See Crisis Center Activation Checklist, section 3.2 • Write up boards during briefing • Request the CMT leader provide a recorder, if necessary • Pass logs to recorder for transcription and retention • Print action/event log when complete and pass to recorder for transcription into a word-processing document • Work with Logistics—identify and track resources
Brief recorder on arrival.
Establish and maintain the official CMT Log of Events: • Mark the information on the Log of Events and the relevant CMT wallboards
Ensure all boards and displays are kept up to date: • Request a time out/update from CMT leader if unsure of situation or if information thought to be missing • During updates, stop briefing if you need clarification
Supervise the recorder and ensure the log is typed accurately: • Answer any queries the recorder might have
Ensure that the Log of Events is as follows: • Printed off • Copied and distributed to CMT personnel • Copied to keep an extra copy of the Log of Events for the CMT leader as a permanent record • Used for update messages (e-mails) when appropriate

Table 4.12. Action Checklist: Documentation/Recorder Representative (District Secretary/Delegated Authority)

Key roles:
1. Work with the log keeper and maintain full records of the response

Action
• Recognize significant events and ensure they are properly recorded
• Maintain a log of all activities and information
• Document CMT decisions—liaise with coordinator if any questions or if clarification required
• Maintain a record of contacts made with government and other external authorities/agencies made by the CMT
• File all incoming and outgoing documents and ensure their traceability
• Assist the coordinator in the preparation of status reports
• Preserve all documentation that may be required for future insurance and legal claims
• Recover documents and notes from all CMT members (on a regular basis)
• Keep the minutes of CMT updates
• Monitor the accuracy of visual displays
• Manage the e-mail interface between the CMT and other response team elements and involved parties

Table 4.13. Action Checklist: Logistics Representative (Coordinator, Business Support Services/Delegated Authority)

Key roles:
1. Provide logistics support to the CMT and other response elements
2. Resource appropriate transportation for teams
3. Identify additional resources required
4. Supply contract management
5. Track and account for all personnel members

Action
Register arrival with Crisis Center.
Initiate and maintain contact with CMT, remote team coordinators, and other response team elements as appropriate: • Get an update/establish facts • What does the CMT need? • Ensure response is appropriate and fully resourced • Agree that Logistics call schedules with teams (if required)
Work with CMT and evaluate status of emergency: • Agree on priorities • Take care of people • Protect environment • Protect assets • Business continuity • Casualty evacuation to a safe place for medical treatment • Personnel evacuation /shelter-in-place/student/personnel care and custody issues

Ensure appropriate resources are available:
• Consider need for transportation for:
  — CMT and support staff
  — Students
  — Employees
  — Equipment, supplies, food, sanitation, and other materials

Ensure assistance to personnel evacuated:
• Staging area reception (Consider need for postincident debriefing counseling support)
  — Medical treatment
  — Cold/inclement weather protection
  — Cash
  — Food/water
  — Accommodations
  — Others

Control the logistics of technical support sent by the CMT: • Identify/maintain/record the location and movements of people and other support resources dispatched • Maintain a record of all assets available in the field to provide support
Assist CMT in procuring resource drawings, plans, charts, photographs, and other technical support.
Provide advice to the CMT on the availability of additional contracts/logistics advice.
Establish requirements for emergency equipment supplies and other logistical support resources.

Table 4.14. Action Checklist: Human Resources Representative (Director, Human Resources/Delegated Authority)

Key roles:
1. Identify and track all personnel members involved in incident
2. Coordinate and provide feedback to employers
3. Ensure consistent messages are conveyed to all concerned
4. Provide advice on union issues
5. Provide student, employee, and family support counseling services where required

Action
Register arrival with Crisis Center.
Work with CMT to establish the facts: • Casualties/numbers/severity of injury/location, and so forth
Mobilize SS counselors (and/or contract counselors) as appropriate: • Brief supervisor(s) • Keep supervisor(s) updated at regular intervals • Consider appropriate staffing levels
Track casualties: • Ensure Human Resources Casualty Board is kept up to date • Check names of casualties against students/employee/visitor lists to ensure that names are correct • Verify discrepancies
Ensure appropriate resources are available. Consider the following: • Alerting all employers of non-SS personnel working at the site and/or within the operation • Arrangements for handling/assisting employees, contractors, next of kin, and those affected by the emergency • Appropriate systems in place for managing Human Resource issues • Telephone Response Team briefed to direct relatives' calls to Human Resource–designated representatives • Liaise across all SS operations, as appropriate • Grief/support counseling available where needed
Communicate factual student/personnel information on the incident to counselors/team: • Share all press releases as soon as possible • Identify other agencies/stakeholders and ensure close liaison with counselors/team • Verify and maintain a record of location and status of persons involved in the incident • Verify details of fatalities, casualties, missing people, and survivors • Determine the nature, tone, and format of communication with students, employees, and families • Conduct postincident debriefing as soon as possible • Transportation for families • Accommodation • Consider need for cash/clothing/communications with families, and so on • Establish call schedules as appropriate
Facilitate visits to hospitals by relatives.

Provide support for families. Consider the following:
- Transportation to hospital/point of arrival
- Child care
- Accommodation
- Passport/visa issues
- Financial support
- Counseling support
- Reassurance as appropriate

Provide advice to CMT:
- Student, family, employee, and union relations
- SS Human Resources Policy

Monitor stress levels of the CMT and support teams.

Ensure adequate debriefing of all responders and assist in recommending the form and scope of the postincident investigation:
- Arrange postincident support debriefing at first opportunity
- Remember families

Strategic issues for consideration:
- What are impacts on
  - Students/employees? Provide compassionate assistance to injured persons and bereaved families, counseling/travel assistance/accommodation/practical help/loans/cash
  - SS contractors and other key third parties?
- Concern at loss of employment, guilt—keep all employees informed/reaffirm positive aspects of SS
- What effect on morale of district personnel? Reinforce district morale
- What are the likely effects of the incident on the workforce and its relationship with the district?
- Stress—who might be affected?
- Monitor for stress at site and in teams
- Response/telephone teams—arrange relief where signs of serious stress are detected
- Students/families/third-party witnesses—put in place a stress counseling program
- Look for and build on positive aspects of incident/response

Table 4.15. Action Checklist: Finance Representative (Treasurer/Delegated Authority)

Key roles:
1. May not be an initial core team member but should be mobilized as soon as practicable
2. Tracking and forecasting of costs
3. Identification of financial impacts on stakeholders

Action
Work with CMT leader and evaluate impact of emergency relating to • Students, employees, families, local community, and the general public • Partners • Government • Special interest groups • Unions • Others
Contact appropriate financial advisor. Ensure appropriate resources are available for • Tracking financial liabilities associated with the emergency • Advising SS representatives for impact on SS District Operations • Checking the status of reporting to external agencies • Arranging the calculation of financial impacts
Liaise with SS financial and insurance departments.
Ensure appropriate controls, systems, and audit procedures are implemented with respect to emergency expenditures: • Make arrangements for cash and currency when necessary • Work with Risk to set up a claims hotline as soon as possible • Estimate increases in cost of working • Estimate costs of reinstatement • Advise the CMT on financial liabilities concerning the incident and ways to minimize them
For major incidents: • Determine payment strategy for any casual labor (day rates, and so forth)
Ensure appropriate resources are available for • Cash/credit cards at scene if required • Tracking financial liabilities associated with the emergency • Checking the status of reporting to external agencies • Arranging the calculation of financial impacts
Liaise with CMT Risk and Legal representatives: • Establish what SS insurance policies are relevant. Who are the insurers? • Determine what format/information will be required to substantiate SS claims and gather financial information in that format if possible • Estimate potential financial impact of any shutdown and report to CMT
Ensure appropriate controls, systems, and audit procedures are implemented in respect of emergency expenditure: • Make arrangements for cash and currency when necessary • Estimate potential cost of response operations/impacts as requested • Advise the CMT on financial liabilities concerning the incident and ways to minimize them
Brief CMT:

- Issues
- Current and planned tasks
- Actions and concerns

Strategic issues for consideration:
- What insurance cover is applicable and how should costs be tracked to maximize returns?
- Cost of repair/replacement
- Cost of response to emergency
- Cost of clearance/recovery. Installation/spill contamination cleanup/own resources/other resources
- Cost of liabilities, claims, fines, and compensation. Significant claims to be expected?
- Penalties/fines/damages to be expected? Are actions likely?
- Cash flow implications
- Impact on SS?
- Any other financial impacts?
- How will legislators/agencies and the community react?
- How will students, employees, families, unions, and others react?

Table 4.16.   Action Checklist: CMT Update Briefing

Action
Preparation: • CMT coordinator to give ten-minute warning • CMT coordinator to advise CMT members; ensure log keeper and recorder are in place • Conduct roll call prior to commencing brief from site

CMT Brief:
• Review of any outstanding action items from previous meeting
• Identify new issues and actions from update call. Delegate responsibility and track actions
• CMT members to present progress and provide short status report including, where appropriate,
   — Planning for worst-case scenarios
   — Triggers to assist in the proactive recognition of escalation toward the worst-case scenario
   — Indicators of improvement
   — How to make best of situation, and what are positives for SS?
   — Identification of stakeholders and issues
   — Strategies for dealing with stakeholders and issues
• Confirm date and time of next meeting and note on board

Postmeeting actions: • Log keeper captures information • Update complete • CMT leader to update executive team and other senior management, as appropriate

Table 4.17.   Action Checklist: Role Handover

Action
• In the event that the CMT is likely to be required to sit for longer than eight hours, team members will have to be replaced by alternates to avoid fatigue. • When it is obvious that an incident is likely to run for an extended period, it is recommended that the initial handover commence early (and at an appropriate time). • For reasons of information continuity and familiarization with the incident, consideration should be given to initiating the transition after the first six hours.

Table 4.18.   Action Checklist: CMT Stand-down

Action
Questions for consideration prior to termination of operations: • Have facilities been tested and confirmed operational and safe? • Have relevant emergency services acknowledged that normal activities can commence? • Have relevant government agencies/departments acknowledged that normal activities can commence? • Could students and employees be suffering from the effects of the incident?

CHAPTER FIVE

Crisis Response Team Job Descriptions

The job descriptions included in this section are provided as job aids to assist school system (SS) Crisis Response Team members that may be mobilized to a specific school or SS facility to participate in on-site emergency response operations. These procedures conform to protocols established within the framework of the National Incident Management System and are based upon the Incident Command System.

These protocols describe roles and responsibilities for various responders that may comprise the on-site Crisis Response Team. Safety (fire or police) will assume command of operations during the initial stages of the incident response. The extent of activation of the team and specific actions will depend upon the type and magnitude of the incident and will be decided and agreed to between Safety and the SS district Crisis Management Team.

Various positions during the initial stages of response may be supported and/or staffed by the safety agency personnel.

These procedures supplement immediate response actions that are described within the incident-specific Emergency Response Flip Charts included in chapter 7. Copies of flip charts are maintained by all teachers, site administrators, and support staff members (see figure 3.2 for organization chart).

5.1. Command Section

5.1.1. INCIDENT COMMANDER

Responsibilities

The incident commander (IC) is solely responsible for emergency/disaster operations and shall remain at the Command Post to observe and direct all operations.

Ensure the safety of students, staff members, and others on campus. Lead by example: your behavior sets the tone for staff members and students.

Start-up Actions

- Obtain your personal safety equipment (i.e., hard hat, vest, and clipboard with job description sheet).
- Assess the type and scope of emergency.
- Determine the threat to human life and structures.
- Implement the emergency plan and hazard-specific procedures.
- Develop and communicate an Incident Action Plan with objectives and a time frame to meet those objectives.

- Activate functions and assign positions as needed.
- Fill in the Incident Assignments form (refer to the Site Crisis Response Team Assignment Form in appendix D for a blank copy).
- Appoint a backup or alternate IC.

Ongoing Operational Duties

- Continue to monitor and assess the total school situation:
  - View the site map periodically for search and rescue progress and damage assessment information.
  - Check with chiefs for periodic updates.
  - Reassign personnel members as needed.
- Report (through Communications) to the school district on the status of students, staff members, and facility, as needed (Site Status Report).
- Develop and communicate revised Incident Action Plans as needed.
- Begin student release when appropriate.

NOTE: No student should be released until student accounting is complete. Never send students home before the end of the regular school day unless directed by the superintendent, except at the request of parent/guardian.

- Authorize the release of information.
- Utilize your backup; plan and take regular breaks (five to ten minutes per hour). During break periods, relocate away from the Command Post.
- Plan regular breaks for all staff members and volunteers. Take care of your caregivers!
- Release teachers as appropriate and per district guidelines.
- Remain on and in charge of your campus until redirected or released by the superintendent.

Closing Down

- Authorize deactivation of sections, branches, or units when they are no longer required.
- At the direction of the superintendent, deactivate the entire emergency response. If the fire department or other outside agency calls an "all clear," contact the district before taking any further action.
- Ensure that any open actions not yet completed will be taken care of after deactivation.
- Ensure the return of all equipment and reusable supplies to Logistics.
- Close out all logs. Ensure that all logs, reports, and other relevant documents are completed and provided to the Documentation Unit.
- Announce the termination of the emergency and proceed with recovery operations if necessary.

Command Post Equipment/Supplies

- Campus map
- Master keys
- Staff and student rosters
- Crisis response forms (refer to appendix D)
- Emergency plan
- Duplicate rosters (two sets)
- Tables and chairs (if Command Post is outdoors)
- Vests (if available)
- Job description clipboards
- Command Post tray (pens, etc.)
- Two-way radios
- AM/FM radio (battery)

5.1.2. SAFETY OFFICER

RESPONSIBILITIES

The safety officer ensures that all activities are conducted in as safe a manner as possible under the existing circumstances.

Start-up Actions

- Check in with the IC for a situation briefing.
- Obtain necessary equipment and supplies from Logistics.
- Put on a position identifier, such as a vest, if available.
- Open and maintain a position log (refer to the Sample Log in appendix D for a blank copy). Maintain all required records and documentation to support the history of the emergency or disaster.
- Document the following:
  - Messages received
  - Action taken
  - Decision justification and documentation
  - Requests filled

Operational Duties

- Monitor drills, exercises, and emergency response activities for safety.
- Identify and mitigate safety hazards and situations.
- Stop or modify all unsafe operations.
- Ensure that responders use appropriate safety equipment.
- Think ahead and anticipate situations and problems before they occur.
- Anticipate situation changes, such as cascading events, in all planning.
- Keep the IC advised of your status and activity and on any problem areas that now need or will require solutions.

Closing Down

- When authorized by the IC, deactivate the unit and close out all logs. Provide logs and other relevant documents to the Documentation Unit.
- Return equipment and reusable supplies to Logistics.

Equipment/Supplies

- Vest or position identifier, if available
- Hard hat, if available
- Clipboard, paper, and pens
- Two-way radio, if available

5.1.3. PUBLIC INFORMATION OFFICER (PIO)

Personnel

Available staff members with assistance from available volunteers.

Policy

The PIO has the right and needs to know important information related to an emergency/disaster at the school site as soon as it is available.

The PIO acts as the official spokesperson for the school site in an emergency situation. If a school district PIO is available, he/she will be the official spokesperson. A school site–based PIO should be used only if the media is on campus and the district PIO is not available.

News media can play a key role in assisting the school in getting emergency/disaster-related information to the parents.

Information released must be consistent, accurate, and timely.

Start-up Actions

- Determine a possible "news center" site as a media reception area (located away from the Command Post and students). Get approval from the IC.
- Identify yourself as the PIO (by vest, visor, sign, etc.).
- Consult with the district PIO to coordinate information release.
- Assess the situation and obtain a statement from the IC. Tape record it if possible.
- Advise arriving media that the site is preparing a press release and the approximate time of its issue.
- Open and maintain a position log (refer to the Sample Log in appendix D for a blank copy) of your actions and all communications. If possible, tape media briefings. Keep all documentation to support the history of the event.

Operational Duties

- Keep up to date on the situation.
- Statements must be approved by the IC and should reflect the following:
  ○ Reassurance (EGBOK—"Everything's going to be OK")
  ○ Incident or disaster cause and time of origin
  ○ Size and scope of the incident
  ○ Current situation—condition of school site, evacuation progress, care being given, injuries, student release location, and so on. Do not release any names.
  ○ Resources in use
  ○ Best routes to the school, if known and if appropriate
  ○ Any information the school wishes to be released to the parents
- Read statements if possible.
- When answering questions, be complete and truthful, always considering confidentiality and emotional impact. Avoid speculation, bluffing, lying, talking "off the record," arguing, and so forth. Avoid using the phrase "no comment."
- Remind school staff members and volunteers to refer all questions from the media or waiting parents to the PIO.
- Update information periodically with the IC.
- Ensure that announcements and other information are translated into other languages as needed.
- Monitor news broadcasts about the incident. Correct any misinformation heard.

Closing Down

- At the IC's direction, release PIO staff members when they are no longer needed. Direct staff members to sign out through Timekeeping.
- Return equipment and reusable supplies to Logistics.
- Close out all logs. Provide logs and other relevant documents to the Documentation Unit.

Equipment/Supplies

- ID vest
- Battery-operated AM/FM radio

- Paper/pencils/marking pens
- Notebook
- Forms:
  - Sample Public Information Release
  - School Profile Information

5.1.4. LIAISON OFFICER

RESPONSIBILITIES

The liaison officer serves as the point of contact for agency representatives from assisting organizations and agencies outside the school district and assists in coordinating the efforts of these outside agencies by ensuring the proper flow of information.

Start-up Actions

- Check in with the IC for a situation briefing.
- Determine your personal operating location, and set it up as necessary.
- Obtain the necessary equipment and supplies from Logistics.
- Put on a position identifier, such as a vest, if available.
- Open and maintain a position log (refer to the Sample Log in appendix D for a blank copy). Maintain all required records and documentation to support the history of the emergency or disaster.

Operational Duties

- Brief agency representatives on the current situation, priorities, and Incident Action Plan.
- Ensure coordination of efforts by keeping the IC informed of agencies' action plans.
- Provide periodic update briefings to agency representatives as necessary.

Closing Down

- At the IC's direction, deactivate the liaison officer position and release staff members who are no longer needed. Direct staff members to sign out through Timekeeping.
- Return equipment and reusable supplies to Logistics.
- Close out all logs. Provide logs and other relevant documents to the Documentation Unit.

Equipment/Supplies

- Vest or position identifier, if available
- Two-way radio, if available
- Clipboard, paper, and pens

5.2. Operations Section

5.2.1. OPERATIONS SECTION CHIEF

Responsibilities

The Operations chief manages the direct response to the disaster, which can include

- Site facility check/security
- Search and rescue
- Medical
- Student care
- Student release

Start-up Actions

- Check in with the IC for a situation briefing.
- Obtain necessary equipment and supplies from Logistics.
- Put on a position identifier, such as a vest, if available.

Operational Duties

- Assume the duties of all operations positions until staff members are available and assigned.
- As staff members are assigned, brief them on the situation, and supervise their activities, using the position checklists.
- If additional supplies or staff members are needed for the Operations Section, notify Logistics. When additional staff members arrive, brief them on the situation, and assign them as needed.
- Coordinate search and rescue operations if it is safe to do so. Appoint a Search and Rescue Team leader to direct operations, if necessary.
- As information is received from Operations staff members, pass it on to situation analysis and/or the IC.
- Inform the Planning Section chief of operations tasks and priorities.
- Make sure that Operations staff members are following standard procedures, using appropriate safety gear, and documenting their activities.
- Schedule breaks and reassign staff members within the section as needed.

Closing Down

- At the IC's direction, release Operations staff members no longer needed. Direct staff members to sign out through Timekeeping.
- Return equipment and reusable supplies to Logistics.
- When authorized by the IC, deactivate the section and close out all logs. Provide logs and other relevant documents to the Documentation Unit.

Equipment/Supplies

- Vest or position identifier, if available
- Search and rescue equipment
- Two-way radio
- Job description clipboard, paper, and pens
- Maps:
  - Search and rescue maps
  - Large campus map

5.2.2. SITE FACILITY CHECK/SECURITY

Personnel

Staff as assigned. Work in pairs.

Responsibilities

Take no action that will endanger yourself.

Start-up Actions

- Wear hard hat and identification vest, if available.
- Take appropriate tools, job description clipboard, and radio.
- Put batteries in flashlight, if necessary.

Operational Duties

As you complete the following tasks, observe the campus and report any damage by radio to the Command Post.

- Remember: If you are not acknowledged, you have not been heard. Repeat your transmission, being aware of other simultaneous transmissions.
- Lock gates and major external doors.
- Locate, control, and extinguish small fires as necessary.
- Check gas meter, and if gas is leaking, shut down the gas supply.
- Shut down electricity only if building has clear structural damage or if advised to do so by Command Post.
- Post yellow caution tape around damaged or hazardous areas.
- Verify that the campus is "locked down" and report the same to the Command Post.
- Advise the Command Post of all actions taken for information and proper logging.
- Be sure that the entire campus has been checked for safety hazards and damage.
- No damage should be repaired before full documentation, such as photographs and video evidence, is complete unless the repairs are essential to immediate life safety.
- Route fire, rescue, and police as appropriate.
- Direct all requests for information to the information officer.

Closing Down

- Return equipment and reusable supplies to Logistics.
- When authorized by the IC, close out all logs. Provide logs and other relevant documents to the Documentation Unit.

Equipment/Supplies

- Vest, hard hat, work gloves, and whistle
- Two-way radio, master keys, and clipboard with job description
- Bucket or duffel bag with goggles, flashlight, dust masks, yellow caution tape, and shutoff tools—for gas and water (crescent wrench)

5.2.3. STUDENT CARE

Personnel

Classroom teachers, substitute teachers, and staff members as assigned.

Responsibilities

Ensure the care and safety of all students on campus.

Start-up Actions

- Wear an identification vest, if available.
- Take a job description clipboard and radio.
- Check in with the Operations Section chief for a situation briefing.
- Make personnel assignments as needed.
- If evacuating,
  - verify that the assembly area and routes to it are safe.
  - count or observe the classrooms as they exit, to make sure that all classes evacuate.
  - initiate the setting up of portable toilet facilities and hand-washing stations.

Operational Duties

- Monitor the safety and well-being of the students and staff members in the assembly area.
- Administer minor first aid as needed.
- Support the student release process by releasing students with the appropriate paperwork.
- When necessary, provide water and food to students and staff members.
- Make arrangements for portable toilets if necessary, ensuring that students and staff members wash their hands thoroughly to prevent disease.
- Make arrangements to provide shelter for students and staff members.
- Arrange activities and keep students reassured.
- Update records of the number of students and staff members in the assembly area (or in the buildings).
- Direct all requests for information to the PIO.

Closing Down

- Return equipment and reusable supplies to Logistics.
- When authorized by the IC, close out all logs. Provide logs and other relevant documents to the Documentation Unit.

Equipment/Supplies

- Vest
- Clipboard with job description
- First aid kit
- Student activities: books, games, coloring books, and so on
- Forms:
  - Student Accounting
  - Notice of First Aid Care
- Two-way radio
- Water, food, and sanitation supplies

5.2.4. STUDENT RELEASE

Personnel

School secretary, available staff members, and disaster volunteers. Use a buddy system. The student release process is supported by designated runners.

Responsibilities

Assure the reunification of students with their parents or authorized adult through separate Request and Release Gates. Refer to section 9.12 Student/Family Reunification for details.

Start-up Actions

- Obtain and wear a vest or position identifier, if available.
- Check with the Operations Section chief for assignment to the Request Gate or Release Gate.
- Obtain necessary equipment and forms from Logistics.
- Secure the area against unauthorized access. Mark the gates with signs.
- Set up the Request Gate at the main student access gate. Use alphabetical grouping signs to organize parent requests.
- Have Student Release Forms available for parents outside of the fence at the Request Gate. Assign volunteers to assist.
- Set up the Release Gate some distance from the Request Gate.

Operational Duties

Follow the procedures outlined below to ensure the safe reunification of students with their parents or guardians:

- *Refer all requests for information to the POI. Do not spread rumors!*
- If volunteers arrive to help, send those with disaster volunteer badges with photo ID to Logistics. If they are not registered (i.e., do not have badges), direct them to the Operations Section chief.

Procedures

- The requesting adult fills out a Student Release Form, gives it to a staff member, and shows identification.
- The staff member verifies the identification, pulls the Emergency Card from the file, and verifies that the requester is listed on the card.
- The staff member instructs the requester to proceed to the Release Gate.
- If there are two copies of the Emergency Cards (one at each gate), the staff member files the Emergency Card in the out-box. If there is only one copy, a runner takes the card with the Student Release Form, and the staff member files a blank card with the student's name on it in the out-box.
- The designated runner takes the form(s) to the designated classroom.

Note: If a parent refuses to wait in line, don't argue. Note the time with appropriate comments on the Emergency Card and place it in the out-box.

If the student is with the class,

- a designated runner shows the Student Release Form to the teacher.
- The teacher marks the box "Sent with Runner."
- If appropriate, the teacher sends the parent copy of the First Aid Form with the runner.
- The runner walks the student(s) to the Release Gate.
- The runner hands the paperwork to the release personnel.
- Release staff members match the student to the requester, verify proof of identification, ask the requester to fill out and sign the lower portion of the Student Release Form, and release the student. Parents are given the Notice of First Aid Care Given, if applicable.

If the student is not with the class,

- the teacher makes the appropriate notation on the Student Release Form:
  - "Absent" if the student was never in school that day.
  - "First Aid" if the student is in the medical treatment area.
  - "Missing" if the student was in school but now cannot be located.
- The runner takes the Student Release Form to the Command Post.
- The Command Post verifies the student's location, if known, and directs the runner accordingly.
- If the designated runner is retrieving multiple students and one or more are missing, the runner walks the available students to the Release Gate before returning forms to the Command Post for verification.
- The parent should be notified of the missing student's status and escorted to a crisis counselor.
- If the student is in First Aid, the parent should be escorted to the safety emergency medical personnel.
- If the student was marked absent, the parent will be notified by the principal or designated staff member.

Closing Down

- At the direction of the Operations Section chief, return equipment and unused supplies to Logistics.
- Complete all paperwork and turn it in to the Documentation Unit.

Equipment/Supplies

- Job description clipboards
- Pens and stapler
- Box(es) of Emergency Cards
- Signs to mark Request Gate and Release Gate
- Signs for alphabetical grouping to organize the parents (A–F, etc.)
- Empty file boxes to use as out-boxes
- Student Release Forms (copies for every student)

5.3. Planning Section

5.3.1. PLANNING SECTION CHIEF

Responsibilities

This section is responsible for the collection, evaluation, documentation, and use of information about the development of the incident and the status of resources. Maintain accurate records and site map. Provide ongoing analysis of situation and resource status.

Start-up Actions

- Check in with the IC for a situation briefing.
- Obtain necessary equipment and supplies from Logistics.
- Put on a position identifier, such as a vest, if available.

Operational Duties

- Assume the duties of all Planning Section positions until staff members are available and assigned.
- As (or if) staff members are assigned, brief them on the situation and supervise their activities, utilizing the position checklists.
- Assist the IC in writing action plans.

Closing Down

- At the IC's direction, deactivate the section and close out all logs.
- Verify that the closing tasks of all Planning Section positions have been accomplished.
- Return equipment and reusable supplies to Logistics

Equipment/Supplies

- Two-way radio
- File box(es)
- Dry-erase pens
- Large laminated site map of campus
- Forms:
  - Emergency Time/Situation Report
  - Sample Log
  - Student Accounting Form
- Paper and pens

- Job description clipboard
- Tissues

5.3.2. DOCUMENTATION

Responsibilities

This section is responsible for the collection, evaluation, documentation, and use of information about the development of the incident and the status of resources.

Start-up Actions

- Check in with the Planning Section chief for a situation briefing.
- Obtain necessary equipment and supplies from Logistics.
- Put on a position identifier, such as a vest, if available.
- Determine whether there will be a Finance/Administration Section. If there is none, the Documentation clerk will be responsible for maintaining all records of any expenditures as well as all personnel timekeeping records.

Operational Duties

Records

- Maintain a time log of the incident, noting all actions and reports. (See the Sample Log in appendix D.)
- Record content of all radio communication with the district emergency operations center (EOC).
- Record verbal communication for basic content.
- Log in all written reports.
- File all reports for reference (file box).
- Important: A permanent log may be typed or rewritten at a later time for clarity and better understanding. Keep all original notes and records—they are legal documents.

Student and Staff Accounting

- Receive, record, and analyze Student Accounting Forms (refer to appendix D for a blank copy).
- Check off staff roster. Compute the number of students, staff members, and others on campus for the Situation Analysis. Update periodically.
- Report missing persons and site damage to the Command Post.
- Report first aid needs to the Medical Team leader.
- File forms for reference.

Closing Down

- Collect and file all paperwork and documentation from deactivating sections.
- Securely package and store these documents for future use.
- Return equipment and reusable supplies to Logistics.

Equipment/Supplies

- Two-way radio
- File box(es)
- Forms:
  - Emergency Time/Situation Report
  - Student Accounting Form
  - Sample Log
- Paper and pens
- Job description clipboard

5.3.3. SITUATION ANALYSIS

Responsibilities

This section is responsible for the collection, evaluation, documentation, and use of information about the development of the incident and the status of resources. Maintain accurate site map. Provide ongoing analysis of situation and resource status.

Start-up Actions

- Check in with the Planning Section chief for a situation briefing.
- Obtain necessary equipment and supplies from Logistics.
- Put on a position identifier, such as a vest, if available.

Operational Duties

Situation Status (Map)

- Collect, organize, and analyze situation information.
- Mark the site map appropriately as related reports are received, including but not limited to search and rescue reports and damage updates, giving a concise picture of the status of the campus.
- Preserve the map as a legal document until it is photographed.
- Use an areawide map to record information on major incidents, road closures, utility outages, and so on. (This information may be useful to staff members for planning routes home, etc.)

Situation Analysis

- Provide current situation assessments based on analysis of information received.
- Develop situation reports for the Command Post to support the action planning process.
- Think ahead and anticipate situations and problems before they occur.
- Report only to the Command Post personnel. Refer all other requests to the PIO.

Closing Down

- Close out all logs and turn all documents in to the Documentation Unit.
- Return equipment and reusable supplies to Logistics.

Equipment/Supplies

- Two-way radio
- Paper, pens, dry-erase pens, and tissues
- Job description clipboards
- Large laminated site map of campus
- File box(es)
- Map of county or local area

5.4. Logistics Section

5.4.1. LOGISTICS SECTION CHIEF

Responsibilities

The Logistics Section is responsible for providing facilities, services, personnel, equipment, and materials in support of the incident.

Start-up Actions

- Check in with the IC for a situation briefing.
- Open the supplies container or other storage facility.
- Put on position identifier, such as a vest, if available.
- Begin distribution of supplies and equipment as needed.
- Ensure that the Command Post and other facilities are set up as needed.

Operational Duties

- Assume the duties of all Logistics positions until staff members are available and assigned.
- As (or if) staff members are assigned, brief them on the situation and supervise their activities, utilizing the position checklists.
- Coordinate supplies, equipment, and personnel needs with the IC.
- Maintain security of the cargo container, supplies, and equipment.

Closing Down

- At the IC's direction, deactivate the section and close out all logs.
- Verify that closing tasks of all Logistics positions have been accomplished. Secure all equipment and supplies.

Equipment/Supplies

- Two-way radio
- Job description clipboard
- Paper and pens
- Cargo container or other storage facility and all emergency supplies stored on campus
- Clipboards with volunteer sign-in sheets
- Forms:
  - Inventory of emergency supplies on campus
  - Site Status Report
  - Communications Log
  - Message forms

5.4.2. SUPPLIES/FACILITIES

Responsibilities

This unit is responsible for providing facilities, equipment, supplies, and materials in support of the incident.

Start-up Actions

- Check in with the Logistics Section chief for a situation briefing.
- Open the supplies container or other storage facility if necessary.
- Put on a position identifier, such as a vest, if available.
- Begin distribution of supplies and equipment as needed.
- Set up the Command Post.

Operational Duties

- Maintain security of the cargo container, supplies, and equipment.
- Distribute supplies and equipment as needed.

- Assist team members in locating appropriate supplies and equipment.
- Set up the staging area, Sanitation Area, Feeding Area, and other facilities as needed.

Closing Down

- At the Logistics Section chief's direction, receive all equipment and unused supplies as they are returned.
- Secure all equipment and supplies.

Equipment/Supplies

- Two-way radio
- Job description clipboard
- Paper and pens
- Cargo container or other storage facility and all emergency supplies stored on campus
- Form: Inventory of emergency supplies at school/facility

5.4.3. STAFFING

Responsibilities

This unit is responsible for coordinating the assignment of personnel (staff members, students, and disaster volunteers) in support of the incident.

Start-up Actions

- Check in with the Logistics Section chief for a situation briefing.
- Put on a position identifier, such as a vest, if available.
- Open logs to list staff members, volunteers, and students who are awaiting assignment.

Operational Duties

- Deploy personnel as requested by the IC.
- Sign in volunteers, making sure volunteers are wearing their ID badges and are on the site disaster volunteer list. Unregistered volunteers should be sent to the Operations Section chief for instructions.

Closing Down

- Ask volunteers to sign out.
- At the Logistics Section chief's direction, close out all logs and turn them in to the Documentation Unit.
- Return all equipment and supplies.

Equipment/Supplies

- Two-way radio
- Job description clipboard
- Paper and pens
- Cargo container or other storage facility and all emergency supplies stored on campus
- Clipboards with volunteer sign-in sheets
- Forms:
  - Inventory of emergency supplies at school/facility
  - List of registered disaster volunteers

5.4.4. COMMUNICATIONS

Responsibilities

This unit is responsible for establishing, coordinating, and directing verbal and written communications within the school disaster site and with the school district. If the school district cannot be contacted, communications may be made with outside agencies when necessary.

Personnel

A school staff member with a campus two-way radio, supported by disaster volunteer runners.

Start-up Actions

- Set up the Communications station in a quiet location with access to the Command Post.
- Turn on radios and advise the Command Post when ready to accept traffic.

Operational Duties

- Communicate with the district EOC per district procedure. At the direction of the IC, report the status of students, staff members, and campus, using the Site Status Report form (refer to appendix D for a blank copy).
- Receive and write down all communications from the district EOC.
- Use designated runners to deliver messages to the IC with copies to the Planning Section chief.
- Maintain the Communications Log: date/time/originator/recipient.
- Follow Communications protocol. Do not contact the city directly if the district EOC is available.
- Direct the media or the public to the PIO.
- Monitor local emergency news:
  - Radio:
    - _____
    - _____
    - _____
    - _____
    - _____
    - _____
  - TV:
    - _____
    - _____
    - _____
    - _____
    - _____
  - Internet:
    - www.xxx.com

Closing Down

- Close out all logs, message forms, and so forth, and turn them over to the Documentation Unit.
- Return all equipment and unused supplies to Logistics.

Equipment/Supplies

- Two-way radios with spare batteries for each
- Job description clipboard

- Paper and pens
- Table and chairs
- AM/FM radio
- File boxes and tote tray for outgoing messages
- Forms:
  - Site Status Report
  - Message forms

5.5. Finance/Administration Section

5.5.1. FINANCE/ADMINISTRATION SECTION CHIEF

Responsibilities

The Finance/Administration Section is responsible for financial tracking, procurement, and cost analysis related to the disaster or emergency. It maintains financial records and tracks and records staff hours.

Start-up Actions

- Check in with the IC for a situation briefing.
- Put on a position identifier, such as a vest, if available.
- Locate and set up work space.
- Check in with the Documentation clerk to collect records and information that relate to personnel timekeeping and/or purchasing.

Operational Duties

- Assume the duties of all Finance/Administration positions until staff members are available and assigned.
- As (or if) staff members are assigned, brief them on the situation and supervise their activities, utilizing the position checklists.

Closing Down

- At the IC's direction, deactivate the section and close out all logs.
- Verify that the closing tasks of all Finance/Administration positions have been accomplished. Secure all documents and records.

Equipment/Supplies

- Job description clipboard
- Paper and pens
- Form: Staff Duty Log

5.5.2. TIMEKEEPING

Responsibilities

This unit is responsible for maintaining accurate and complete records of staff hours.

Start-up Actions

- Check in with the Finance/Administration Section chief for a situation briefing.
- Put on a position identifier, such as a vest, if available.

- Locate and set up work space.
- Check in with the Documentation clerk to collect records and information that relate to personnel timekeeping.

Operational Duties

- Meet with the Finance/Administration Section chief to determine the process for tracking regular and overtime hours of the staff.
- Ensure that accurate records are kept of all staff members, indicating the hours worked.
- If district personnel members not normally assigned to the site are working, be sure that records of their hours are kept.

Closing Down

- Close out all logs.
- Secure all documents and records.

Equipment/Supplies

- Job description clipboard
- Staff Duty Log

5.5.3. PURCHASING

Responsibilities

This unit is responsible for maintaining accurate and complete records of purchases. Most purchases will be made at the district level; however, in emergency situations, it may be necessary for school sites to acquire certain items quickly.

Start-up Actions

- Check in with the Finance/Administration Section chief for a situation briefing.
- Put on a position identifier, such as a vest, if available.
- Locate and set up work space.
- Check in with the Documentation clerk to collect records and information that relate to purchasing.

Operational Duties

- Meet with the Finance/Administration Section chief to determine the process for tracking purchases.
- Support Logistics in making any purchases that have been approved by the IC.

Closing Down

- Close out all logs.
- Secure all documents and records.

Equipment/Supplies

- Job description clipboard
- Paper and pens

CHAPTER SIX

Response Resources

This section provides a summary of supplementary emergency preparedness and response resources within the school system (SS).

6.1. Personnel

Tables 6.1 through 6.5 identify the following:

- Listing of staff members with specialty skills (e.g., language) that could/would render assistance to persons with special needs.
- Listings of students and staff members with special needs requiring special assistance during emergencies, including pertinent support needs and "buddy" arrangements.

6.2. External Agencies and Response Teaming Partners

Table 6.6 provides a listing of external emergency response and support agencies and organizations, including brief summaries of respective roles and capabilities that could/would respond to emergency events associated with SS operations and events.

6.3. Emergency Operations Center

Table 6.7 identifies the primary and backup SS district emergency operations center (EOC) locations and contact information.

6.4. Emergency Evacuation/Receiving Facilities

Table 6.8 provides a comprehensive listing of school emergency evacuation receiving sites and staging information.

6.5. Contact List for Charter and Parochial Schools

Table 6.9 provides a comprehensive listing of emergency contacts for charter and parochial schools located within the school district.

6.6. Emergency Equipment and Supplies

Tables 6.10 to 6.12 provide suggested listings of emergency equipment and supplies to be positioned throughout SS district facilities, including in the district EOC, schools, and buses, to support emergency response operations.

Table 6.1. Staff Members with Skills in Medical Care

Name	School/Facility	Room #	Training/Certification	Cell Phone #

Table 6.2. Bi/Multilingual Staff Members

Name	School/Facility	Room #	Language(s)	Cell Phone #

Table 6.3. Staff Members with Sign Language Skills

Name	School/Facility	Room #	Cell Phone #	Comments

Table 6.4. Students Needing Special Assistance in an Emergency

Name	Homeroom # Bus #	Description of Assistance Needed	Person(s) Assigned to Assist

Table 6.5. School System Staff Member Needing Special Assistance in an Emergency

Name	Location Room #	Description of Assistance Needed	Person(s) Assigned to Assist

Table 6.6. Local, County, State, and Federal Agency Supplemental Contacts and Support Information

Agency	Role	24-Hour Phone No.
Emergency Medical Service	• Emergency medical response	
Fire Department	• Fire response • Hazardous material spill/release response • Search and rescue • Emergency medical response • Evacuation • Assistance for special needs groups • Damage assessment • Terrorism response	911
Police Department	• Law enforcement • Traffic control • Area control • Evacuation • Search and rescue • Communications	911
Transit System	• Mass transportation	
American Red Cross	• Student shelter operations • Student care and release operations • First aid shelters • Responder food services	
Bureau of Alcohol, Tobacco, Firearms, and Explosives	• Lead agency for arson and nonterrorist bombings • Arson and Bomb Crime Lab	
Centers for Disease Control and Prevention	• Source for general information on disease-related issues • Manages the National Strategic Stockpile • Responds to biological attacks and epidemics • Activated via safety in consultation with health department	
City of Office of the Mayor	• Safety support • Works support	
Federal Bureau of Investigation	• Lead agency for terrorism and weapons of mass destruction incidents • High-level crime scene investigations • Lead agency for most federal crimes • Coordinates requests for federal resources—military and civilian • Activated via Safety	
Federal Emergency Management Agency	• Coordinates federal disaster assistance • Provides disaster-related funding assistance	
Food and Drug Administration	• Source for general information on food safety and related issues • Food contamination • Food borne illnesses and surveillance	

Agency	Role	24-Hour Phone No.
Hospitals — _____ — _____ — _____ — _____	• Medical Support	
Local Radio — _____ — _____ — _____ — _____	• Broadcast emergency information and instructions	
Local TV — _____ — _____ — _____ — _____	• Broadcast emergency information and instructions	
Internet — www.xxx.com	• Broadcast and observe emergency information and news	
National Response Center	• Regulatory reporting of hazardous materials spill in excess of Reportable Quantities (RQs)	
State Emergency Management Agency	• Activation of state and multi-county emergency resources (equipment and personnel)	
State Environmental Protection Agency	• On-scene direction of hazardous materials spills cleanup	
State National Guard	• Disaster Recovery Assistance • Law Enforcement Support • Civil Support Team • Activation via Safety	
State Patrol	• Law enforcement on state property • Traffic control on state highways	
Department of Health	• Health response and coordination • Infectious disease surveillance • Quarantine matters	
County Emergency Management Agency	• Coordination with officials in affected jurisdictions • Activation and coordination of local, county, regional, and state agency, personnel, and equipment resources • Activated via safety agency	

(continued)

Table 6.6. (*continued*)

Agency	Role	24-Hour Phone No.
County Sheriff	• Law enforcement	
US Environmental Protection Agency	• Management of hazardous materials spills • Conducts investigations regarding environmental matters	

Table 6.7. Contacts: School System Emergency Operations Center

Primary Emergency Operations Center	
Secondary Emergency Operations Center	

Table 6.8. Evacuation Partners School Facility

Evacuating School/Facility	Receiving School/Facility	Evacuating School/Facility	Receiving School/Facility	Evacuating School/Facility	Receiving School/Facility

Note: If it becomes necessary to evacuate school/facility buildings, the principal/building manager, in consultation with the SS superintendent/designee, may decide to evacuate and transport students and staff members to another SS school/facility. The designated partner schools/facilities are listed above.

This partnership is designed to avoid problems and liability of dismissing young children home early without proper supervision. This decision will be influenced by many related conditions at the time of the incident including time of day, season of the year, urgency of the evacuation, and weather or civil conditions within the community.

The receiving location will be the gymnasium, cafcteria, library, or othcr common arcas, as indicated, to house and care for evacuated students for the remainder of the school day.

Bus schedules must be adjusted to accommodate these circumstances.

Table 6.9. Contact List for Charter and Parochial Schools

School	Contact	Phone	Fax	E-mail

Table 6.10.   Emergency Operations Center Emergency Kit

The following items should be maintained in the SS emergency operations center and should be available for transport to any designated incident site and/or alternate command:
1. SS Crisis Management Plan
2. Crisis and Crisis Response Team responsibilities checklists
3. Master keys to all school facility doors
4. MSS of evacuation routes showing all primary and alternate routes and staging areas
5. Aerial photos of schools/campus including surrounding areas
6. MSS of schools/campus and surrounding areas showing transportation routes and major traffic patterns
7. School/facility layout drawings showing classroom layouts, floor plans, and exits of the building and grounds, including information about main leads for water, gas, electricity, cable, telephone, telephone wall jacks, computer locations, alarm and sprinkler systems, hazardous materials location, elevators, and entrances. Possible threat areas (e.g., chemistry laboratory, biology laboratory, and welding and wood shop areas that could also become a haven for weapons, etc.), locations of fire alarm turnoff, sprinkler system turnoff, utility shutoff valves, cable television shutoff, and emergency response supplies and first aid supply boxes.
8. Fire alarm turnoff procedures
9. Sprinkler system turnoff procedures
10. Utility shutoff procedures
11. Cable television satellite feed shutoff procedures
12. Student photos
13. Incident and Crisis Management Team member contact information
14. Maps showing Designated Command Post and staging areas
15. Emergency Resource Listing (Copy of Crisis Management Plan in section 5; see table 4.3)
16. Student Disposition Forms and Emergency Data Cards
17. Student attendance roster
18. List of students with special needs
19. Faculty/staff roster with the following: a.   list indicating those with first aid, CPR, and/or EMT training   b.   list of mobile/cellular telephone numbers
20. Emergency communication equipment (two-way radio, cellular telephones, and fully charged battery-operated bullhorn)
21. Phone lists: a.   Community Emergency Numbers   • General emergency number—911   • Police department/sheriff   • Rescue/ambulance   • Fire department   • Poison Control Center   • Local hospitals   b.   School Numbers: • Central Office telephone and fax numbers   • List of portable telephones and beeper numbers of division staff members   • Extension numbers for school security, school health nurse, guidance service, and other support staff   c.   Other Resource Numbers: • Home/work telephone numbers of parent networks, school volunteers, local clergy, and other resources previously identified   • Student roster including home and emergency phone numbers
22. Master schedule
23. Name tags and sign-in sheet for Crisis Response Team members and community resource people
24. Sample statements/letters for use in notifying faculty members, students, and parents about crisis incident

Table 6.11. Bus Emergency Equipment

Each SS bus should be equipped with the following emergency equipment:	
AM Portable Radio	First Aid Book
District Radio	First Aid Supplies
Emergency Blanket	Food Bars
Flashlight	Safety Lightsticks
Extra Batteries (flashlight/radio)	Sanitation Supplies

Table 6.12. Suggested School Emergency Supplies

Item	Quantity
Blankets	10
Large battery-operated radio with batteries	1
Heavy-duty flashlights with batteries and bulbs	4
Whistles (for communicating with staff members and students)	4
Clipboards	4
Ink pens	6
Medium garbage bags	4 packages (40 count)
Large 3-ply garbage bags	4 packages (20 count)
Plastic buckets—5 gallon	6
Pads of paper	4
Scotch tape	4 rolls
Bed sheet strips (to be used as optional bandages)	4

CHAPTER SEVEN

Emergency Response Flip Charts

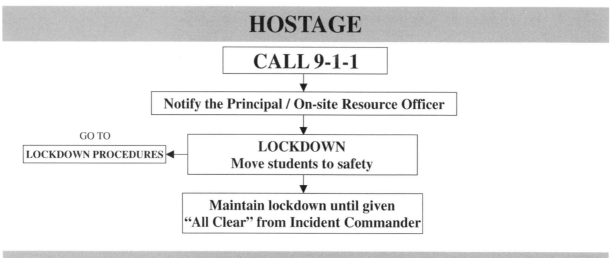

CALL 9-1-1

↓

Notify the Principal / On-site Resource Officer

↓

GO TO
LOCKDOWN PROCEDURES ◄—— **LOCKDOWN**
Move students to safety

↓

**Maintain lockdown until given
"All Clear" from Incident Commander**

HOSTAGE

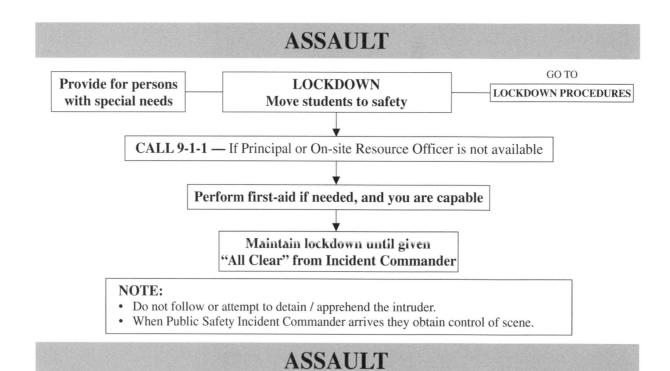

**Provide for persons
with special needs** —— **LOCKDOWN**
Move students to safety —— GO TO
LOCKDOWN PROCEDURES

↓

CALL 9-1-1 — If Principal or On-site Resource Officer is not available

↓

Perform first-aid if needed, and you are capable

↓

**Maintain lockdown until given
"All Clear" from Incident Commander**

NOTE:
- Do not follow or attempt to detain / apprehend the intruder.
- When Public Safety Incident Commander arrives they obtain control of scene.

ASSAULT

Reverse Evacuation is the process of moving all students and staff inside the building because there is a threat outside the building.

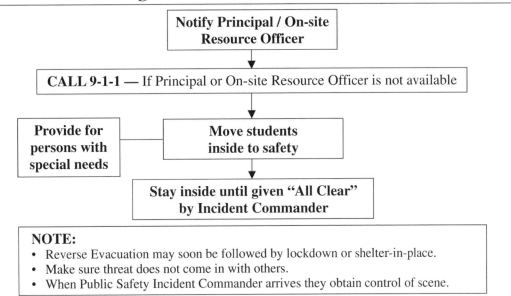

Notify Principal / On-site Resource Officer

↓

CALL 9-1-1 — If Principal or On-site Resource Officer is not available

↓

Provide for persons with special needs — Move students inside to safety

↓

Stay inside until given "All Clear" by Incident Commander

NOTE:
- Reverse Evacuation may soon be followed by lockdown or shelter-in-place.
- Make sure threat does not come in with others.
- When Public Safety Incident Commander arrives they obtain control of scene.

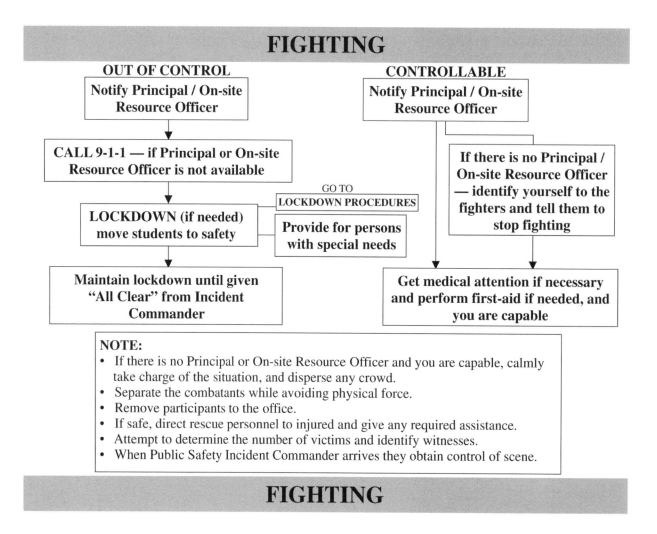

OUT OF CONTROL

Notify Principal / On-site Resource Officer

↓

CALL 9-1-1 — if Principal or On-site Resource Officer is not available

↓

LOCKDOWN (if needed) move students to safety

GO TO
LOCKDOWN PROCEDURES

Provide for persons with special needs

↓

Maintain lockdown until given "All Clear" from Incident Commander

CONTROLLABLE

Notify Principal / On-site Resource Officer

If there is no Principal / On-site Resource Officer — identify yourself to the fighters and tell them to stop fighting

↓

Get medical attention if necessary and perform first-aid if needed, and you are capable

NOTE:
- If there is no Principal or On-site Resource Officer and you are capable, calmly take charge of the situation, and disperse any crowd.
- Separate the combatants while avoiding physical force.
- Remove participants to the office.
- If safe, direct rescue personnel to injured and give any required assistance.
- Attempt to determine the number of victims and identify witnesses.
- When Public Safety Incident Commander arrives they obtain control of scene.

WEAPONS

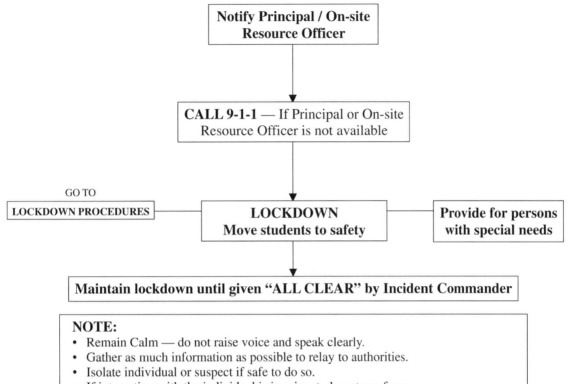

Notify Principal / On-site Resource Officer

↓

CALL 9-1-1 — If Principal or On-site Resource Officer is not available

↓

GO TO
LOCKDOWN PROCEDURES — **LOCKDOWN** Move students to safety — Provide for persons with special needs

↓

Maintain lockdown until given "ALL CLEAR" by Incident Commander

NOTE:
- Remain Calm — do not raise voice and speak clearly.
- Gather as much information as possible to relay to authorities.
- Isolate individual or suspect if safe to do so.
- If interaction with the individual is imminent, do not use force.
- When Public Safety Incident Commander arrives they obtain control of scene.

WEAPONS

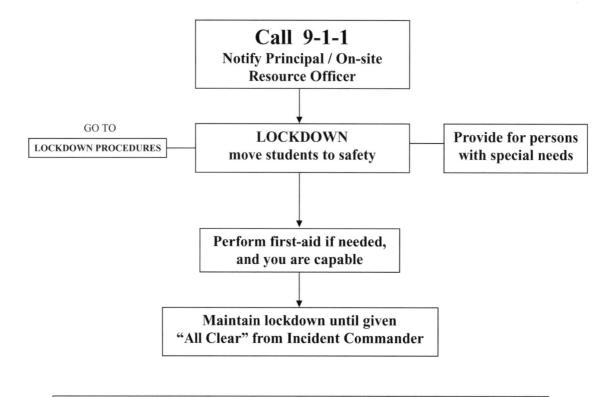

Call 9-1-1
Notify Principal / On-site
Resource Officer

GO TO
LOCKDOWN PROCEDURES

LOCKDOWN
move students to safety

**Provide for persons
with special needs**

**Perform first-aid if needed,
and you are capable**

**Maintain lockdown until given
"All Clear" from Incident Commander**

NOTE:
- If safe, direct rescue personnel to injured and give any required assistance.
- When Public Safety Incident Commander arrives they obtain control of scene.
- Keep students away from doors and windows.

GAS LEAK / CHEMICAL / HAZMAT SPILL

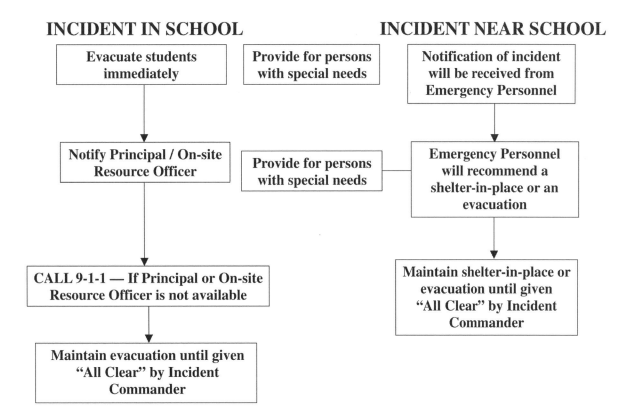

INCIDENT IN SCHOOL

INCIDENT NEAR SCHOOL

Evacuate students immediately

Provide for persons with special needs

Notification of incident will be received from Emergency Personnel

↓

Notify Principal / On-site Resource Officer

Provide for persons with special needs

Emergency Personnel will recommend a shelter-in-place or an evacuation

↓

CALL 9-1-1 — If Principal or On-site Resource Officer is not available

Maintain shelter-in-place or evacuation until given "All Clear" by Incident Commander

↓

Maintain evacuation until given "All Clear" by Incident Commander

NOTE:
- Keep students and staff from going near the area of contamination.
- If evacuation is necessary take attendance regularly.
- When Public Safety Incident Commander arrives they obtain control of scene.

GAS LEAK / CHEMICAL / HAZMAT SPILL

Evacuation should occur when there is some kind of a threat that can directly affect those in the school facility. Direction should be given as to how far evacuees need to go.

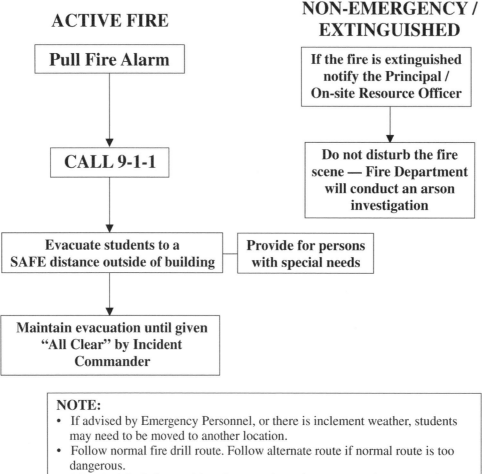

ACTIVE FIRE

Pull Fire Alarm

↓

CALL 9-1-1

↓

Evacuate students to a SAFE distance outside of building —— **Provide for persons with special needs**

↓

Maintain evacuation until given "All Clear" by Incident Commander

NON-EMERGENCY / EXTINGUISHED

If the fire is extinguished notify the Principal / On-site Resource Officer

↓

Do not disturb the fire scene — Fire Department will conduct an arson investigation

NOTE:
- If advised by Emergency Personnel, or there is inclement weather, students may need to be moved to another location.
- Follow normal fire drill route. Follow alternate route if normal route is too dangerous.
- When Public Safety Incident Commander arrives they obtain control of scene.
- False alarms should be called in to Student Services / Security.
- If the principal is not available, non-emergency fires that have been extinguished should be reported to the Fire Department at xxx-xxx-xxxx.

Shelter-in-Place provides refuge for students, staff and public within a school building during an emergency. Shelters are located in areas that maximize the safety of inhabitants. Safe areas may change depending on emergency.

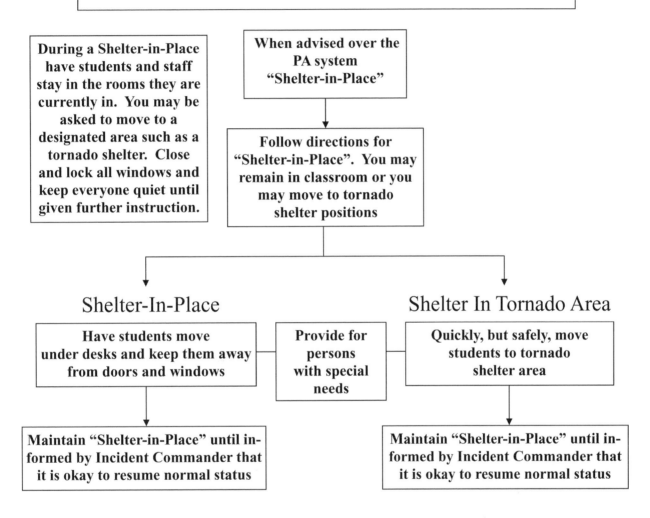

During a Shelter-in-Place have students and staff stay in the rooms they are currently in. You may be asked to move to a designated area such as a tornado shelter. Close and lock all windows and keep everyone quiet until given further instruction.

When advised over the PA system "Shelter-in-Place"

Follow directions for "Shelter-in-Place". You may remain in classroom or you may move to tornado shelter positions

Shelter-In-Place

Have students move under desks and keep them away from doors and windows

Provide for persons with special needs

Maintain "Shelter-in-Place" until informed by Incident Commander that it is okay to resume normal status

Shelter In Tornado Area

Quickly, but safely, move students to tornado shelter area

Maintain "Shelter-in-Place" until informed by Incident Commander that it is okay to resume normal status

NOTE:
- Keep everyone calm.
- Keep away from doors and windows.
- When Public Safety Incident Commander arrives they obtain control of scene.
- Sheltering-in-Place may need to happen in many situations and often should be done if deemed necessary before the announcement is given.

LOCKDOWN PROCEDURES

Lockdown - those conditions requiring complete separation and protection of school staff and students from any situation regarding an existing internal or external situation that could directly threaten their safety.

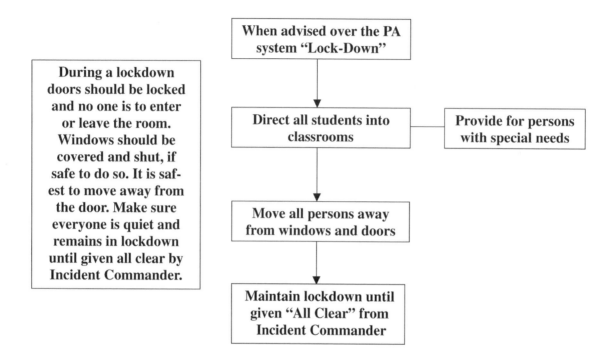

During a lockdown doors should be locked and no one is to enter or leave the room. Windows should be covered and shut, if safe to do so. It is safest to move away from the door. Make sure everyone is quiet and remains in lockdown until given all clear by Incident Commander.

When advised over the PA system "Lock-Down"

↓

Direct all students into classrooms —— Provide for persons with special needs

↓

Move all persons away from windows and doors

↓

Maintain lockdown until given "All Clear" from Incident Commander

---

NOTE:
- PA announcement will be in plain language and provide as much information about the incident as possible.
- Under lockdown, conditions in a specific classroom can be communicated using color coded cards. A card, either posted in the window, or slipped under the door, can alert emergency responders to the status of students in individual classrooms:
    - Green Card —— NO injuries
    - Yellow Card —— Injuries have occurred but are minor.
    - Red Card —— Injuries have occurred and medical assistance is needed immediately.
- When Public Safety Incident Commander arrives they obtain control of scene.

LOCKDOWN PROCEDURES

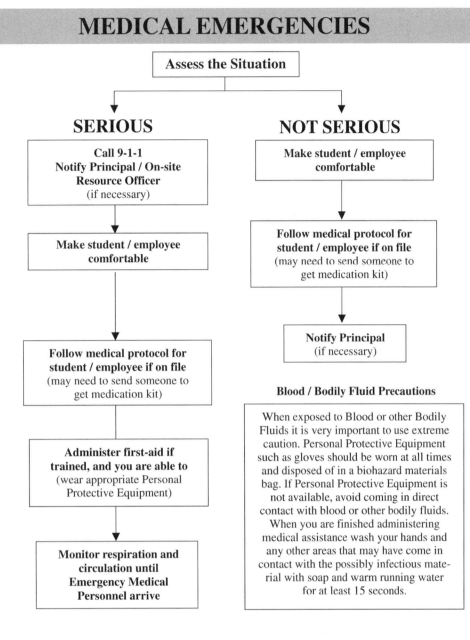

Assess the Situation

SERIOUS

Call 9-1-1
Notify Principal / On-site
Resource Officer
(if necessary)

Make student / employee
comfortable

Follow medical protocol for
student / employee if on file
(may need to send someone to
get medication kit)

Administer first-aid if
trained, and you are able to
(wear appropriate Personal
Protective Equipment)

Monitor respiration and
circulation until
Emergency Medical
Personnel arrive

NOT SERIOUS

Make student / employee
comfortable

Follow medical protocol for
student / employee if on file
(may need to send someone to
get medication kit)

Notify Principal
(if necessary)

Blood / Bodily Fluid Precautions

When exposed to Blood or other Bodily
Fluids it is very important to use extreme
caution. Personal Protective Equipment
such as gloves should be worn at all times
and disposed of in a biohazard materials
bag. If Personal Protective Equipment is
not available, avoid coming in direct
contact with blood or other bodily fluids.
When you are finished administering
medical assistance wash your hands and
any other areas that may have come in
contact with the possibly infectious material with soap and warm running water
for at least 15 seconds.

NOTE:
- Stay Calm!
- **ONLY** move the person if there is a question of their, or your, safety.
- If poisoning suspected, call the Poison Control Center, 1-800-222-1222 and follow medical direction.
- Record time and site of insect sting, ingestion of food, exposure to other allergen; and name of medicine, dosage and time; if appropriate.
- When Public Safety Incident Commander arrives they obtain control of scene.
- For clean up of bodily fluids refer to the guidelines regarding clean-up of potentially infectious materials.

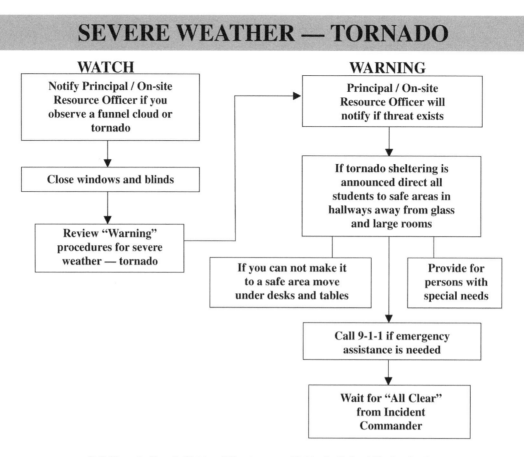

WATCH

Notify Principal / On-site Resource Officer if you observe a funnel cloud or tornado

↓

Close windows and blinds

↓

Review "Warning" procedures for severe weather — tornado

WARNING

Principal / On-site Resource Officer will notify if threat exists

↓

If tornado sheltering is announced direct all students to safe areas in hallways away from glass and large rooms

If you can not make it to a safe area move under desks and tables

Provide for persons with special needs

↓

Call 9-1-1 if emergency assistance is needed

↓

Wait for "All Clear" from Incident Commander

Definitions of a Tornado Watch and Warning as provided by the National Weather Service:

Tornado Watch

This is issued by the National Weather Service when conditions are favorable for the development of tornadoes in and close to the watch area. Their size can vary depending on the weather situation. They are usually issued for a duration of 4 to 8 hours. They normally are issued well in advance of the actual occurrence of sever weather. During the watch, people should review tornado safety rules and be prepared to move to a place of safety if threatening weather approaches.

Tornado Warning

This is issued when a tornado is indicated or sighted by spotters; therefore, people in the affected area should seek safe shelter immediately. They can be issued without a Tornado Watch being already in effect. They are usually issued for a duration of 30 minutes.

NOTE:
- Stay Calm!
- Remind teachers to take class rosters.
- Remain in safe areas until warning expires or until incident commander has issued an "All Clear" signal.
- Keep everyone away from doors, windows and rooms with high ceilings.
- When Public Safety Incident Commander arrives they obtain control of scene.

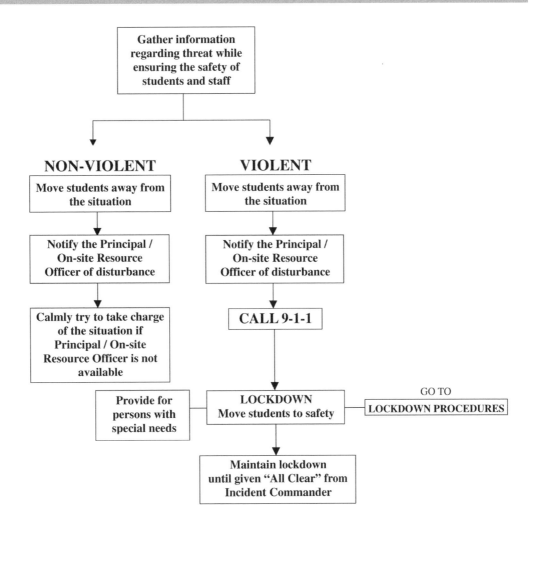

Gather information regarding threat while ensuring the safety of students and staff

NON-VIOLENT

Move students away from the situation

Notify the Principal / On-site Resource Officer of disturbance

Calmly try to take charge of the situation if Principal / On-site Resource Officer is not available

VIOLENT

Move students away from the situation

Notify the Principal / On-site Resource Officer of disturbance

CALL 9-1-1

Provide for persons with special needs

LOCKDOWN
Move students to safety

GO TO
LOCKDOWN PROCEDURES

Maintain lockdown until given "All Clear" from Incident Commander

NOTE:
- If safe, direct rescue personnel to injured and give any required assistance.
- When Public Safety Incident Commander arrives they obtain control of scene.
- Take class attendance to see who is accounted for and who is not.

A biological or bioterrorism incident is an event where an infectious agent (viral or bacterial) has been used to threaten harm to an individual(s).

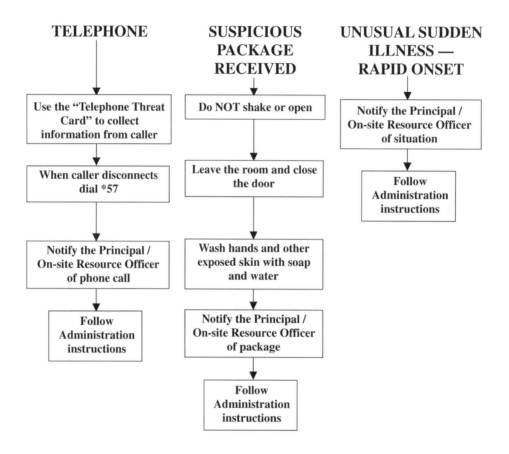

TELEPHONE

Use the "Telephone Threat Card" to collect information from caller

↓

When caller disconnects dial *57

↓

Notify the Principal / On-site Resource Officer of phone call

↓

Follow Administration instructions

SUSPICIOUS PACKAGE RECEIVED

Do NOT shake or open

↓

Leave the room and close the door

↓

Wash hands and other exposed skin with soap and water

↓

Notify the Principal / On-site Resource Officer of package

↓

Follow Administration instructions

UNUSUAL SUDDEN ILLNESS — RAPID ONSET

Notify the Principal / On-site Resource Officer of situation

↓

Follow Administration instructions

NOTE:
- Isolate the area.
- Do not touch or move the object.
- Do not attempt to cover or hide the device.
- Avoid using any electrical devices around the object—as they could trigger the device.
- When Public Safety Incident Commander arrives they obtain control of scene.

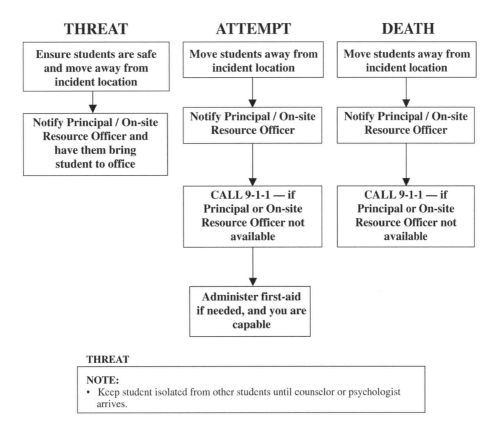

THREAT	ATTEMPT	DEATH
Ensure students are safe and move away from incident location	Move students away from incident location	Move students away from incident location
Notify Principal / On-site Resource Officer and have them bring student to office	Notify Principal / On-site Resource Officer	Notify Principal / On-site Resource Officer
	CALL 9-1-1 — if Principal or On-site Resource Officer not available	CALL 9-1-1 — if Principal or On-site Resource Officer not available
	Administer first-aid if needed, and you are capable	

THREAT

NOTE:
- Keep student isolated from other students until counselor or psychologist arrives.

ATTEMPT

NOTE:
- DO NOT divulge the fact that death has/may have occurred — This is the role of Public/Hospital medical officials.
- When Public Safety Incident Commander arrives they obtain control of scene.

DEATH

NOTE:
- Move students and staff away from victim and close off the area.
- DO NOT touch the victim or anything at the scene.
- When Public Safety Incident Commander arrives they obtain control of scene.

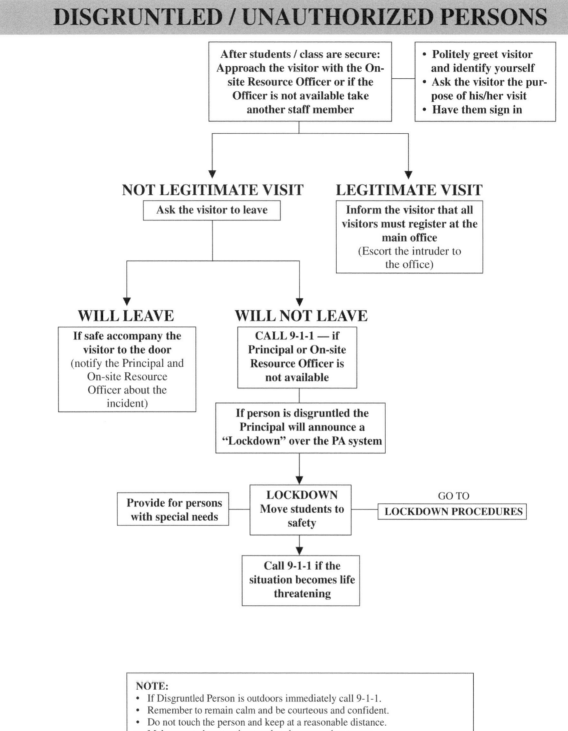

After students / class are secure:
Approach the visitor with the On-site Resource Officer or if the Officer is not available take another staff member

- Politely greet visitor and identify yourself
- Ask the visitor the purpose of his/her visit
- Have them sign in

NOT LEGITIMATE VISIT
Ask the visitor to leave

LEGITIMATE VISIT
Inform the visitor that all visitors must register at the main office
(Escort the intruder to the office)

WILL LEAVE
If safe accompany the visitor to the door
(notify the Principal and On-site Resource Officer about the incident)

WILL NOT LEAVE
CALL 9-1-1 — if Principal or On-site Resource Officer is not available

If person is disgruntled the Principal will announce a "Lockdown" over the PA system

Provide for persons with special needs

LOCKDOWN
Move students to safety

GO TO
LOCKDOWN PROCEDURES

Call 9-1-1 if the situation becomes life threatening

NOTE:
- If Disgruntled Person is outdoors immediately call 9-1-1.
- Remember to remain calm and be courteous and confident.
- Do not touch the person and keep at a reasonable distance.
- Make sure to be attentive to what the person has to say.
- When Public Safety Incident Commander arrives they obtain control of scene.

BOMB / BOMB THREAT

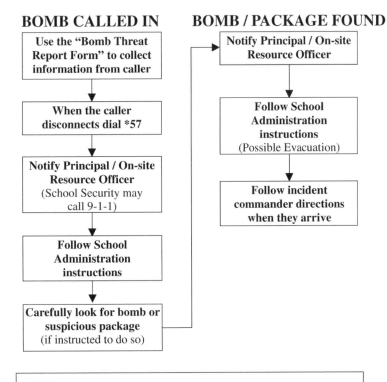

BOMB CALLED IN

Use the "Bomb Threat Report Form" to collect information from caller

↓

When the caller disconnects dial *57

↓

Notify Principal / On-site Resource Officer
(School Security may call 9-1-1)

↓

Follow School Administration instructions

↓

Carefully look for bomb or suspicious package
(if instructed to do so)

BOMB / PACKAGE FOUND

Notify Principal / On-site Resource Officer

↓

Follow School Administration instructions
(Possible Evacuation)

↓

Follow incident commander directions when they arrive

NOTE:
- Isolate area.
- Do not touch or move the object.
- Do not attempt to cover or hide the device.
- Avoid using any electrical devices around the object — as they could trigger the device.
- When Public Safety Incident Commander arrives they obtain control of scene.

BOMB THREAT REPORT FORM

Number at which call is received:

(   ) _____

Time: _____ pm / am   Date: ___ / ___ / ___

Sex of Caller: ___ M / F ___   Race: _____

Length of Call: min. _____ sec. _____ Age: _____

Exact Wording of the Threat:
(Place on another sheet)

QUESTIONS TO ASK?

When is the bomb going to explode?

Where is it right now?

What does it look like?

What kind of bomb is it?

What will cause it to explode?

Did you place the bomb?

Why?

What is your address?

What is your name?

CALLER'S VOICE

_____ Calm	_____ Nasal
_____ Angry	_____ Stutter
_____ Excited	_____ Lisp
_____ Slow	_____ Raspy
_____ Rapid	_____ Deep
_____ Soft	_____ Ragged
_____ Loud	_____ Clearing throat
_____ Laughter	_____ Deep breathing
_____ Crying	_____ Cracking voice
_____ Normal	_____ Disguised
_____ Distinct	_____ Accent
_____ Slurred	_____ Familiar

If voice is familiar, whom did it sound like?

_____

_____

Background sounds:

_____ Street noises	_____ Machinery
_____ Animal noises	_____ Clear
_____ Voices	_____ Static
_____ PA System	_____ Local
_____ Music	_____ House
_____ Motor	

Other Noises:

_____

_____

_____

Threat Language:

_____ Foul	_____ Taped
_____ Irrational	_____ Incoherent
_____ Message read by threat maker	
_____ Well spoken (educated)	

Remarks: _____

_____

_____

Report call immediately to:
Principal
(Principal will begin Notification Chart)

Date: ___ / ___ / ___   Phone: (   ) _____

Name: _____

NOTE: WHEN CALL IS OVER—HANG UP AND IMMEDIATELY DIAL *57

BOMB / BOMB THREAT

CHAPTER EIGHT

District Incident-Specific Response Protocols

Emergency response protocols supplement emergency procedures encompassed within the Emergency Response Flip Charts maintained at each school and within each classroom. The flip charts distill emergency actions into minimal clear and concise steps to ensure maximum effectiveness during times of need.

These procedures provide expanded action items and considerations for use by the district Crisis Management Team (CMT) and the Crisis Response Team (CRT) leaders in response to operations planning. These procedures further provide key information for incorporation into emergency preparedness and response training sessions and exercises.

8.1. Accidents at School

Accidents can happen at any time during school activities, for example, on the playground, in the building or classroom, in physical education, and so forth. Responding appropriately to the needs of victims of the accident is of utmost importance.

MINOR ACCIDENTS AND INJURIES

For minor accidents, have student/staff member taken to the school clinic by a responsible person for assistance.

MORE SERIOUS ACCIDENTAL INJURY

The following procedures should be taken in the event of a more serious accidental injury to students and staff members:

- The first adult staff member on the scene assumes responsibility for appropriate procedures to be taken until an administrator arrives.
  —Keep injured person still and quiet.
  —Check for breathing and bleeding; administer immediate first aid if necessary and if trained to do so.
  —Call 911 if appropriate; give necessary information.
  —Send someone to get victim's medical sheet/card, if available.
  —Call for administrative assistance, nurse.
  —Collect the facts of the cause or nature of the injury.

- The administrator or designee will do as follows:
  —Initiate notification per the flow chart shown in figure 2.2.
  —Contact parent/guardian or relative/spouse for student/employee, if needed.
  —Complete necessary forms: accident report, insurance forms, and so on.

8.2. Accidents to and from School

In the event of accidents involving an employee or student who is on the way to or from school, first determine whether or not help is on the way. If help is not on the way, do as follows:

- Call 911.
- Notify principal.
- Initiate notification per the flow chart shown in figure 2.2.
- Notify parents, spouse, or individual on Emergency Card.

If help is on the way, do as follows:

- If not reached earlier, continue to try to notify parents, spouse, or named individual.
- If parents, spouse, or closest relatives are not available, discuss situation with an associate at the place of employment of the parents, guardian, spouse, or closest relative.
- Send an appropriate staff member (security, counselor, or person trained in emergency preparedness/response skills) to observe the situation and report back as directed.
- Assess need to activate the school system (SS) CMT.
- Conduct incident assessment to determine need to activate the SS CRT. Refer to incident assessment protocols included in tables 2.1 and 2.2.

8.3. After-School Events

The school may experience an emergency during an after-school event (i.e., sports event, concert, etc.). These may be outdoor or indoor events. This plan addresses those possibilities. There will be a school representative on duty at each event. The school representative will be familiar with these procedures and will be responsible for initiating their implementation. The school representative will carry a walkie-talkie, a cell phone, a building master key, and these instructions.

FOR ALL SERIOUS INCIDENTS OR THREATS

- Call 911.
- Initiate SS notifications per the flow chart shown in figure 2.2.

FOR OUTDOOR EVENTS

- Severe weather conditions (heavy rain, hail, high winds, lightning, tornado, and so on):
  —Instruct all personnel to enter the designated and posted storm shelter area on the bottom floor of the school. The school representative will have the building master key and be able to unlock the entrances to be used. All school representatives will be familiar with light switches that may be needed. Use the small classrooms and interior hallways that have been designated as storm shelters. Do not allow individuals to enter/remain in the auditorium, cafeteria, and other spaces with large roof expanses; they are not safe under these conditions.

—If the building principal is not present, notify the building principal of the situation by calling her or him at home. The superintendent will in turn be notified.

- Group fight, disturbance:
  —Notify the police.
  —Use the public address (PA) system to announce that all persons need to return to the bleachers/seats and that anyone creating a disturbance will be arrested.
  —The school representative should be ready to sign a police complaint if necessary to conduct an arrest.
  —If the building principal is not present, notify the building principal of the situation by calling her or him at home. The superintendent will in turn be notified.
- Gun fire:
  —Notify the police and ask that an ambulance be dispatched as well. Be specific about the location of the threat and the best approach to the incident site.
  —Use the PA system to give the following instructions: Please remain where you are, get down on the ground or the floor of the bleachers, remain quiet, and await further instructions. Help is on the way. Do not panic.
  —Open any closed gates to facilitate the orderly exit from the danger area.
  —If the building principal is not present, notify the building principal of the situation by calling her or him at home. The superintendent will in turn be notified.

FOR INDOOR EVENTS

- Group fight, disturbance:
  —Notify the police.
  —Use the PA system to announce that all persons need to return to the bleachers/seats and that anyone creating a disturbance will be arrested.
  —The school representative should be ready to sign a police complaint if necessary to effect an arrest.
  —If the building principal is not present, notify the building principal of the situation by calling her or him at home. The superintendent will in turn be notified.
- Gun fire:
  —Notify the police and ask that an ambulance be dispatched as well. Be specific about the location of the threat and the best approach to the incident site.
  —Use the PA system to give the following instructions: Please remain where you are, get down on the floor, remain quiet, and await further instructions. Help is on the way. Do not panic.
  —If the shooters are still in the area, try to have people move into safe locations away from the shooters and secure the doors to those locations. Individuals should be instructed to wait inside secure locked areas until released by the police.
  —Open any closed exit doors to facilitate the orderly exit from the danger area.
  —If the building principal is not present, notify the building principal of the situation by calling her or him at home. The superintendent will in turn be notified.
- Tornado conditions:
  —Instruct all personnel to enter the designated and posted storm shelter area on the bottom floor of the school. The school representative will have the building master key and be able to unlock the entrances to be used. All school representatives will be familiar with light switches that may be needed. Use the small classrooms and interior hallways that have been designated as storm shelters. Do not allow individuals to enter/remain in the auditorium, cafeteria, and other spaces with large roof expanses; they are not safe under these conditions.

—If the building principal is not present, notify the building principal of the situation by calling her or him at home. The superintendent will in turn be notified.

8.4. Aircraft Disaster

AIRCRAFT CRASH INTO OR NEAR BUILDING WITH DAMAGE TO BUILDING

- Call 911 and report incident.
- Initiate SS notifications per the flow chart shown in figure 2.2.
- Implement emergency evacuation plan (modified as appropriate to the incident) to maximize safety of students.
- Assemble students and staff members in an area as far from the crash scene as possible; uphill and upwind from the crash.
- Provide for treatment and removal of injured building occupants.
- Account for all building occupants and determine extent of injuries.

AIRCRAFT ON OR NEAR SCHOOL SITE BUT NO DAMAGE TO BUILDING

- Call 911 and report incident.
- Seek advice from fire department regarding evacuation versus sheltering in place.
- Initially, shelter-in-place until advised by fire officials.
- Initiate SS notifications per the flow chart shown in figure 2.2.
- If directed by fire department, keep all students and staff members in the building(s). Any students and staff members outside should report immediately to their classroom or designated area until further instructions are received.
- If directed to evacuate by fire officials, follow procedures noted above or as otherwise provided by fire officials.

8.5. Allergic Reaction

Possible symptoms: General feeling of impending doom or fright, weakness, sweating, sneezing, shortness of breath, nasal itching, hives, vomiting, cough, restlessness, shock, hoarseness, swollen tongue, and severe localized swelling.

FIRST ACTIONS

- Assess situation, remain calm, and make student/employee comfortable.
- Only move person for safety reasons.
- Send for immediate help and medication kit (in cases of known allergies).
- Follow medical protocol for student, if on file.
- Notify 911, depending on circumstances.
- Notify parent or guardian.
- Administer medication, by order of a doctor, if appropriate. Apply ice pack, keep warm, as appropriate.
- Observe for respiratory difficulty.
- Record time and site of insect sting, ingestion of food, or exposure to other allergen; record name of medicine, dosage, and time, if appropriate.
- Depending on circumstances, initiate SS notifications per the flow chart shown in figure 2.2.

8.6. Angry and Disgruntled Parents, Employees, and Patrons

Strategies may be adapted to use with angry parents, employees, and patrons:

- Be courteous and confident.
- Remain calm.
- Do not touch.
- Keep at a reasonable distance.
- Listen.
- Allow the opportunity to vent.
- Meet in a neutral, protected location.
- Leave door open or have another staff member join you.
- Avoid blame—focus on what can be done.

Approach the intruder with the resource officer, if available. Otherwise approach with another staff member.

ASK

- "How can I help you get the services you/your child needs?"
- "How can we work together?"
- "What kinds of support can we put in place to help your child succeed?"

IF SITUATION ESCALATES

- Notify site resource officer (if assigned/present).
- Notify principal.
- Notify 911 if situation becomes threatening.
- Initiate SS notifications per the flow chart shown in figure 2.2.

8.7. Assault by Intruder

- Call 911 and notify the on-site local police resource officer if assigned and available.
- Initiate SS notifications per the flow chart shown in figure 2.2.
- Determine the extent of crisis.
- Do not follow or attempt to detain or apprehend the assailant.
- If continued danger, move other potential victims from area.
- Provide first aid.
- Question victim—make reasonable notes for potential court case:
  —Description of assailant
  —Details of the assault
- Initiate SS notifications per the flow chart shown in figure 2.2.
- Determine if a threat still exists, and if so, move others to safety.
- If the assailant has not been contained and continues to be a threat to others, institute lockdown procedures.
- Inform the staff of potential plans as soon as possible.
- The SS CMT Public Information Office will handle all media and community inquiries into the event(s).

- The parents (or spouse) of the victim should be notified as soon as possible.
- The staff should be informed of the situation as soon as possible.
- The SS CMT will consult with the superintendent regarding the need for early dismissal. The Transportation Department can, at the direction of the SS CMT, provide buses for early dismissal.
- Inform students of the facts as soon as possible so they can deal with the situation by being informed, rather than receiving their "facts" through rumors.
- Inform other schools, via the public information officer (PIO), of basic information as soon as possible, since siblings/neighbors will quickly learn of the disturbance.
- Prepare a statement for the individuals who answer the telephones to read. Instruct them that any further inquiries should be made to the PIO. Provide the telephone number to the caller for use as a reference.

8.8. Bomb Found on School Premises

- Isolate the area.
- Call 911 and notify the site resource officer.
- Evacuate the building. Evacuate by room, starting with rooms nearest the device.
- Do not use cell phones or other electronic devices.
- Do not turn light switches, computers, televisions, or other electronic devices on or off.

EVACUATION PROCEDURES

Note: Use of fire drill procedures to evacuate a school immediately upon receipt of a bomb threat can be dangerous if an actual explosive device is involved and, unknowingly, students are evacuated past its location.

DEVICE FOUND

- Handling of any suspected explosive device must be left to experts.
- Do not touch or move the device.
- Do not attempt to cover or hide the device.
- If evacuation is needed, communicate information verbally from person to person since any electrical device could trigger the device.
- Complete evacuation as quickly and as orderly as possible.
- Members of the police department may be used to direct evacuation away from possible bomb area.

DETONATION

If a bomb or other explosive device detonates prior to it being located, or detonates without warning, the following steps will be taken:

- All students, staff members, and faculty members should be instructed to DROP–COVER–HOLD.
- Call 911.
- Render first aid to victims.
- Do not evacuate until advised by the public safety incident commander (possibility of a secondary device), but remove all students from areas of obvious danger (fire, gas, etc.).
- Initiate SS notifications per the flow chart shown in figure 2.2.
- Consider the area to be a crime scene; do not touch or move anything except to provide first aid and/or rescue of victims.

- Account for all students and staff members.
- Do not reenter the building or evacuated areas.
- Do not allow students or staff members to circulate.
- Follow the directions of the public safety incident commander (IC).

8.9. Bomb Threats/Telephone Threats

All bomb threats will be taken seriously. Bomb and other threats may be originated in writing, in person, or over the telephone, or related through a second source.

THE PERSON RECEIVING THE BOMB THREAT WILL . . .

- Attempt to gain as much information as possible when the threat is communicated.
- Use the Bomb Threat Report Form as a guide to collect the information needed. Don't be bashful about asking direct, specific questions about the threat. Keep the caller on the phone as long as possible, if the threat is received by phone; attempt to gain more information.
- The most important information is as follows:
  —When will the bomb explode?
  —Where is the bomb located?
- Immediately after receiving the bomb threat, the person receiving the call will verbally notify the building administrator of the threat received. Complete the Bomb Threat Report Form.
- Turn off cellular phone and/or walkie-talkie (transmits radio waves—could trigger a bomb).
- Immediately upon call disconnection, press *57 on the telephone set to facilitate tracing of the call by the telephone company.

BUILDING ADMINISTRATOR WILL (IF NECESSARY) . . .

- Call 911 and notify the site resource officer.
- Initiate SS notifications per the flow chart shown in figure 2.2.
- Implement a quiet inspection of the facilities, if directed to do so by police.
- Execute fire drill procedure via word of mouth to evacuate students, staff members, and other building occupants:
  —*Do not use the PA system or turn lights on or off.*
  —Following the signal, the SS Bomb Threat Team will support the Police Bomb Squad in conducting a thorough search of assigned areas as outlined below. If anything is found, it should not be touched in any way. Information should be immediately reported to the Police Bomb Squad.
- Instruct search team not to touch or move any foreign object located! If the object doesn't belong there, leave it alone.
- Maintain an open telephone line for communications.
- Secure all exits to prevent reentry to buildings during the search period.
- Be certain people stay clear of all buildings; a bomb(s) may be planted against an outside wall. The blast will be directed in large part away from the building.
- Reoccupy buildings only when clearance is given by proper authorities.
- Fill out Bomb Threat Report Form and send to the SS executive director, Business Affairs.

Responsibilities for search efforts are delineated in table 8.1. These actions will be undertaken with support of the Police Bomb Squad.

Table 8.1.   School Personnel Responsibilities for Search Efforts

School Rooms	School Personnel
Custodial closets	Lead custodian
Girl's toilet	Principal, assistant principal, or designee
Boy's toilet	Principal, assistant principal, or designee
Mechanical room	Lead custodian/HVAC tech.
Library, office, and audiovisual room	Librarian
Food service area, dining room	Cafeteria manager
Principal's office and other administrative areas	Office personnel
Outdoor storage	Lead custodian
Outdoor school/facility grounds	Maintenance manager

8.10. Bus Accidents

In the event that a bus accident occurs and the school has been contacted for assistance, the principal or designee determines and coordinates the appropriate responses. Interventions may include the following.

AT THE SCENE

- Provide emotional support.
- Be available and attend to the injured, as directed by emergency medical personnel.
- Be available and attend to the uninjured and account for all.

AT THE SCHOOL

- Provide emotional support and coordination.
- Provide emotional support and attend to the affected students.
- Provide information to the faculty.
- Call counselors for mental health assistance, as needed.
- Contact parents of students involved.

IMMEDIATE RESPONSE ACTIONS: BUS ACCIDENT—NONINJURY

- Driver reports details of accident by radio or second party.
  —Who? Bus number and driver name.
  —Where? Exact location and direction of travel.
  —What? Describe incident.
- Transportation Department notified of incident. Call 911 with information.
  —Who? Name of district department.
  —What? Describe briefly the vehicles involved/nature of accident.
  —Where? Exact location/address.
  —When? Time of incident.
- Transportation Department dispatches bus, mechanic, and replacement driver with route information and camera.
- Transportation initiates SS notifications per the flow chart shown in figure 2.2.
- Supervisor should go to scene of accident.
- Transportation notifies schools regarding accident and delay or change in routes.
- Transport students to their destination.

IMMEDIATE RESPONSE ACTIONS: BUS ACCIDENT—INVOLVING SERIOUS INJURY OR DEATH

- Driver response: Use a prearranged code to notify office by radio. (The reason for using a code is to avoid unnecessary curious onlookers/ambulance chasers and anticipation, confusion, and stress to those who may be monitoring the radio frequency.)
  —Who? Bus number and driver name.
  —What? Code.
  —Where? Exact location, address, and direction of travel.
  —Office announces over radio to all district vehicles to lower the volume on their radio. (This is to avoid unnecessary stress to students.)
- District response:
  —Call 911 with information.
  —Who? Name of SS and department.
  —What? Describe briefly the facts as known.
  —Where? Exact location/address.
  —When? Time of accident.
  —Dispatch bus with driver and a mechanic with all route information and camera.
  —Initiate SS notifications per the flow chart shown in figure 2.2.
  —Supervisor should go to scene of accident.
  —Complete student roster.
  —School will notify parents/legal guardians.
  —Activate support group for students.
- District CMT will follow up with an investigation of the accident and respond to the media.

8.11. Chemical/Hazmat Spill

INSIDE THE BUILDING

Accidental spillage or release of chemicals and other hazardous materials (hazmat) can result in harmful exposure and injury to people and physical damage to property. These incidents can occur during activities associated with on-site maintenance and cleaning operations, on-site construction and remodeling, classroom chemistry labs, and materials storage.

In the Event of a Spill or Airborne Release

- Evacuate the area immediately.
- Call 911.
- Initiate SS notifications per the flow chart shown in figure 2.2.
- Notify the principal/building manager of the spill/release.
- Check the Material Safety Data Sheet (MSDS) to determine the specific hazards, risks, precautions, and urgency of the situation.
- The principal/building manager will call the manager, Energy, Environmental, Health, and Safety Department or the fire department, if deemed necessary, for consultation regarding personal protective equipment, cleanup, and disposal of recovered materials and other contaminated supplies and debris.

OUTSIDE THE BUILDING

SS schools and facilities can be adversely impacted by incidents occurring on properties and along transportation corridors outside and adjacent to the public school scope of operations, for example, large-scale accident/chemical release in neighborhood industrial facilities, railway accident/incident with chemical release, highway accident/release involving chemical carriers, and so forth. These incidents may result in the airborne release of hazardous materials requiring sheltering of persons in place and reverse evacuation of persons from the outside to indoors.

In the Event of a Spill or Airborne Release

- The school staff may be advised of the situation by the fire department and directed to act accordingly.
- Initiate shelter-in-place procedures if you are made aware of the incident and potential impact to your facility and you are not alerted to the situation by division personnel or outside agencies (e.g., police and fire).
  —Ensure that all students, staff members, and others remain in the building.
  —Move any students, staff members, and others back indoors as warranted.
  —Shut off all outside air ventilators.
  —Close all windows and doors.
  —Await further instructions from the fire or police department.
- Initiate SS notifications per the flow chart shown in figure 2.2.

8.12. Child Missing/Kidnapping

Any report of a lost student brought to the attention of the school staff should be considered serious. When the student is reported missing coming to or going from school functions, school personnel will become involved.

WHEN A STUDENT IS REPORTED LOST

- Notify resource office/notify police by calling 911, especially if foul play is suspected.
- Initiate SS notifications per the flow chart shown in figure 2.2.
- Call parent/guardian and encourage them to call 911. Establish a communication plan with them, if necessary.
- Activate school CRT and the district CMT to work on the issue as deemed appropriate.
- Conduct immediate search of school building and grounds, as appropriate.
- Gather the following information for the police:
  —Who made the report?
  —Time last seen, where, and with whom?
  —Physical description and how dressed?
  —Playmates, friends' names, addresses, and phone numbers.
  —Student normal path, mode of transportation to and from school. (Contact Transportation to track possible information.)
  —Contact teachers or counselors to see if student shared any information with them that might be helpful.
  —Provide counselor with information regarding those who may be distraught over the situation.

WHEN A STUDENT IS REPORTED KIDNAPPED

- Upon report of kidnapping, call parent/guardian and 911. Relay available information to the dispatcher. Establish a communication plan with parent/guardian, if necessary.
- Initiate SS notifications per the flow chart shown in figure 2.2.
- Activate school CRT and the district CMT to work on the crisis.
- Gather witnesses in a private area to meet with police.
- Obtain description of suspect(s) and vehicle, if possible.
  —Suspect: Height, weight, hair color, race, facial hair, and clothing.
  —Vehicle: Color, make, year, license plate number, and noticeable damage.
- Clarify type of kidnapping—custodial or other.
  —If suspect is custodial problem, obtain information from legal guardian/parent and relay to 911 dispatcher/police.
  —Suspect is "other" if person other than parent/guardian.
- Obtain name of kidnapped victim's best friend who may know ex-boyfriend or ex-girlfriend of the person kidnapped. He/she should be available for police.
- Obtain photograph of victim—from yearbook, personnel files, or parent/guardian.
- Cooperate with police.

8.13. Death of a Student or Staff Member

- Initiate SS notifications per the flow chart shown in figure 2.2.
- Prepare a fact sheet giving accurate, up-to-date information.
- Hold a faculty meeting as soon as possible. Review the procedures for the day, availability of support services, and referral process for at-risk students.
- Contact family of the deceased. Preferably an administrator and CRT member should visit the family at their home and offer assistance.
- Hold a faculty meeting at the end of the day to review the day's events.
- Notify all bus drivers by written memo to be alert for students who show signs of emotional distress, along with a telephone number for drivers to use to reach a guidance counselor.
- Personal contact should be made with the driver of the bus that goes into the neighborhood of the student who has died. Supply a school staff member to ride the bus if that seems necessary.

8.14. Disaster—Destruction of Part/Whole of Building (e.g., Tornado, Plane Crash, or Bomb)

ACTIONS

- Call 911 for immediate help.
- Initiate SS notifications per the flow chart shown in figure 2.2.
- Inspect extent of damage and injuries.

EVACUATION

- If there is no danger outside the building, use fire alarm to evacuate building.
- Safe areas: Identify areas away from problem area and route to be taken by classes in going to safe areas. Designate which classes/groups of students should go to which area.

ATTEND TO INJURED

- Assign one adult designated as "in charge"; assign available adults to attend to injured.
- Meet rescue personnel.
- Have staff members direct rescue personnel to problem area and assist in providing access as needed by rescue personnel.
- Make head custodian available to assist rescue personnel.

DISMISSAL

- Arrange for dismissal with executive director, Business Affairs Office.
- Public Information Office should be notified of emergency closing so that radio and TV stations can be contacted.

INFORMATION

- Consider briefly summarizing the situation for all students and adults, either via PA or preferably by informing teachers and having them explain to students, prior to dismissal.
- If time permits, prepare a written memo to parents detailing the situation and how it was handled, including plan for follow-up, to be sent home with students or distributed the following day.
- Call an emergency staff meeting after students leave to explain the situation and any plans for follow-up.
- Involve PIO in all information being prepared and distributed, and refer media and other calls from the general public to that office.

8.15. Disaster—Preventing Dismissal/Evacuation (e.g., Tornado, Sniper, or Plane Crash)

ACTIONS

- Call 911 for immediate help.
- Initiate SS notifications per the flow chart shown in figure 2.2.
- Inspect extent of damage and injuries.

Information may be received from a variety of sources:

- Telephone call
- Superintendent's office
- Radio or television
- Visual observation: Ascertain specifics such as extent of immediate danger and possible length of time danger may exist.
- Safe areas: Consider large areas at the interior of the building that have a reliable source of lighting away from numerous windows and outside walls. Designate which classes/groups of students should go to which area. Evacuate trailers to main building or safe area.
- Move students: Use the PA, if working, or a system of notes sent by messengers, to inform teachers and other adults of the situation and where to bring students.
- Superintendent: Notify of plan being implemented; call police and maintain contact as necessary.
- All "clear": Monitor situation to ascertain when danger is removed; direct teachers and other adults to escort students back to class when situation is clear.

- If crisis interferes with normal dismissal, arrange with Transportation and Superintendent's Office to dismiss students following normal procedures. Elementary schools will want to inform Extended Day personnel in advance of dismissal.

INFORMATION

- Consider briefly summarizing the danger and its resolution for all students, either via PA or preferably by informing teachers and having them explain to students, prior to dismissal.
- Consider preparing a written memo to parents detailing the situation and how it was handled; send home with students or distribute the next day.
- Prepare written memo to the staff summarizing the situation and how it was handled.
- Handle all distribution of information through the Public Information Office.

8.16. Disturbance/Demonstration/Unlawful Assembly

STUDENT INVOLVEMENT

- Secure the classroom, notify office to secure building, and keep students in classrooms and away from windows or areas of possible danger.
- Call 911 to alert police to situation and possible future needs.
- Alert the CRT.
- Initiate SS notifications per the flow chart shown in figure 2.2.
- Principal should request to meet with a group of three to five students who either witnessed or were directly involved in the incident to discuss concerns, encouraging others to return to class.
- Students should not be released until it is determined by the principal that they will not be at risk of harm.
- If necessary, students should be removed from the school grounds via an alternate route.

NONSTUDENT INVOLVEMENT

- Secure the classroom, notify office to secure building, and keep students in classrooms and away from windows or areas of possible danger.
- Call 911 to alert police to situation and possible future needs.
- Initiate lockdown procedures, if considered appropriate.
- Alert the CRT.
- Initiate SS notifications per the flow chart shown in figure 2.2.
- Inform employees and students as necessary. Calm fears and keep operations as normal as possible. Passing times may be adjusted for student protection.
- District administrator or school principal should inform demonstrators of laws and policies regarding unauthorized assembly.
- Demonstrators should be asked to leave school grounds. The administrator should offer to meet with a spokesperson.
- If negotiations fail, the authorities should be called to the scene.
- The district administrator should be a spokesperson for the media.
- Students should not be released until it is determined by the principal that they will not be at risk of harm.
- If necessary, students should be removed from the school grounds via an alternate route.

STAFF GUIDELINES

- Exercise good judgment and reasonable action to guard against escalating the disturbance/demonstration.
- Record observations of any incidents, including date, time, place, names, and actions of those involved, and any intervention attempts. Report to the principal.
- Maintain normal classroom operations as much as possible.
- If the disturbance/demonstration is outside the building, keep students away from windows and keep shades down in order to keep students as safe as possible.

8.17. Earthquake

Because earthquakes can strike without warning, the immediate need is to protect lives by taking the best available cover.

ACTIONS

- Principal should provide instructions to teachers via the PA system, intercom, or megaphone.
- Call 911.
- Initiate SS notifications per the flow chart shown in figure 2.2.

The teacher should follow these guidelines:

- Instruct the students to drop to the floor and secure protection beneath a desk or table.
- After the tremor subsides, usher the students out of the building according to the established route for fire evacuation. Leave through the nearest accessible door if the planned route is inaccessible.
- Call roll to be sure all students have exited safely; notify the administration if a student is missing.
- Instruct students to stay clear of the buildings and power lines.

8.18. Emergency School Closure/Bad Weather

When the superintendent is advised by emergency service authorities during school hours to close schools or decides to close schools early, principals will be notified by telephone or the district emergency radio system. The procedures listed below will be implemented in the event of an emergency situation.

8.19. Emergency Situation (Police or Fire) Near or on School Grounds

ACTIONS

- Principal should convene the CRT.
- Initiate SS notifications per the flow chart shown in figure 2.2, depending upon seriousness and magnitude of the incident.
- Determine what additional personnel are needed for such activities as crowd control, answering telephones, and dealing with media.
- Consideration should be given to the following:
  —Safety of students: Are the students safer at school, at a different location, or at home?
  —Making arrangements for the safety of students who live at or near where the emergency situation is occurring

—Providing additional help at the school to answer phones or for crowd control

—Providing extra counseling

- The public safety IC (police or fire) will be responsible for making recommendations for school response and procedures. In the absence of clear direction, the principal will consult with the district Crisis Team.
- If students are kept at school, maintain as normal a routine as possible.
- Parents may need to be informed and told of alternate arrangements for dismissal or transportation. This may be done through the PIO.

8.20. Evacuation Procedure

Exit the building when an alarm sounds or the instruction "leave the building" is announced.

EVACUATION INSTRUCTIONS

Teachers

- Take along class lists or rolls.
- Make special provisions to assist handicapped students.
- Exit the building through assigned exit or nearest unblocked exit.
- Lead the class out of the building to predesignated area at least three hundred feet from building. Area must be free from hazards such as overhead power lines, gas lines, and motor vehicle traffic.
- Call roll and report any missing students (by name) to the principal or designee at predesignated location away from building.

Students

With Homeroom Classes

- Leave *all* personal items in classroom.
- Follow teacher and exit in a quiet and orderly manner.

Not with Homeroom Classes

- Leave *all* personal items in classroom.
- Exit with supervisor.

If Alone

- Exit the nearest unblocked exit.
- Join homeroom class outside.

Staff Members Not Assigned to Classrooms

- Check restrooms, common areas, and kitchen as predesignated by school principal.
- Keep children out of vehicle traffic areas and other hazardous areas.
- Assist as directed by principal or designee.

Principal or Designee

- Report any missing persons to emergency response personnel.
- Determine if building is safe to reenter.
- Determine *when* it is safe to reenter.
- Notify teachers by megaphone, flag, hand signal, or runner. *Do not use fire alarm signal* for reentry.

- *If building is unsafe to reenter, evacuate the school site, using predetermined plan.*
- Instruct teachers to release students to responsible adults using predetermined procedure.

8.21. Fighting—Violence between Two or More Students

PROCEDURES FOR HANDLING FIGHTS IN SCHOOL SETTINGS

Intervening and managing physical altercations and/or fights require making a judgment call. There may be several goals at one time, and individual circumstances will determine the priorities of your interventions.

- Walk briskly—don't run.
- Notify the site resource officer, if present.
- Announce lockdown over PA system, if needed.
- Call 911 if the situation is escalating and/or serious harm or injury is becoming apparent or imminent.
- If 911 is called and/or if serious injury occurs, initiate SS notification per the flow chart shown in figure 2.2.
- Get help along the way; send responsible students for help from the closest source.
- Assess and evaluate the following:
  —Number of students involved
  —Size of students involved
  —Any weapons involvement
  —Proximity of individuals who can assist
- Recognize that there may be several subtle things going on simultaneously that are being tangibly expressed in the conflict.
  —Is there gang involvement?
  —What other alliances might exist?
- Identify yourself to the fighters and tell them to stop fighting in a firm, authoritative voice. If known, call the students by name.
- Calmly take charge of the situation, and disperse any crowd.
- Separate the combatants; avoid physical force.
- Remove participants to the office.
- Get medical attention if necessary.
- Debrief relevant teacher(s).
- Provide protection and support for victims.
- Report incident to law enforcement and other child-serving agencies who may be serving the youngster.

8.22. Fire

ACTIONS

- Sound alarm. Evacuate building if serious threat of danger.
- Call 911 and ask for required emergency services.
- Advise 911 of any known injuries. Provide first aid through school personnel, such as school nurse, nurse's aide, and athletic trainer.
- Initiate SS notifications per the flow chart shown in figure 2.2.

- In all probability, school will have to be dismissed and arrangements for transportation will have to be made. Students and staff members will have to be informed. A portable bullhorn should be available to make announcements to students and staff members who have evacuated the building.
- If the building is damaged, several different steps may have to be taken. Severe damage will require repair work—another location for classes will have to be scheduled through the Business Affairs Office.
- Prepare written memo for the staff to advise of follow-up procedures.
- Send letter to parent's home with students.
- Consider issuing announcements through the media.

8.23. Food-Borne Illness/Communicable Disease Outbreak

In the event of an incident suspected to be due to a food-borne illness or communicable disease, action must be taken to ensure the health and safety of students/staff members and to prevent further potential spread of the problem.

- If students or staff members are getting ill while school is in session, do the following:
  —Evacuate facility if an environmental reason is suspected.
  —Call 911 if anyone appears in need of medical attention.
  —Initiate SS notifications per the flow chart shown in figure 2.2.
- If it appears that food or beverage may be involved, do the following:
  —Discontinue food services.
  —Lock/isolate food service areas including drinking fountains and vending machines.
  —Do not throw away any remaining food or beverage that had been served that day; package in leak-proof containers, and store in a refrigerated area until removed by authorities for testing if necessary.
  —Announce that all persons should refrain from using drinking fountains and any consumption of food or water, regardless of source.
  —Notify other school principals. Advise termination of food services until further notice.
  —Implement the SS Food Safety Management Plan.
- Notify the Health Department Office of Epidemiology of a possible disease outbreak and ask about appropriate actions.
- Consult with public safety officials regarding appropriate actions.
- Document times illness began, numbers and names of persons affected, type of symptoms experienced, locations of persons becoming ill, and any unusual odors, tastes, or other changes. The Health Department will work with the schools and other agencies to develop the appropriate investigation, testing, follow-up, student/staff member/parent education, and recommendations for a sudden outbreak of illness.
- If foul play or terrorism is suspected, incident management will be assumed by public safety officials. The SS CMT will cooperate/support follow-on response actions and longer term strategy development and implementation.
- If the school notices a larger-than-usual absentee rate with similar illnesses or the school is notified by the Health Department of an unusual occurrence of illness, do the following:
  —Notify the Health Department Office of Epidemiology of the increasing number of illnesses.
  —The Health Department will work with the schools and other agencies to develop the appropriate investigation, testing, follow-up, student/staff member/parent education, and recommendations depending on the nature of the illness.
  —Initiate SS notifications per the flow chart shown in figure 2.2.

8.24. Gas Leak

Natural gas leaks, with odor in the building, may occur and present danger of explosion. Natural gas is mixed with mercaptan to give it odor.

If a leak is discovered in or near the building, do the following:

- Call 911 to notify fire department.
- Evacuate the building immediately, following the local building evacuation plan. Move students a safe distance from the building.
- Call gas company.
- Turn off the main gas valve.
- Initiate SS notifications per the flow chart shown in figure 2.2.
- Keep students at a safe distance until the problem has been corrected or instructions are received from the fire department and/or the district CRT.

8.25. Hostage Situation—School Building

All hostage situations are dangerous events. A hostage taker might be a terrorist, fleeing felon, disgruntled employee (past or present), spouse or significant other, drug or alcohol abuser, emotionally disturbed person, trespasser, or on occasion, a parent, student, or citizen who is usually angry about some situation and decides to resolve it by taking hostages and making demands to achieve some resolution. Likewise, the dynamics of a hostage situation vary greatly, and no two incidents will be the same.

ACTIONS

- Call 911 and notify the site resource officer.
- Institute lockdown procedures.
- Initiate SS notifications per the flow chart shown in figure 2.2.
  —Activate the CMT.
  —Place the Transportation Department on standby status to provide buses for evacuation of students to a safer location or to their homes.
  —Provide basic information to the other schools as soon as possible since siblings/neighbors will quickly learn of the disturbance.
- Activate the CRT.
- Staff members should keep students in safe and secure areas: students should not be released for any reason until told to do so by the police.
- Do not allow personnel to circulate around the premises.
- Prepare a statement to be read by individuals who will be answering the telephones. Instruct them that any further inquiries should be made to the Public Information Office. Provide the telephone number for the caller to call.
- Persons familiar with the entire building should be available to discuss the interior room arrangements, and so forth. These individuals should be available to meet with police at a designated location. Maps and building blueprints should be made available.
- Remain in lockdown mode and follow the instructions of the public safety IC.

8.26. Hostage Situation—School Bus

All hostage situations are dangerous events. A hostage taker might be a terrorist, fleeing felon, disgruntled employee (past or present), spouse or significant other, drug or alcohol abuser, emotionally disturbed person, trespasser, or on occasion, a parent, student, or citizen who is usually angry about some situation and decides to resolve it by taking hostages and making demands to achieve some resolution. Likewise, the dynamics of a hostage situation vary greatly, and no two incidents will be the same.

PLAN OF ACTION: SCHOOL BUS

Consideration must be given to the possibility of a hostage situation occurring on a bus operated by the public schools. If such an incident occurs, the following procedures should be implemented.

BUS DRIVER

The bus driver must assume a position of heightened responsibility for the welfare of the students on the bus as well as his/her own safety. Sound judgment, good decision making, knowledge of school and police procedures in handling such incidents, and training will be of greatest assistance to drivers should she/he become a victim.

ACTIONS

- If safe to do so, evacuate as many students as possible from the bus and direct them to move to a position out of sight of the bus.
- If possible, call 911.
- Be compliant and follow the orders/directions of the hostage taker.
- Do not attempt to apprehend or interfere with the hostage taker.
- Clear the area of as many students and others as is safely possible.
- Notify the Transportation Radio Dispatcher of as much information as possible regarding your situation and location. If allowed to maintain radio contact, do so. All radio transmissions must be disciplined.
- The CRT and CMT will be activated and follow the same procedures as for a building hostage situation.

TRANSPORTATION DEPARTMENT

The Dispatch Office should do the following:

- Call 911.
- Initiate SS notifications per the flow chart shown in figure 2.2.
- Implement procedures set out in the plan of action for buildings.

8.27. Intruder/Trespasser

ACTIONS

- Determine whereabouts of the intruder.
- Determine extent of the problem or potential crisis.
- Call 911 and notify the site resource officer.
- Consider instituting the lockdown procedure.
- Trespasser with no safety hazard may be dealt with by informing the intruder of the offense being committed. If trespasser refuses to leave, wait for police to intervene. If the trespasser has previously been warned (placed on notice), trespass charges may be filed.
- Trespass with threat to others' safety will require assistance from the police.
- Make notes. Record what has occurred to provide information important to the police and in potential subsequent court cases.

- Initiate SS notifications per the flow chart shown in figure 2.2, depending upon seriousness of the incident.
   —Activate the CMT.
   —Place the Transportation Department on standby status to provide buses for evacuation of students to a safer location or to their homes.
   —Provide basic information to the other schools as soon as possible since siblings/neighbors will quickly learn of the disturbance.
- Staff members should keep students in present areas: students should not be released for any reason until told to do so by the police.
- Do not allow personnel to circulate around the premises.
- Prepare a statement to be read by individuals who will be answering the telephones. Instruct them that any further inquiries should be made to the Public Information Office. Provide the telephone number for the caller to call.
- Police information for charges: The police will need to be sure of details from persons involved in the incident as well as from others interviewed. Trespassing is a misdemeanor or felony, depending upon the location of the intrusion.

8.28. Life-Threatening Crisis

(Major) life-threatening injury to individual: When a life-threatening situation is perceived to exist, a building administrator or principal/delegate in charge of a building should do the following:

- Call 911.
- Notify site resource officer, if assigned to facility.
- Apply first aid and life-sustaining techniques using trained persons on staff.
- Initiate SS notifications per the flow chart shown in figure 2.2.
- Call parent/guardian immediately.

Implement lockdown procedures if it is determined that the safety and health of students and staff members are in jeopardy.

TEACHERS/STAFF MEMBERS

- Teachers should quickly check halls and get students into classrooms.
- Lock doors and close blinds.
- Teachers will keep all students in the classroom until an all clear has been sounded.
- Teachers will maintain (as best they can) a calm atmosphere in the classroom, keeping alert to the emotional needs of students.
- Staff members without students will report to the office for instruction.
- The secretary will maintain the phones. Administrative staff member/delegate will deliver messages as needed and work with the principal and security.
- The staff is *not* to use remote controls, telephones, or radios during a lockdown unless assigned/delegated by the principal.
- Staff members will not leave their assigned area unless authorized by principal, security, or police.
- When the emergency is over, an all clear will be announced.
- Each staff member will document exactly what occurred in their area of responsibility. This will be done as soon as possible. These will be turned into district security.

If intruder(s) are on playground or at lunch time, the following should occur:

- Outdoor supervisor should move all students into cafeteria/gym.
- Lock exit doors to cafeteria/gym.
- Advise principal of actions taken.
- Ask all students to sit on floor.
- Indoor supervisor, aides, and so on, should help supervise students and personnel members.

8.29. Lockdown Procedure

When a dangerous person or condition exists on or near the school, the primary objective is to protect students from the danger.

In cases of an emergency requiring lockdown, the following procedure will be followed by staff members and students:

- The principal or his designee will announce over the PA system that a lockdown is in effect.
- One of the secretaries will be directed to call 911 and notify the police of the emergency and the need for immediate police assistance.
- Initiate SS notifications per the flow chart shown in figure 2.2.
- Provide for persons with special needs.

The following announcements will be made:

Class in Session (No Lunches in Progress)

Students and staff members, it is necessary at this time to begin a schoolwide lockdown. All students are to remain in class. Students in the hall report immediately back to your room. Teachers lock your classroom doors. No one is to leave the classroom until an all clear announcement is made by an administrator. Ignore a fire alarm. If we need to evacuate the building, an announcement will be made.

Class Change in Progress

Students and staff members, it is necessary at this time to begin a schoolwide lockdown. All students and teachers report immediately to your next class. Teachers, be at your classroom door and lock it as soon as the students have arrived. Ignore a fire alarm. If we need to evacuate the building, an announcement will be made.

During Lunch

Students and staff members, it is necessary at this time to begin a schoolwide lockdown. Students in the cafeteria are to report immediately to the [gym or auditorium, whichever is appropriate]. Teachers lock your classroom doors. Students outside of their classroom at this time are to report back to your class immediately. No one is to leave the classroom or designated area until an all clear announcement is made by an administrator. Ignore a fire alarm. If we need to evacuate the building, an announcement will be made.

During the lockdown announcement, the administrator and head custodian may lock the exit doors to prevent entry into the building.

- Teachers are to do the following:
  —Lock the classroom door.
  —Tell the students that there is an emergency and you don't know what it is.

—Get the students to go to an area of the room that is away from the door and away from any windows.

—Have students stay there until an announcement is made. Members of the crisis team will come to your room and update you. Communications among administrators will be by two-way radio to assess the situation and plan the next course of action.

The school nurse and attendance clerk will report immediately to the main office during the lockdown announcement. Security monitors will report to the nearest classroom and maintain radio contact with administrators.

Under lockdown, conditions in a specific classroom can be communicated using color-coded cards.

A card, either posted in the window or slipped under the door, can alert emergency responders to the status of students in individual classrooms:

- Green card: No injuries.
- Yellow card: Injuries have occurred but are relatively minor; assistance can be delayed.
- Red card: Injuries have occurred. Medical assistance is needed immediately.

8.30. Perceived Crises

Perceived crises are conditions or situations, often community based, that are perceived as potentially affecting a large number of people. Examples of perceived crises include racial events, school rivalry situations, events in which a group feels left out or not represented, introduction of new school procedures without adequate warning, real or perceived unsafe conditions such as toxic fumes or food poisoning, gang-related activities, or rumors about people with HIV/AIDS or other contagious conditions.

It is the task of those in charge to defuse any irrational response. It is also incumbent upon school and administration officials to maintain situational awareness, and to the maximum extent practicable, to do the following:

- Identify situations in advance that may be perceived crises.
- Maintain open lines of communication with students and staff members.
- Maintain procedures for dealing with the public and the media.

ACTIONS

- Consult with the resource officer.
- For any health or safety condition or credible threat, immediately call 911 and contact appropriate health authorities.
- Initiate SS notifications per the flow chart shown in figure 2.2, depending upon the seriousness of the incident.
- Don't panic. Project a sense of calm and control.
- Gather detailed and accurate information about the perceived crisis.
- If necessary, call a team meeting to assess the situation and make decisions on what actions to take.
- Provide appropriate faculty members, staff members, and those individuals or groups affected by the situation with specific information.
- Designate someone who would act as a single point of contact for controlling rumors. Keep lines of communication open; a feeling that secrets are being kept can increase the sense of crisis.

- Have trained individuals available to speak with small groups of students/staff members.
- Take all actions that you have determined necessary to prevent a more serious situation from developing.

8.31. Poisoning

In the event of the poisoning or suspected poisoning of a student or an employee, take the following actions.

IMMEDIATE ACTIONS

- Call 911.
- Call the Poison Control Center for advice: (800) 222-1222 (nationwide number).
- Initiate SS notifications per the flow chart shown in figure 2.2.

8.32. Power Failure/Lines Down

If there has been a power failure at a school, or if lines are reported down in the area of the school, do the following.

POWER FAILURE

- Initiate SS notifications per the flow chart shown in figure 2.2.
- SS Energy, Environmental, Health, and Safety Department will contact power company.

LINES DOWN IN AREA

- Have an adult posted in the area of the downed lines to prevent children and other people from going near them.
- Call 911 and request assistance in securing the area.
- Initiate SS notifications per the flow chart shown in figure 2.2, as appropriate.
- SS Energy, Environmental, Health, and Safety Department will contact power company.

Note: Telephone notification may require the use of a cellular phone, depending on whether the building telephone is set up to rely on electricity.

8.33. School Shootings

IMMEDIATE RESPONSE

Immediate responses in the event of a school shooting include the following:

- Call 911 and notify the site resource officer, if one is assigned to the school.
  —Relay additional information on the location of the perpetrator and number of victims as it becomes available.
- Determine if the perpetrator is still on premises.
- Institute lockdown and/or evacuation procedures.
- Initiate SS notifications per the flow chart shown in figure 2.2.
- Attempt to determine the number of victims and identify witnesses.

- Implement necessary first aid procedures through trained staff members, the school nurse, the nurse's aide, the physical education department, and/or the athletic trainer. Direct rescue personnel to the injured and give any required assistance. Designate a staff member to accompany victim(s) in ambulance.

LOCKDOWN OR EVACUATION?

When a dangerous person or condition exists on or near the school, the primary objective is to protect students from the danger. Many site-specific factors, including the types of communication systems available, layout of the school, and types of construction, are taken into consideration in determining whether lockdown or evacuation should occur. For example, a classroom with block walls and a locked steel door provides a more secure environment than a portable classroom. Because of these site-specific variables, individual schools should establish internal procedures unique to their location.

Options Include
- Full school lockdown.
- Full evacuation.
- Lockdown of designated areas and evacuation of other areas.

In general, if the perpetrator remains at large in the building or his/her location is not known, lockdown is likely to be the better choice.

If some students are not secured in a locked location and are in the path of danger, then an evacuation of those students may be required.

8.34. Securing and Restoring the Crime Scene

Immediately following an incident involving criminal activity, law enforcement officials will assume responsibility for the scene. However, before they arrive, it is important that anything that might be considered physical evidence be preserved "as is."

- Do not touch or move anything, unless necessary to do so for safety or to provide first aid.
- Do not allow anyone to pick up items such as the weapon, ammunition casings, or items belonging to the perpetrator.
- When law enforcement officials take over, be prepared to assist them in keeping students, staff members, and any other onlookers out of the area of the crime scene.
- Be aware that investigation of the crime scene can take from one to several days.

When law enforcement investigators have completed their work and released the area for cleanup, the worst damage should be cleaned, the area generally straightened, and the victims' possessions gathered.

Experience with school shootings has taught that it is better to not immediately remove all signs of the incident such as patching bullet holes because students, parents, and others in the community will want to see the scene in the days immediately following the incident and such evidence helps people understand what happened.

According to the National Education Association's "Crisis Communications Guide and Toolkit," "There is a strong and significant psychological connection to death sites that needs to run its full course and should never be ignored or discounted."

8.35. Sexual Assault

When a school is notified that a sexual assault has occurred to a student or staff member, the school CRT and the school must protect the identity and right to privacy of the victim and the alleged perpetrator. News of the incident should be contained as much as possible. Appropriate responses by school staff members will be directed at minimizing the fear of fellow students and quelling the spread of rumors. All services provided to the victim and his/her family should be kept confidential and should be coordinated with outside providers, such as the police, physicians, and hospital emergency room personnel.

A sexual assault will likely be a crisis to be managed by the school when one or more of the following conditions exist:

- The sexual assault occurs in the school, on the school grounds, on the way to or from the school, during a school activity, and so on.
- A member of the victim's family requests school intervention.
- The victim's friends request intervention.
- Students witness police action or the emergency services response.

When one or more of the above conditions exists, the following should be implemented:

- Call 911.
- The area where the assault occurred should be treated as a crime scene.
- Initiate SS notifications per the flow chart shown in figure 2.2.
- If office staff members heard the report, tell them not to repeat or give out any information within or outside the school unless they are specifically told to do so.
- Activate the district CMT.
- The principal/administrator activates the site CRT.
- Designate the site CRT member closest to the victim to talk to him/her about the types of support he or she and the closest friends need, and the person(s) the victim would like to provide that support.
- Provide a quiet space in the school for the victim and identified peers to receive support services.
- Coordinate response actions with police officials.
- Encourage the victim to seek additional support from a community-based crisis agency.
- Ensure that all records related to the sexual assault and follow-up services are kept confidential.

8.36. Shelter-in-Place

Shelter-in-place is one of the basic instructions public safety officials may issue during a chemical or hazmat emergency in the community, (e.g., chemical or manufacturing plant accident, or highway or railway transportation accident with hazmat release). Shelter-in-place may also be appropriate in the event of chemical attack or threat at or in the vicinity of a school facility. It is critical that communications be maintained with public safety officials (police and/or fire) in order to receive vital information and instructions.

Sheltering in place offers immediate protection for a short period of time and requires that students and staff members diligently adhere to the following procedures to ensure the maximum protection of people.

IMMEDIATE ACTIONS

At School

- The principal/administrator makes an announcement over the PA system to shelter-in-place.
- Call 911.
- Activate the CRT.
- Initiate SS notifications per the flow chart shown in figure 2.2.
- Communicate with public safety officials to receive further directions and guidance.
- Establish a Command Post in the principal's office/conference room.
- Follow reverse evacuation procedures to bring students, faculty members, and staff members indoors.
- If there are visitors in the building, provide for their safety by asking them to stay—not leave.
- Provide directions to close and lock all windows, exterior doors, and any other openings to the outside.
- If told there is a danger of explosion, direct that window shades, blinds, or curtains to be closed.
- Immediately tune to the radio or the television and listen for emergency broadcasts.
- Have employees familiar with the building's mechanical systems turn off all fans, heating, and air-conditioning systems. Some systems automatically provide for exchange of inside air with outside air. These systems, in particular, need to be turned off, sealed, or disabled.
- Shut off elevators.
- Gather essential disaster supplies, such as nonperishable food, bottled water, battery-powered radios, first aid supplies, flashlights, batteries, duct tape, plastic sheeting, and plastic garbage bags.
- Deploy nonclassroom personnel to assist in the classrooms and in the halls.
- Advise all classroom personnel members stationed inside to prepare their rooms for those coming from the outside. They will remain in their classrooms and follow the direction given over the PA system.
- Deploy administrators to their supervisory zones to secure and supervise their areas.
- Select interior room(s) above the ground floor, with the fewest windows or vents. The room(s) should have adequate space for everyone to be able to sit in. Avoid overcrowding by selecting several rooms if necessary. Classrooms may be used if there are no windows or the windows are sealed and cannot be opened. Large storage closets, utility rooms, meeting rooms, and even a gymnasium without exterior windows will also work well.
- Provide for persons with special needs.
- It is ideal to have a hard-wired telephone in the room(s) you select. Call emergency contacts and have the phone available if you need to report a life-threatening condition. Cellular telephone equipment may be overwhelmed or damaged during an emergency.
- Bring everyone into the room(s). Shut and lock the door.
- Use duct tape and plastic sheeting (heavier than food wrap) to seal all cracks around the door(s) and any vents into the room.
- Place plastic sheeting, towels, or carpets at the bottom of the outside doors and use tape to seal these exterior doors to minimize air intrusion and to neutralize outside air.
- Write down the names of everyone in the room, and call your schools' designated emergency contact to report who is in the room with you.
- Listen for an official announcement from school officials via the PA system, and stay where you are until you are told all is safe or you are told to evacuate.
- Provide for answering telephone inquiries from concerned parents by having at least one telephone with the school's listed telephone number available in the room selected to provide shelter for the school secretary or person designated to answer these calls. This room should also be sealed.

There should be a way to communicate among all rooms where people are sheltering in place in the school.

- If students have cell phones, allow them to use them to call a parent or guardian to let them know that they have been asked to remain in school until further notice and that they are safe.
- If the school has voice mail or an automated attendant, change the recording to indicate that the school is closed and that students and staff members are remaining in the building until authorities advise that it is safe to leave.
- Send anyone exposed to hazardous materials to the health room or clinic room for attention.
- If exposure should happen, those exposed should be given a change of clothes (or a gown) and an opportunity to wash the exposed areas with soap and water.
- Advise public safety officials of any injuries and/or exposures.
- Place a sign on the front door making notification of a "Shelter-In-Place Emergency."
- Do not open doors until public safety officials arrive.
- Ensure availability of preauthorized prescription medicines to students and staff members as necessary.
- Supervise and make bathroom facilities available to staff members and students.
- Make bottled water and cups available in each administrative zone.
- Make noncontaminated and nonperishable food available as necessary.
- Establish sign-out procedures once permission is given to release students to their parent/guardian. Use main office to facilitate student pickup, if appropriate.
- Update staff members and students as appropriate and permitted.
- Sound all clear signal when appropriate.
- Parent notifications should be sent home on the day of an event or the next day.

KEY REMINDERS

Do

- Wait for official notification *before* going to shelter-in-place status.
- Lock exterior doors and assign a staff member at the front door.
- Establish a student release area with an exterior door specific to your school, and have it staffed.
- Have a student sign-out procedure in place.
- Place signs at the locked entrances directing parents to your established student release area.
- Comply with responding emergency officials' directions.

Do Not

- Use a bell system (use voice instead) to announce shelter-in-place.
- Permit students or staff members to leave the building, until cleared.
- Evacuate unless ordered to do so by authorized emergency personnel.
- Panic—assistance will be at your school as soon as possible.

8.37. Shootings/Woundings/Assaults

ACTIONS

- Quickly assess the situation with the primary goal of not placing any additional students or staff members in harm's way.
- Call 911 and notify the site resource officer.

- Initiate either an announced or quiet lockdown.
- If safe to do so, determine if the perpetrator is still on premises; determine the number of victims and identify witnesses.
- The emergency signal to staff members and students should convey the seriousness of the situation. Follow-up announcements will be necessary to keep everyone informed.
- Initiate SS notifications per the flow chart shown in figure 2.2.
- Activate the district CMT.
- Activate the CRT members and assign duties.
- If safe to do so, implement first aid procedures until emergency services personnel arrive.
- If safe to do so, have a member of the school/facility CRT meet the emergency services personnel when they arrive. Designate a staff member to accompany victim(s) in the ambulance(s).
- Establish a school/facility Command Post for use by the site CRT. If the crisis requires you to evacuate the school/facility, consult with the police and the district CMT regarding an alternate location.
- When emergency services personnel arrive, they assume command and control of the scene.
- No school personnel should circulate through the building.
- If students and staff members are evacuated by emergency services personnel, no individuals should be allowed to enter or reenter the building.
- Instruct any person answering phones to direct all requests to the district CMT PIO.
- Keep telephone lines, including pay telephones, open for emergency services use.
- Throughout the crisis, maintain a chronology of events. Record all significant events, actions, and individuals that are involved.
- Maintain open, nondefensive communication with students, staff members, parents, the media, and the community at large. Keep staff members, students, and parents fully informed throughout the crisis. Information centers and crisis counseling for students, staff members, and parents should begin immediately, even if located away from the school.

8.38. State of Emergency (City or County)

Public SS schools may be used as community shelters in the event that public safety officials mandate mass evacuation and sheltering of residents due to a local or regional emergency or disaster. A request for use of school facilities may originate from the Mayor's Office, police or fire department, or the county's Emergency Management Agency.

ACTIONS

- If contacted directly by a local emergency preparedness official who is known and who requires the use of a school as an emergency reception site, and so on, school officials must cooperate fully.
- Initiate SS notifications per the flow chart shown in figure 2.2.
- The executive director, Business Affairs, notifies the district CMT. The CMT consults to determine the need to activate a district emergency operations center and the extent of site support required.
- Principal/facility manager notifies the school/facility CRT members and assigns duties.
- Determine the actions necessary to maintain the safety of students and staff members as they relate to the crisis.

Note: A minimum of three school division employees are to be on duty at each school shelter.

THEY INCLUDE

- Building Administrator—either the principal or assistant principal. Duties include coordinating building use with the appropriate emergency personnel and safeguarding school property. The principal may ask teachers to volunteer to assist at the shelter.
- School Custodian—duties include maintaining the facility, cleaning appropriate areas, supplying necessary restroom supplies, and cooperating with emergency personnel. The custodian should secure areas not to be used by evacuees.
- Cafeteria manager—either the cafeteria manager or other person designated by the school district. Duties include supervising safe operation of the kitchen and safeguarding school property. Supplies of food will be delivered to the shelter by the school support staff, city, and/or emergency personnel or their designate.

City and county emergency officials will assume command and control of community emergency evacuation and care of persons sheltered at school facilities. Care and feeding of people will be supported by the Red Cross and other predesignated community social service organizations. The SS may be requested to provide additional support, which will be determined and jointly agreed to between SS and emergency services at the time of the event.

8.39. Stranded Students and/or Staff Members

Prior to leaving on an extended (out-of-city) or overnight field trip, including all extracurricular activities, the staff supervisor will do the following:

- Provide the bus driver with the completed List of Participants form before departure.
- If a van is used, the List of Participants form must be given to the Transportation Department prior to keys being issued.
- The List of Participants form is to be kept in an emergency folder in the vehicle.

ACTIONS

In the event that school personnel become stranded, the following should take place:

- The teacher/advisor/coach is to contact his/her supervisor, who will start an emergency phone tree.
- If a district van or bus is used, the teacher/advisor/coach is to contact the Transportation Department.
- As the situation warrants, initiate SS notifications per the flow chart shown in figure 2.2.
- Depending on the situation, do as follows:
  —Call 911 if foul play is suspected.
  —The Transportation Department will make arrangements for alternate transportation.
  —The principal will convene a CRT.
  —The executive director, Business Affairs, or superintendent will convene the district CMT.
- When telephone lines are down or inaccessible, and it is difficult to give and get information to the district, the responsible adults are to keep students safe and secure until contact can be made with the district.

8.40. Suicide/Attempted Suicide

Any suicide attempt should be taken seriously.

IMMEDIATE RESPONSE ACTIONS

Suicide Attempt—No Injury

- Call 911 if a weapon is involved.
- Notify resource officer.
- *Do not leave person alone.*
- Notify principal, who will activate the CRT.
- Initiate SS notifications per the flow chart shown in figure 2.2.
- Call the parent/legal guardian.
- The principal and/or counselor will provide a verbal and written report to the executive director, Business Affairs Office.

Suicide Attempt—Injury

- Call 911 immediately.
- Notify resource officer.
- Administer first aid.
- Notify the nurse and principal, who will activate the CRT.
- Initiate SS notifications per the flow chart shown in figure 2.2.
- Call parent/legal guardian, specify what is going to happen and where to go (office or hospital), and have someone ready to meet parent/legal guardian.
- The principal and/or counselor should provide a verbal and written report to the executive director, Business Affairs Office.

Completed Suicide

- Call 911 immediately.
- Notify nurse and principal, who will activate the CRT.
- Initiate SS notifications per the flow chart shown in figure 2.2.
- Call parent/legal guardian. Inform of an attempted suicide. *Do not divulge* the fact that death has/may have occurred—this is the role of public/hospital medical officials. Advise where to go (office or hospital), and have someone ready to meet parent/legal guardian.
- Call emergency staff meeting. As much factual information as possible will be presented to disconnect the rumor mill and to provide consistent data to share with students when school convenes. The principal will tell the staff about the strategy for the day.
- An intervention area will be available for counseling for staff members and students.

Note: The CMT's PIO is the only person authorized to talk to the media/press.

Suicide Threats

In the event that a staff member has reason to believe that a student may be suicidal, the following actions are to be taken:

- Take all comments about suicide seriously, especially if details of a suicide plan are shared.
- Immediately report any concerns to an administrator, the counselor, and the psychologist.

Do Not Delay!

- Under no circumstances should an untrained person attempt to assess the severity of suicidal risk; all assessment of threats, attempts, or other risk factors must be left to appropriate mental health professionals.
- If the student is in the school, ensure they are immediately placed under adult supervision and not allowed to leave the school.
- Call a school CRT meeting if possible.
- Initiate SS notifications per the flow chart shown in figure 2.2.
- Designate a case manager. When possible, the school CRT members should quickly gather to designate the case manager, usually the school counselor or school psychologist.
- Conduct an initial interview with the student. The case manager, normally with at least one other staff person present, should interview the student on the day of the referral. They will determine the extent of suicidal thinking, the potential plan of suicide, the lethality of the plan, and the history of the student's suicidal thinking and attempts. For severe cases, ensure the safety of the student by continuing to provide adult supervision.
- Develop an initial plan of action. The case manager and other members of the school CRT should quickly meet to formulate a plan of action. Depending on the seriousness of the case, the CRT may wish to consult with other staff persons not initially involved or discuss the case with external professionals (e.g., physician, mental health worker, etc.), some of whom may have had prior involvement with the student. Plans formulated by the team might range from no further involvement, to monitoring by a specific staff member, to referral for follow-up counseling within the school setting, and to asking the parents or guardians to immediately come to the school to be part of the planning process.
- Notify parents or guardians. The case manager must contact the parents of all interviewed students on the same day of the referral and interview. Parents will be told of the reason for the referral, the outcome of the interview, and if the parents have not been part of the planning to date, the initial actions taken by the team. When the potential for suicide is significant, the case manager needs to ensure that the parents accept responsibility to follow through with the team's recommendations.
- When parents or guardians are not available: If the student presents as being in immediate danger of hurting himself or herself, the case manager, with support from other team members, must ensure the immediate safety of the student. In extreme situations, the family doctor may be contacted, the student may be taken to the emergency room at the general hospital, or the involvement of the police may be requested.
- Follow-up with the student: Follow-up with the student remains the responsibility of the case manager, unless explicitly transferred to another team member. The case manager should document the case and regularly share information with other team members.
- Follow-up with others: Assess the need for providing follow-up to staff members, classmates, friends, peer helpers, and so forth, who may have come forward with information. Depending on the actions taken, staff members may need to be advised on a need-to-know basis.

8.41. Suspicious or Threatening Letter or Package Handling

- Do not open any letter or package until it has been inspected thoroughly. According to the U.S. Postal Service, some typical characteristics that ought to trigger suspicion include letters or parcels that show the following characteristics:
  —Have any powdery substance on the outside.
  —Are unexpected or from someone unfamiliar.

—Have excessive postage, handwritten or poorly typed address, incorrect titles or titles with no name, or misspellings of common words.

—Are addressed to someone no longer with your organization or are otherwise outdated.

—Have no return address, or have one that can't be verified as legitimate.

—Are of unusual weight, given their size, or are lopsided or oddly shaped.

—Have an unusual amount of tape.

—Are marked with restrictive endorsements, such as "Personal" or "Confidential."

—Have strange odors or stains.

- Contact your principal or supervisor, who will call the appropriate public safety officials and describe the situation. The school division central office is to be notified also.
- If a suspicious or threatening letter is received, the Postal Service advises the following:

  —Handle with care.

  —Don't shake or bump the package.

  —Don't open, smell, touch, or taste the letter or package or its contents.

  —Isolate the suspicious item.

- Anyone in the immediate vicinity of the letter must remain in the area. Take steps to admit no additional persons to the area. The room and adjoining rooms should be secured.
- The custodian/maintenance staff will shut off the HVAC system.
- Depending on the advice of public safety officials, the building may need to be evacuated and/or quarantined.
- The Postal Service also recommends that, if a letter/parcel is opened and/or a biological or chemical threat is identified, the following should take place:

  —Isolate the letter/parcel—don't handle it.

  —Evacuate the immediate area.

  —Wash hands with soap and warm water.

  —Call the police.

  —Contact postal inspectors.

  —Call the local fire department/hazmat unit.

8.42. Utility and Operational Failure

Operational failures include the following:

- Breakdown of the heating/air-conditioning system.
- Broken water, steam, or gas lines.
- Loss of electrical, sewer, or water service.
- Breakdown of elevators.

ACTIONS

- Notify the principal of operational failure that endangers building occupants or buildings.
- Principal/delegate will do as follows:

  —Notify custodian and/or support services.

  —Notify utility/service company(ies) serving the school.

  —Alert employees/staff members and students to evacuate, if warranted.

  —Call 911.

  —Initiate SS notifications per the flow chart shown in figure 2.2.

  —Check and turn off gas (custodian) if gas can be smelled or other damage is evident.

—Check and turn off electricity (custodian) if electricity damage is evident.

—Check and turn off water (custodian) if pipes are broken or leaking.

- Fire department, district maintenance, and utility personnel will attempt to correct the problem.
- Consult with the executive director, Business Affairs/CMT manager regarding decisions on whether or not to dismiss students.

SPECIAL NOTE—ELEVATOR FAILURE

- If school personnel members are in an elevator that stops between floors or the doors will not open, they should use the elevator phone or alarm button to call for help.
- They should never attempt to pry open the doors or overhead hatch of a stopped elevator. Such actions by unskilled personnel may result in injury.
- Call 911 for help in extricating trapped persons.

8.43. Vandalism

- Photograph any willful and malicious destruction of school property (e.g., graffiti, broken windows, etc.), for insurance and law enforcement purposes.
- For minor damage, simply note the time, date, and type of damage for record keeping.
- For serious acts of vandalism (e.g., hate crimes, gang-related activity, damage to property, and equipment presenting health and safety hazards and/or disruption to school operations), report them to the school security officer and the police.
- Clean up and repair the damage as soon as possible to avoid encouraging future acts of vandalism.
- Aggressively prosecute all vandals to convey that you will not tolerate this type of offense.
- Collect restitution by having the offender pay money or provide labor to clean and/or repair the damage he or she has caused.

8.44. Weapons Situation

ACTIONS

- Assess the situation.
- Notify the site resource officer.
- Call 911. Provide as much information as possible. Be prepared to act as a resource and liaison between school and police. If necessary, have a map of the school available for police.
- Initiate SS notifications per the flow chart shown in figure 2.2.
- Gather as much detailed information as possible. Try to determine the following:
  —Location, identity, and detailed description of the individual.
  —Location and description of weapon.
  —Any pertinent background information on the individual, including a possible reason for carrying a weapon.
- Isolate individual or suspect if safe to do so. (If weapon is in a locker or elsewhere, prevent access to it.)
- Confer with police when they arrive. They will advise you how they intend to proceed.
- If interaction with the individual is imminent, do not use force or touch the person or weapon. Avoid sudden moves or gestures.
- Remain calm. Try not to raise your voice—but, if this becomes necessary, do so decisively and with clarity. Your tone and demeanor will strongly influence the outcome of the crisis.

- Be certain that at least one other administrator (or designee) is aware of the situation, but limit information to staff members and students on a need-to-know basis.
- Use emergency signal (define SS signal) to notify teachers of the threatening situation, and have teachers keep students in classroom until all is clear.
- Refer media questions to the district PIO.
- Call emergency staff meeting. It is important that staff members leave with accurate information about the incident and subsequent actions to be taken.

8.45. Weather (Tornado or Other Inclement Weather)

DEFINITIONS

- Severe Weather Watch: Forecast of severe weather in area; normal activities continue; no schoolwide announcement; and principal or designee monitors the situation.
- Severe Weather Warning: Severe and dangerous weather situation approaching. Be prepared.

ACTIONS

- Alert the staff of the impending weather conditions.
- Advise all students and staff members who are outside to reenter the school/facility.
- Call the school/facility CRT members together, and assign duties, for example, monitor building's cable television and Internet weather service; monitor weather radio; and observe sky for threatening weather conditions.
  —TV Stations: Channels _____
  —Radio Weather Station: _____
  —Internet Weather Channel: _____
- If danger is imminent, move students quickly and quietly to a designated area, underground shelter if available, or interior hallways on first floor. Avoid windows, auditoriums, gyms, and any wide span or overhead structure. Close windows and blinds.
- Have students/staff members sit in fetal position with face and head protected. Review "drop and tuck" command.
- Provide for students and staff members with special assistance needs. Persons in wheelchairs or other persons with special needs who are unable to assume this position should assume whatever position that affords them the most protection. It is recommended that those in wheelchairs not be removed from their wheelchairs, as this will limit their mobility.
- When sent to designated areas, teachers should (if possible) carry their roll book and, if time permits, identify each student present in the area.
- Students in portable or temporary classrooms must be evacuated to designated shelter areas or predetermined exterior areas such as ditches, culverts, or ravines. They must be instructed to assume the protective position.
- School buses should not be operated during a period of tornado warning. If a tornado warning is issued or severe weather is observed at dismissal time, students should be moved to designated tornado shelter areas in the school. Bus drivers should be prepared to move students to predesignated shelters along the various bus routes. In the event there is no immediate shelter, students should evacuate the bus to a ditch, culvert, ravine, or low-lying area and assume the protective position until the threat of weather has passed.
- If a tornado or other storm should hit the building, persons should remain in the sheltered area until it passes. The area should then be carefully inspected for downed electrical lines and other hazards.

Before leaving, the area should be checked for injured persons. If possible, one staff member should remain with the injured while others direct the remainder to predesignated assembly areas.

- Compile a list of students/staff members who are present, those known to be injured, and those that cannot be located.
- If a tornado appears so quickly that the above actions cannot be followed, all occupants should seek cover at once. For those inside the building, heavy furniture provides good protection. Interior closets also provide shelter. Once inside the sheltered area, persons should assume the protective position.

IF DAMAGE AND INJURY OCCUR

- Call 911 to ensure that emergency help is summoned.
- Initiate SS notifications per the flow chart shown in figure 2.2.
- Mobilize the school/facility CRT members and assign duties.
- Check for and provide first aid until emergency medical personnel arrive.
- Account for all students and staff members.
- Evacuate if there is a possibility of injury by staying in the school.
- Do not allow anyone back into the building until instructed by emergency services personnel that it is safe to do so.

CHAPTER NINE

General Response Procedures

These general response procedures should be considered by the Crisis Management Team (CMT) to supplement and help sustain initial response actions and operations addressed in chapter 8.

9.1. Cleaning Up

A damage assessment must be done first. Refer to section 9.4 for information on how to perform one.

Good record keeping is a must. Refer to section 9.3, "Cost Accounting"; section 9.5, "District—Community Emergency Resource Coordination"; and section 9.9, "Reports and Record Keeping" for information on how to keep records.

ACTIONS

- Take pictures of the area before and after cleaning up; record date, time, and location.
- Track hours of employees and volunteers:
  —Name
  —All hours worked by date
  —Job performed
- Track equipment used:
  —Type of vehicle
  —License plate number (or serial number)
  —Number of hours used
- Track supplies used:
  —Name of material
  —Amount of material
  —Cost of material (if known)
- Use caution while performing task so you don't do more damage to persons or property.
- Use a separate project number for each site.

9.2. Communications

In any emergency or disaster, people need information. The larger the emergency/disaster, the more information will be needed. It is important to organize the gathering and dissemination of information.

For communications to be successful, a plan must be followed. When releasing information to the media, parents, or others outside the district, follow the procedures in section 9.8, "Public Relations and the Media." This section deals with handling information within the building or with the District Office.

METHODS OF COMMUNICATIONS

The following are examples of communications options and tools that can be considered during any response operations:

- Telephone
  —Normal communications will be by telephone throughout the crisis period. All schools and district buildings will establish telephone answering and communicating procedures.
  —The volume of calls will be higher than normal. Additional lines may be required.
  —The Telecommunications Department will be responsible for keeping phones and lines functional.
- Cordless telephone
  —Good when the speaker is mobile.
  —Will not work when the electricity is not working.
- Cell phone
  —Good when the speaker is mobile, especially when traveling from site to site.
  —Will not work if the cell sites have gone down.
  —Cell towers may be overloaded during emergencies; cell phones may not always be reliable.
  —Good as a backup system for school phones.
- Mobile phone
  —Strong signals when traveling in a vehicle.
  —Will not work when the phone lines are down.
- Intercom
  —Good for two-way communication from classroom to office.
  —Short messages are best.
- Fire alarm
  —Good for evacuating building population.
- Megaphone
  —Good system for talking to a crowd outside but limited in its uses.
- Bullhorn
  —Will work better than a megaphone but still limited in its use.
- FM/AM radio
  —Good way to get information from weather and news stations.
- Bus radios
  —Good secondary method of communication.
  —Will not work if there is no electricity.
  —Can only talk bus to bus or with the dispatcher.
- Maintenance radios
  —Good secondary method of communication.
  —Will not work if there is no electricity.
  —Can only talk vehicle to vehicle or with the dispatcher.
  —900 MHz radios.
  —Can communicate with the emergency management personnel.
- Police department radios
  —Will work if you have the same crystals.
  —Will work for departments that have not gone to 900 MHz radios.

- Fire department radios
  —Will work if you have the same crystals.
  —Will work for departments that have not gone to 900 MHz radios.

COMMUNICATING WITH THE DISTRICT EMERGENCY OPERATIONS CENTER

- The CMT will require timely information.
- Information needed includes, but is not limited to, the following:
  —Type of emergency/disaster
  —Cause
  —Names, number injured, and types of injuries
  - ☐ Students
  - ☐ Employees
  - ☐ Visitors
  —Time emergency/disaster happened
  —Who has responded?
  —Who has been called?
  —What is being done?
  —Extent of damage
  —Location where parents can meet students
  —Estimates of cost of repairs

Specific information needs, protocols, and reporting formats are addressed in chapter 3.

9.3. Cost Accounting

The school system (SS) should be self-insured for most minor types of loss and damage. Casualty insurance is maintained to cover extraordinary damage and loss to persons, buildings, and property. Employee injuries are covered under the State Workers' Compensation. In the event of a significant incident, the SS will file a claim with its insurance broker. Claims for damage loss and recovery will be coordinated through SS Risk Management. The SS may maintain the following types of insurance, each subject to varying limits and deductibles (details of coverage are administered through SS Risk Management): property, content, flood/earthquake, inland marine, general liability, education legal liability, employment practice liability, employee benefits, state stop gap, crime coverage, business auto, boiler/machinery, and student health.

All damage and loss claims must be substantiated with detailed record keeping documenting the nature of the loss. The SS must initiate detailed cost accounting procedures to ensure appropriate documentation of the incident, response actions, and cost impacts associated with damage, response, and recovery operations.

Furthermore, should the loss be attributable to natural forces, (e.g., tornado, flood, etc.) and the area/region be designated a national disaster as declared by the U.S. president, cost may be covered by federal funds through the Federal Emergency Management Agency (FEMA).

At a minimum, the SS should ensure the incident and cost-related documentation listed below is assembled. The SS should consult with its insurance broker and claims adjusters to determine additional documentation needs. The SS should establish a special account number to track emergency-related expenses. Both Risk Management and FEMA require that all the crisis situation hours, supplies, equipment usage, and so forth, be tracked separately from day-to-day expenses.

The project file must contain but not necessarily be limited to the following records:

- Loss inventory
- Cost/property valuation records
- Computations
- Measurements
- Notes
- Photo documentation of damage/scene
- Blueprints
- Plans
- Maps
- Special considerations include the following:
  —Payroll records
  —Time sheets for volunteers
  —Contractor records/costs
  —Emergency service provider costs/records
  —Equipment used record
  —Materials used record
  —Repair invoices and receipts
  —Police and/or fire reports
  —Internal security reports
  —Other expenses
- Copy of insurance documentation including anticipated insurance settlement or actual insurance settlement (FEMA requirement)
  —Data
  —Declarations
  —Endorsements
  —Exclusions
  —Schedules
  —Any other attachments
  —Copies of the claim
  —Proof of loss
  —Statement of loss

9.4. Damage Assessment

9.4.1. PURPOSE

In the event of a disaster, the SS may be requested to support safety personnel in the conduct of rapid building assessment(s) of the school/facility to evaluate the safe occupation/entry by employees and students. Persons selected should be familiar with the building and possible damage from fires, explosions, earthquakes, and so forth. This section provides forms to aid in building assessment.

9.4.2. SCOPE AND FUNCTIONS

Depending upon the type and severity of the incident, the SS may become involved in the conduct of independent building assessments of school buildings. If substantial damage is experienced, the SS may not conduct assessments but instead rely upon its insurance underwriters and contractors to perform this work. In minor damage situations, SS personnel may conduct these assessments in-house.

The following damage assessment forms can be used by the SS to support initial assessment activities, or they can be replaced by protocols utilized by insurance and contractor professionals providing follow-up support.

When in doubt, the building is to be evacuated and closed.

The Crisis Response Team (CRT) will support this endeavor, which could involve the following functions:

- Conduct evacuation assessment, if time and conditions permit.
- Conduct rapid building assessment of all floors and facilities.
- Close building or cordon off all danger areas.
- Document building damage.
- Request professional help as needed.

Sample Building Assessment Checklist

A. Assemble and Equip Teams

Team Leader

_____

Team Members

_____

_____

_____ 1. Form building assessment teams of at least two persons per team.
_____ 2. Establish communications. Check with the Command Post for information on the status of school and possible hazards.
_____ 3. Equip team members with hard hats, gloves, and tools as needed. Review safety equipment and guidelines.

B. Evacuation Assessment

_____ 1. Check evacuation routes for safety.
_____ 2. Check assembly areas for safety—gas/water pipe ruptures, down power lines, trees, land slide danger, hazardous materials, and so forth.

C. Rapid Building Assessment

_____ 1. Establish an assessment plan. Divide the school into manageable areas prior to starting to evaluate. Use a floor plan area map or a sheet of paper to identify the sections and the problems encountered. Mark the areas evaluated.
_____ 2. Review structures for conditions listed on the forms.
_____ 3. Indicate condition of the building. Close building if necessary, and cordon off dangerous areas with barrier tape, signs, barricades, and so on.
_____ 4. Make recommendations on safety of building and notify Command Post.
_____ 5. Document all activities of the building assessment teams. This should include areas searched, victims found, damage noted, times, team members, and so on. Information regarding victims must be reported to the Crisis Response Team.
_____ 6. Submit Building Rapid Evaluation Form to Command Post.

BUILDING RAPID EVALUATION FORM

Building Description

Name　　　_____

Address　_____

　　　　　_____

　　　　　_____

# of stories _____

Basement: Yes____ No____ Unknown____

Building Type:
_____ School
_____ Office
_____ Ancillary Building
_____ Warehouse
_____ Other (specify) _____

Structural System:
_____ Wood frame
_____ Unreinforced masonry
_____ Reinforced masonry
_____ Tilt up
_____ Concrete frame
_____ Steel frame
_____ Other (specify) _____

Main Occupants:
_____ Students/Staff
_____ Handicapped
_____ Non–English speaking
_____ Staff
_____ Outside agency
_____ Other (specify) _____

Overall Rating (check one)

_____ Inspected (green)
_____ Exterior only
_____ Exterior and Interior

_____ Limited Entry (yellow)
_____ Unsafe (red)

Inspector _____

Department _____

Inspection Date (m/d/y) _____

Inspection Time ____:____ a.m./p.m.

Instructions

1. Review structure for conditions listed below.
2. A "yes" answer to 1, 2, 3, or 4 is grounds for posting the entire structure AREA UNSAFE.
3. If more review is needed, post LIMITED ENTRY.
4. A "yes" answer to 5 requires posting AREA UNSAFE and/or barricading around the hazard.
5. Hazards such as a toxic spill or an asbestos release are covered by 6, and are to be posted and/or barricaded to indicate AREA UNSAFE.

Condition of Building

	Yes	No	More Review Needed
1. Collapse, partial collapse, or building off foundation	_____	_____	_____
2. Building or story noticeably leaning	_____	_____	_____
3. Severe racking of walls, obvious severe damage and distress	_____	_____	_____
4. Severe ground or slope movement present	_____	_____	_____
5. Chimney, parapet, or other falling hazard	_____	_____	_____
6. Other hazard	_____	_____	_____

Recommendations

_____ No further action needed

_____ Detailed evaluation required

_____ Structural

_____ Geotechnical

_____ Other _____

_____ Barricades needed in these areas: _____

_____ Other (specify) _____

Comments: _____

_____

_____

Building Equipment Damage Assessment

	OK	Damaged/ Operable	Damaged/ Inoperable	Comments
Main boilers	___	___	___	_____
Chillers (for HVAC)	___	___	___	_____
Emergency generators	___	___	___	_____
Fuel tanks	___	___	___	_____
Battery racks	___	___	___	_____
Fire pumps	___	___	___	_____
On-site water storage	___	___	___	_____
Communication equipment	___	___	___	_____
Main transformers	___	___	___	_____
Elevators	___	___	___	_____

	OK	Damaged/ Operable	Damaged/ Inoperable	Comments
Other Fixed Equipment	___	___	___	_____
Gas main	___	___	___	_____
_____	___	___	___	_____

(continued)

BUILDING RAPID EVALUATION FORM (*continued*)

Special Concerns

Toxic chemical storage: ___   ___   ___   _____

_____   ___   ___   ___

Other

_____   ___   ___   ___   _____
_____   ___   ___   ___   _____
_____   ___   ___   ___   _____

Comments: _____

_____

_____

Geotechnical Hazards

	OK	No	Unknown	Comments
Slope failure, debris	___	___	___	_____
Ground movement, fissures	___	___	___	_____
_____	___	___	___	_____
_____	___	___	___	_____

Nonstructural Hazards

Parapets, ornamentation	___	___	___	_____
Cladding, glazing	___	___	___	_____
Ceilings, light fixtures	___	___	___	_____
Interior walls, partitions	___	___	___	_____
Elevators	___	___	___	_____
Stairs, exits	___	___	___	_____
Electric, gas, other utilities	___	___	___	_____
_____	___	___	___	_____
_____	___	___	___	_____

SEND COPY OF THIS FORM TO DISTRICT EMERGENCY OPERATIONS CENTER

9.5. District—Community Emergency Resource Coordination

The SS will cooperate with city and county emergency management agencies, and such organizations as the American Red Cross, to provide community emergency relief services. SS support includes, but is not necessarily limited to, the following:

- Use of district schools and facilities for sheltering and feeding of community residents
- Use of district buses to facilitate evacuation and transport of people to and from shelters

BUILDING DETAILED EVALUATION FORM

Building Name and Address

_____

_____

_____

_____

Sketch—draw sketch if appropriate

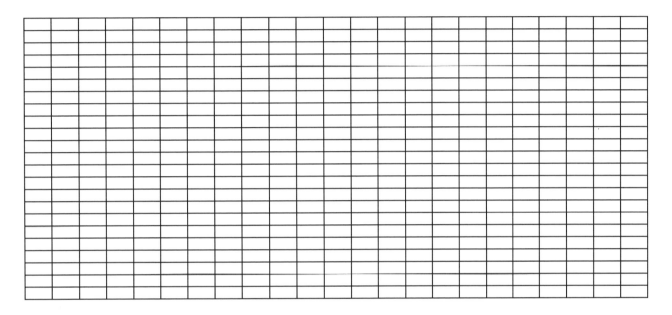

SEND COPY OF THIS FORM TO DISTRICT EMERGENCY OPERATIONS CENTER

- Use of district personnel
- Use of volunteers

Stipulations concerning specific support agreements are maintained in the Offices of the Executive Director, Schools Business Affairs, the mayor, the county Emergency Management Agency (EMA), and the Red Cross. The Red Cross, or another such organization, is the designated agency to operate shelters during emergency situations.

A general summary of SS support capabilities and actions follow below.

ACTIVATION OF SS RESPONSE TEAMS

- The executive director, Schools Business Affairs, will notify and activate the CMT as appropriate.
- The CMT will consult with the on-site SS incident commander (IC) to determine specific on-site support needs.

USE OF DISTRICT FACILITIES

- In terms of descending priority, SS high schools, middle schools, and then elementary schools may be called upon during a major community disaster to provide for the temporary sheltering, feeding, and caring of community residents.
- The county EMA will request use of SS schools by contacting the SS executive director of Business Affairs.
- The SS district will make every effort to accommodate the emergency request. In general, the following is a guide:
  —Cafeterias and gymnasiums will be made immediately available.
  —Designated sheltering areas within individual schools will be isolated to the maximum extent practicable from ongoing school and classroom operations.
  —The SS on-site IC will coordinate additional security provisions to ensure segregation of school activities and sheltering operations.
- Special note: Downtown Evacuation Plan
  —The city has developed an Evacuation Traffic Pattern for use during an emergency downtown evacuation.
  —Nine specific school sites have been designated as emergency shelters to support downtown evacuations (see table 9.1).
- Use of district buses:
  —Mass transportation of community residents to designated shelters during emergencies will be coordinated by the county EMA and will rely predominately on the services of the Metro Regional Transit Authority.
  —The SS may be called upon in certain circumstances to provide additional transportation support using school buses.
- Use of district personnel:
  —The SS will initially provide personnel to support security, custodial, and food service operations and will coordinate with county EMA and the Red Cross to transition those roles and responsibilities to them at a time and in a manner agreed upon at the time.

Table 9.1.   Example of Downtown Evacuation Plan: Designated School Shelter Sites

Area	School	Designated Shelter Population
Northeast Shelters		
	North High School	2,900+
	Firestone High School	3,800+
	Perkins Middle School	1,150+
Southwest Shelters		
	Performing Arts School	2,100+
	West Middle School	750+
	South High School	3,500+
Southeast Shelters		
	East High School	2,000+
	Washington High School	1,400+
	Lincoln Middle School	650

USE OF VOLUNTEERS

—The request/use of volunteers to support school operations during emergency sheltering operations should be reviewed with the SS executive director of Business Affairs/CMT.

—Each school or site will coordinate the use of the volunteers that arrive at their site.

—All volunteers must sign in and out using their name, time in, and time out.

DOCUMENTATION AND RECORD KEEPING

* The SS will document usage of facilities, equipment, supplies, and staff and volunteer labor for purposes of insurance, liability considerations, facility repair, and possible remuneration.
* All hours of volunteers (including regular hours) will be tracked during the event using a special project code for possible reimbursement to the district following the event. Volunteer hours may be used for the "match" under some programs.

9.6. Evacuating People with Special Needs

To meet special evacuation needs, special provisions will be made for students and staff members with disabilities, such as learning and developmental disabilities, visual and hearing impairments, and physical limitations.

* Attention will also be provided for students with limited English proficiency to make sure they understand the emergency procedures.
* During emergency evacuations, blind persons should keep physical contact with their aides by placing a hand on the aide's shoulder.

The following procedures will be implemented to ensure that persons with special needs are supported and cared for during any and all types of emergency situations and incidents that may require actions and physical activities beyond the norm.

* The school nurse or medical service provider will be responsible for maintaining a roster of students and staff members who have sight, hearing, language, mobility, and other impairments. Tables 6.4 and 6.5 provide templates for rosters that can be used to list these individuals.
* Persons with special needs should have in their possession, or on file, an individual Emergency Card describing their special needs. The cards should list information such as disability, medications and their application frequencies, mobility constraints, attendant needs, allergies, primary physician, and so forth.
* The building administrators will assign "buddy rooms" to ensure that a teacher with impairments is partnered with a teacher who can assist under emergency conditions.
* Classroom teachers will be provided the roster of students with impairments prior to the beginning of each semester, along with a copy of any existing individual Emergency Action Plans for assigned students. It is recommended that these rosters be retained within the Emergency Flip Chart binders.
* A "buddy system" will be employed that pairs each student with special needs with an individual who will locate and be responsible for her/him in an emergency. Responsibilities include ensuring their awareness of an emergency and may extend to carrying or leading them down stairs. Pairing a disabled person with two aides is preferable.
* Alternate aides will be designated in the event that there is an emergency and the person(s) responsible for assisting a handicapped individual is not available.

- Rescue teams will be made aware of the best way to rescue special needs students. As an example, mobility-impaired students should be allowed to instruct rescue team members on the best way to move them from the hazardous area. For example, the fireman's method of carrying an impaired individual may be dangerous to someone with respiratory problems.
- Administrators will maintain procedures for rapid access of the following documents and equipment to support on-site initial response actions:
  —A printout listing each student and current significant medical information. This information will remain in the custody of the school nurse or medical service provider in order to ensure confidentiality.
  —Parent permission to provide immediate treatment in the case of a medical emergency.
  —Medications, as necessary.
  —American Sign Language cue cards (as deemed appropriate).
  —Listing of triage area(s) designated for nonambulatory students or those needing specific medical assistance.
  —Listing of any special power requirements for sustaining specialized medical support equipment.
  —Evacuation chairs capable of going down a stairway to be used with large students who have limited or no head control.

9.7. Lockdown or Evacuation?

When a dangerous person or condition exists on or near the school, the primary objective is to protect students from the danger.

Many site-specific factors including the types of communication systems available, layout of the school, and types of construction are taken into consideration in determining whether lockdown or evacuation should occur.

For example, a classroom with block walls and a locked steel door provides a more secure environment than a portable classroom. Because of these site-specific variables, individual schools have/should establish internal procedures unique to their location.

Options include a full school lockdown, a full evacuation, or a lockdown of designated areas and evacuation of other areas.

In general, lockdown is likely to be the better choice if the perpetrator remains at large in the building or his/her location is unknown.

If some students are not secured in a locked location and are in the path of danger, then an evacuation of those students may be required.

9.8. Public Relations and the Media

In any emergency situation there are parties who have a legitimate need for information—families, news media, employees, and the like. If a major emergency occurs, the demand for information will be intense. It is important to organize the gathering and dissemination of information.

Key components that lead to the success of any communications plan include the following:

- Avoiding conflicts in the information given
- Keeping media and families away from the immediate disaster area where they could hamper emergency control efforts
- Getting necessary information to the community while avoiding confusion or panic
- Sending accurate information from the disaster area
- Establishing an information center

KEY CONSIDERATIONS

- Communicating with the media—official spokesperson:
  —Media serve a vital link between the incident at hand, responders, parents, and the community at large. Cooperation with media personnel is very important to ensure that timely and most importantly accurate information is conveyed to the public. The SS will be proactive in establishing good working relationships with safety crisis communications responders and media representatives.
  —In the event of a crisis situation, the superintendent and the SS information officer are the only people to serve as spokespersons to the media. No one else is to talk to the media unless designated by the superintendent or the CMT leader to serve as an official spokesperson. Any and all media requests are to be diverted to the information officer.
- Access to school facilities and property:
  —For reasons of safety, security, and privacy, under no circumstances should any member of the media be allowed on school property unescorted during a crisis situation. The district, working in concert with safety officials, will determine when media representatives will be allowed into a school following a crisis situation.
  —Under certain situations, parents can be given access to the facility in order to meet children, and so forth. Such access and egress should be given in a position away from the media.
- Assess the ability to communicate:
  —Establish the ability of communicating information early by the following means:
    - Telephone
    - Television
    - Radio
    - Fax
    - Mobile or cell telephone
    - District cable channel
    - School Parent-Teacher Association calling networks
    - District Web page
    - District emergency phone line
    - Others
- Establish Communication Center:
  —Establish a media center.
  —Center should be set up as follows:
    - ☐ Near the disaster scene if media are likely to be present
    - ☐ At the SS district office or emergency operations center (EOC) in less serious situations
  —Provide telephone numbers or means of contact and location to key disaster staff immediately.
  —Direct all media representatives to the media center.
  —Ensure availability of accurate and critical information at the center including the following:
    - ☐ Emergency cause, if known
    - ☐ Extent of damage
    - ☐ Status of on-site emergency response actions and resources
    - ☐ Extent/number of injuries and support being provided
    - ☐ Location where parents can meet their children
    - ☐ Critical safety- and security-oriented messaging (as decided upon with the public safety IC)
    - ☐ Estimate of when repairs will be made and if school will be closed
  —The SS information officer, superintendent, or designee will share information with the media about the district's efforts to handle the emergency situation.
  —Information such as missing persons and names, ages, condition, nature of injuries of injured, and so forth, will only be shared with parents or guardians.
  —Media representatives who ask for such information will be directed to law enforcement or hospital spokespersons.
    - ☐ Information regarding the ongoing situation shall be processed and disseminated to families and media.

☐ District hotline numbers will be established and updated with information.

—Using a JIC (Joint Information Center)

☐ A JIC should be established as a central location for the media to work and receive briefings and press releases.

☐ The center will allow various agencies/departments responding to the disaster to verify reports and coordinate their news releases.

☐ All information officers will sign off on each other's press releases to make sure everyone is aware of what information is being released.

• Dissemination of information:

—The CMT will be prepared to initiate an information message that can be activated on the district emergency phone line.

—A district spokesperson shall be identified.

☐ The spokesperson shall be a senior district official who will speak for the district and other agencies involved in the disaster. The spokesperson should be experienced in dealing with the media and knowledgeable about emergency plans.

☐ At least two backups shall be identified for the spokesperson.

☐ Information release shall be coordinated with the CMT.

☐ All schools and departments shall release information only through the spokesperson.

—Establish credibility with media, for successful management.

☐ Honesty is essential.

☐ Provide equal access to information.

☐ Strive to gain accurate, detailed information, then determine what is appropriate for release.

☐ Express concern for tragedy, strength for confidence, assurance for future emergency management, and gratitude for emergency efforts.

☐ Focus on helping citizens cope. Criticism would surely contribute to controversy.

DOS AND DON'TS OF MEDIA RELATIONS

Don't

• Talk about things you know nothing about
• Bluff
• Give the interviewer ammunition—rather, give appropriate response
• Go off the record
• Use negative buzz words (tragedy, disaster, rip-off, etc.)
• Get angry or cry
• Offer personal opinions
• Answer with "no comment"
• Beat around the bush
• Appear mechanical or phony
• Get trapped into statistics
• Look at the monitor
• Speculate
• Let incorrect statements or assumptions just lie there
• Use professional jargon
• Apply pressure to have copy slanted or withheld
• Double-talk—rather, be specific

Do

- Bridge the conversation
  a. Make it go where you want it
  b. Use "I don't know about that, but I do know this . . ."
- Turn a negative into a positive, that is, use "on the contrary, this is working very well"
- Do your homework
- Practice the presentation
- Speak in three-second quotes
- Know your audience
- Keep major points you want to make in mind
- Emphasize your interest in the health and safety of the students and be sincere
- Avoid open animosity
- Carefully examine any documentation shown to you by media personnel
- Participate in one-on-one interviews when time and circumstances allow
- Know to whom you are talking
- Be honest
- If the release of certain information will do any harm, tell the interviewer
- Be courteous and considerate
- Answer, "I'll get back to you on that"
- End with, "Thank you very much. We've run out of time. We will give you another update at _____ (time)."

9.9. Reports and Record Keeping

Whether you are submitting expenses to the SS insurance underwriter or FEMA for reimbursement, proper documentation methods must be used. All records must be kept for three years following reimbursement.

- Tracking sites:
  —Each school or district building will be tracked as a separate project.
  —The site number must appear on all photos, MSS, and other forms of documentation.
- Tracking employee hours:
  —A special account number will be set up for disasters/emergencies. All regular and overtime hours must be tracked using it.
- Tracking volunteer hours:
  —All volunteers must sign in and out using their name, time in, and time out. If possible, employees will work an eight-hour day, with lunch and breaks.
- Taking pictures. Use the following kinds of cameras:
  —35 mm camera with a zoom lens (order a minimum of three copies when developing film)
  —Polaroid-type of camera (take three copies of every image)
  —Digital camera
    □ Can make as many copies of the pictures as you want
    □ Use a color printer for better pictures when printing.
    □ Can store the pictures on a computer
    □ Need a large hard drive for storage space
    □ Easy to add pictures to the Internet

- ☐ Easy to add pictures to your documents
- ☐ Can e-mail pictures when reporting
—VHS video camera
- ☐ Can take an overall shot of the site
- ☐ Can document the event as it is happening
- Taking pictures. Other advice:
—Have a date and time recorded for every picture.
- ☐ Use the built-in time/date stamp if you have it.
- ☐ Put a piece of paper with the time/date on it in the picture.
- ☐ Keep a log of pictures taken, along with the location, time, and date.
—You will need pictures of the site:
- ☐ Before the event (take these images as soon as possible)
- ☐ After the event
- ☐ Following the cleanup
- ☐ Following building restoration
—Subjects to photograph include the following:
- ☐ Entries of building
- ☐ Outside of building
- ☐ Areas of damage
(Make sure to have something [a person, truck, or building] in the photos to give a sense of the scale.)
- Tracking messages:
—Send written messages to anyone with whom you need to communicate.
—Phones tend to get tied up quickly.
—Use paper premade forms or a single piece of paper. See appendix D for a sample message form.
—Use e-mail if you have access to a computer.
—Use fax machine.
- Keep copies of all written messages for documentation.
—You may need them to support a legal case.
—You may need them to answer questions from the CMT.
—Write on the messages any decisions made regarding the messages.
- ☐ After the event, it is hard to remember what you did regarding a message.
- ☐ After the event, it is hard to decide why you chose to react a certain way.
- Using a tape recorder:
—Use to document what you did and why.
- ☐ Use for dictation.
- ☐ It is easier to speak than to write.
- Contract work:
—If there is time to let out the bid, the district system will be used. On each invoice indicate the following:
- ☐ Date paid
- ☐ Amount paid
- ☐ Check number used to pay it
(If you do not accept the low bid, indicate in writing why you didn't, and attach this statement to the invoice.)
- Force account work: some work may be done using district personnel, equipment, and materials.

—You must track the following:
  □ Personnel hours
  □ Equipment used
    · Type of equipment
    · Serial or license number (some type of identification)
    · Hours used (i.e., 9 a.m. to 4 p.m.)
    · Number of hours used
    · Site where used
    · Total cost
- Materials and supplies: materials and supplies, purchased or taken from stock, must be documented. Show the following:
  —Unit price
  —Quantity
  —Total cost
  —Description
  —Date purchase or used
  —Job site
  —Date paid for
  —Amount paid
  —Check number used to pay for it
    □ Claims for materials taken from stock must be supported by either the original purchase invoice or invoice for replacement materials.
- Drawings:
  —Site plans:
    □ All files must contain a copy of the site plan.
    □ Architectural/Construction Services has line drawings of all the buildings in the district. Contact them for a copy if you do not have one.
  —Building plans:
    □ All files must contain a copy of the building plan.
    □ Architectural/Construction Services has line drawings of all the buildings in the district. Contact them for a copy if you do not have one.
- MSS:
  —The district must have a map with all the site numbers of damage plotted.
  —Each site needs a map of the location of the site.
  —Do not give away any original MSS; rather, provide copies.

9.10. Resumption of School

School will not be resumed until the building has been deemed safe by emergency personnel and district building inspectors.

- Things to consider:
  —Building safety
  —Emotional trauma
  —Busing
  —Location

- Things to consider when contemplating an alternate site:
  —Armories
  —Churches (small classrooms)
  —Portables
  —Double sessions
- The CMT will meet, evaluate all the data, and decide the following:
  —When to resume school
  —Where to resume school

9.11. Student and Personnel Tracking

Teachers and administrators will account for all persons on site subsequent to an emergency situation that results in an evacuation, shelter-in-place, lockdown, or any other type of event that requires or causes sudden or unplanned action and movement of students, staff members, and other site personnel members.

Teachers will account for their students and charges, using class rosters, as defined within established evacuation procedures.

Status reports will be provided to the principal/IC. The Student/Staff Accounting Form will be used to identify students/staff members/others requiring special assistance (see table 9.2). This information will be conveyed to on-site police and/or fire officials to support on-site search and rescue operations, as may be warranted.

Search and rescue efforts will be led by fire and/or police officials; the SS staff may be requested to assist.

Site staff/student status reports will be prepared and maintained in the on-scene Command Post.

The SS IC will communicate status reports, using the Site Staff/Student Status Report form, to the SS EOC or other designated location, for review and action by district management and/or the CMT (see table 9.3).

Note: Details relating to fatalities can only be confirmed and released by safety and medical professionals.

9.12. Student/Family Reunification

The Student/Family Reunification Team is responsible for supervising the reunification of students with their parents or guardians in an efficient and orderly manner.

MATERIALS NEEDED

- Radios/pagers
- Cell phones
- Clipboards
- Paper
- Pens
- Markers
- Rosters of school students and staff members
- Student Emergency Medical Cards
- Yellow "caution" tape or portable plastic construction fencing

Table 9.2. Student/Staff Accounting Form

School/Site:	
Room No.:	Date:
Enrolled per register:	Reported by:
Not in School today:	Received by:
Present now:	

1. Students or classroom volunteers elsewhere (off campus, left in room, other location, etc.)

Name	Location	Problem

2. Students on playground/yard needing more first aid than you can handle.

Name	Location	Problem

Additional comments (report fire, gas/water leaks, blocked exits, structural damage, etc.)

Table 9.3.   Site Staff/Student Status Report

To:_____ From: (name) _____ Location: _____

Date: _____ Time: _____ Person in Charge at Site: _____

Message via: **Two-way Radio** _____   **Telephone** _____   **Messenger** _____

EMPLOYEE/STUDENT STATUS

	Absent	Injured	# Sent to Hospital	Dead*	Missing	Unaccounted for (Away from site)	# Released to Parents	# Being Supervised
Students								
Site Staff								
Others								

Comments:

9.12.1. DOUBLE-GATE SYSTEM

- The reunification team will be using a double-gate system. Staff members will be located in two areas.
- The "holding area," the first area, will be where students can wait for their parents.
- The second area will include both the "report point" and the "Student Release Point," where adult caregivers will report and wait for their students to join them.
- These will be two distinctly separate areas, but they will be in close proximity to one another.
- Red Cross assistance, if available, will be utilized to increase staffing, to improve the communications capabilities and the conditions at both areas, and to make refreshments available at both areas.

9.12.2. HOLDING-AREA OPERATION

- Designated classroom teachers will remain with their assigned students in the holding area.
- Each will have the list of the students assigned to their supervision, including the exact name of their parents/guardians.
- Anyone who was absent at the start of the school day or who departed prior to the incident will be noted.

- At the end of the day, teachers will call all those parents/guardians who have not yet picked up their child(ren).
- If the parent cannot be reached, the student will be transported to his or her home by a school district personnel member.

9.12.3. RELEASE POINT OPERATION

- When a parent/guardian arrives at the release point, she or he will be asked for the name of the student(s) being picked up.
- The parent/guardian will then be required to show proof of his or her identification (driver's license or other government-issued photo identification).
- When the staff member confirms the parent's/guardian's identity and authority to pick up the student, the staff member will use a runner or a radio/cellular telephone to notify the staging area that the designated student(s) is to be escorted to the release point.
- When the student(s) reports to the release point, the staff member will have the parent/guardian sign for the student(s) on the Student Release Form and the student(s) is released to the adult caregiver.
- If the parent/guardian must be notified that their child(ren) has been injured or for some other reason is not available for release to them, the staff member at the release point will not indicate the status of the child but rather will ask the parent to report to a nearby room for further processing.
- A "notification room(s)" will be staffed by members of the Mental Health Team to deal with these parents.

9.12.4. NOTIFICATION ROOM OPERATION

- Members of the Mental Health Team (school counselors, chaplains, or other mental health professionals) will be responsible for notifying parents that their child is not available for pickup for any of the following reasons: injury, death (release of fatality-related information must be coordinated with safety and/or medical professionals), arrest, required as a witness, and so forth.
- The staff member will do as follows:
  —Provide available information regarding the child(ren) in a sensitive way.
  —In the event of death, will assure the parent/guardian that everything possible is being done to safeguard their child or their child's remains.
  —Will inform the parent/guardian where they are to await further information about how they will be reunited with their child(ren) or the remains of their child(ren).
  —Will assist the parent/guardian with their trauma.
  —Will make available to the parent/guardian means for communicating with other family members and supporters.
  —Will shelter the parent/guardian from media representatives.

Note: Parents and students have been informed of this procedure in a letter from the principal that is part of the registration package distributed at the start of each school year or whenever the student is registered.

9.12.5. DESCRIPTION OF OPERATIONS

Student Holding Area

The double-gated system to be utilized when laying out the Student/Family Reunification Site is depicted in figure 9.1. The adult picking up a student will report to the Adult Report Point at the upper right. Signs will be posted by the Student/Family Reunification Team, and Security Team members

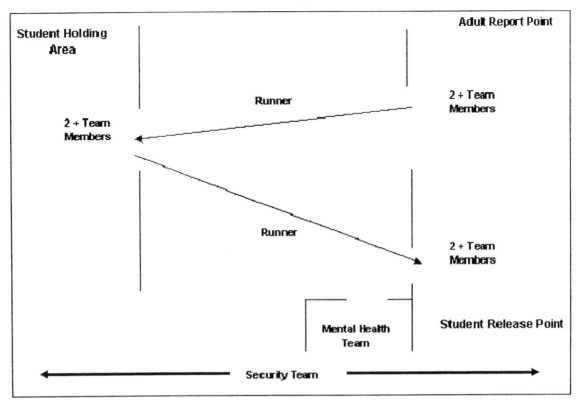

Figure 9.1   Student/Family Reunification Site Layout

will be stationed to assist adults finding their way to the Adult Report Point. The arriving adults will be greeted by two or more members of the Student/Family Reunification Team who are working the report point. The team members will provide the adult with a copy of the Student Release Form, asking the adult to complete the first section. A team member will then confirm the identity of the adult, utilizing a government-issued picture identification (driver's license, military ID, passport, etc.) and confirm that the adult is listed on the emergency data card for the student as being authorized to pick up the student. A team member will then complete the second section of the Student Release Form and hand it to a runner to be carried to the Student Holding Area. The adult will be asked to step around to the Student Release Point and wait for the runner to return. (Note: The Adult Report Point and the Student Release Point may be consolidated if there are too few Student/Family Reunification Team members to run both locations.) The runner will deliver the Student Release Form to the two or more members of the Student/Family Reunification Team who are working at the entrance to the Student Holding Area. They will have the requested student report to them, if the requested student is present in the holding area. A team member will then record on a roster that the student has been released from the holding area, check off the "Sent with Runner" entry in the third section of the Student Release Form, and send the student with a runner to the Student Release Point. If, however, the student was never at school that day (absent), is being attended to at the first aid station, has been taken to the hospital, is not available for pickup due to some other situation, or is missing, the team member will make the appropriate entry in the third section of the Student Release Form and enter comments to clarify the status. The runner will deliver the Student Release Form to the Student Release Point.

When the runner delivers the Student Release Form and the student (if available) to the two or more Student/Family Reunification Team members at the Student Release Point, the team members will call for the adult picking up the student. The adult's identification will again be confirmed, utilizing a government-issued picture identification. The adult will then sign for the student and depart the area

STUDENT RELEASE FORM
First section completed by the adult picking up a student

Please Print

Student's Name _____

Teacher _____ Grade _____

Name of Adult Picking Up the Student _____

To be filled in by the Report Point staff

Proof of ID   Yes _____   No _____

Emergency card gives permission for pickup by this adult   Yes _____   No _____

To be taken by runner

Student's Status
To be filled in by the Holding Area staff

Sent with Runner			
Not Available for Release:	Absent	First Aid	Hospital
	Missing	Other	

Comments: _____
_____
_____

To be filled in by the Release Point staff

Confirm the student is being matched with the correct adult. Have the requesting adult sign for the student.

Parent/Guardian/Caregiver Signature _____

Date_____   Time _____

with the student. If, however, the adult must be notified that the student is not available for pickup, a Student/Family Reunification Team member will take the adult to the notification room where a Mental Health Team member will take over. The Mental Health Team will be responsible for helping the adult and finding answers to the resulting questions.

9.13. Terrorism

Terrorism is a term applied to a specific criminal act based on the motivation of the attacker; it is not a separate incident in and of itself. Acts described as terrorism are legally defined in both federal and state law, and generally include acts of violence, the response to which is set forth in chapter 7. It is not necessary for the SS to determine whether a specific act is legally defined as an act of terrorism, since the actions to be taken at the scene are based on the situation as it occurs, not the motivation of the attacker.

If a threat of or an actual attack is directed at the SS or other assets in the city that might affect the SS, the police department will notify the SS and advise as to specific steps to be taken by either the district or a specific school or facility.

The U.S. Department of Homeland Security issues the Terror Alert Level (color coded) for the nation as a whole but also provides more detailed information on the actual threat risk and potential targets to appropriate local law enforcement (police department).

The SS should convene the CMT if/when the level is raised to Severe (Red) for the region. The CMT should maintain a liaison at the police department to determine appropriate courses of action. If the threat is specific to a school or facility, the CRT should be notified.

In general, actions listed in table 9.4 should be considered at the various established threat levels.

GENERAL BACKGROUND INFORMATION

The terrorist attacks in September 2001 brought to light the need for school Crisis Management Plans to include strategies to protect students and staff members in the event of subsequent attacks. Two key variables in responding to a terrorist attack are the nature of the terrorist threat and how much warning time there is available. In all cases of terrorist threat, school officials should establish and maintain close communication with local safety officials.

TYPES OF TERRORIST ATTACKS

The Federal Bureau of Investigation (FBI) categorizes terrorism in the United States as one of two types—domestic terrorism or international terrorism. Domestic terrorism involves groups or individuals whose terrorist activities are directed at elements of our government or population without foreign direction.

Weapons of mass destruction (WMD) likely to be used by terrorists fall into four categories: (1) conventional, (2) chemical, (3) biological, and (4) nuclear. Specific guidelines for schools have not yet been developed; however, some preliminary considerations are set forth below.

Conventional Weapons

Conventional weapons include bombs and other explosive devices. The goal is to place students and staff members in a protected space and/or to increase the distance from the blast area. Possibilities include the following:

- Move to basement rooms, if possible.
- Move to interior hallways, away from windows, closing doors to exterior rooms.
- Students/staff members assume "duck-and-cover" position.

Table 9.4. Homeland Security Advisory System Recommendations

Threat level	Recommended actions
SEVERE (Red)	❖ Monitor national and local news media for information and possible instructions. ❖ Prepare for evacuation, shelter-in-place, or school closing based on information received from the police department. ❖ Consult with police/school resource officer regarding access control procedures including positive identification checks of all visitors to SS schools and facilities. ❖ Ensure mental health counselors are available for students, staff members, and faculty members. ❖ Advise all teachers and staff members to review the Crisis Management Plan flip charts and the appropriate sections of the Crisis Management Plan.
HIGH (Orange)	❖ Be alert to suspicious activity, and report it to the proper authorities. ❖ Advise all teachers and staff members to review the Crisis Management Plan flip charts and the appropriate sections of the Crisis Management Plan. ❖ Prepare to handle inquiries from anxious parents and media. ❖ Discuss/be prepared to discuss students' fears concerning possible terrorist attacks.
ELEVATED (Yellow)	❖ Be alert to suspicious activity, and report it to the proper authorities. ❖ Ensure all emergency supplies are stocked and ready.
GUARDED (Blue)	❖ Be alert to suspicious activity, and report it to the proper authorities. ❖ Conduct safety training/emergency drills following written emergency plans/procedures.
LOW (Green)	❖ Maintain and distribute emergency response plans and procedures. ❖ Maintain training programs and procedures.

- Shut off gas utilities.
- If school buildings themselves are targeted, evacuation to alternate sites should be considered.
- Release students to their parents/other authorized persons in accordance with emergency release procedures.

Chemical Weapons

Chemical agents are poisonous gases, liquids, or solids that have toxic effects on people, animals, or plants. Most chemical agents cause serious injuries or death.

The goal is to limit exposure to contaminated air.

- In the absence of gas masks, which are not available in sufficient quantity and present other practical problems, move all students into buildings and shelter-in-place: close all windows and doors, and shut off HVAC systems.
- Ground-level spaces are preferable to basement areas because vapors may settle and become trapped in basements.
- Decisions to evacuate should be based on reliable information from safety officials about the location of the chemical release and the direction and speed of winds carrying the agent toward or away from the school.

Biological Weapons

Biological agents are organisms or toxins that have illness-producing effects on people, livestock, and crops. They can be dispersed as aerosols or airborne particles.

Biological weapons present a particular challenge because symptoms may not present for days or weeks following exposure. Schools must rely on medical expertise in the development of procedures for responding to biological attack. Consider the following:

- If an attack is identified while it is occurring, schools should get students into buildings and shelter-in-place: close all doors and windows, and shut down HVAC systems. Just as with chemical weapons, the goal is to prevent or reduce exposure to the substance.
- Release students to their parents/other authorized persons in accordance with emergency release procedures.
- Because diseases caused by the use of many biological weapons are contagious (i.e., smallpox), school will likely be closed after an attack, pending clearance by medical authorities.

Nuclear Weapons

Just as with conventional weapons, the goal is to place students and staff members in a protected space and/or to increase the distance from the blast area. Such weapons present a threat of not only blast effect but also exposure to radiation. Possibilities include the following:

- Move to basement rooms, if possible.
- Move to interior hallways, away from windows, closing doors to exterior rooms.
- Students/staff members assume "duck-and-cover" position.
- Shut off gas utilities.
- Release students to their parents/other authorized persons in accordance with emergency release procedures.

GUIDELINES FOR BIOHAZARD THREATS

Follow procedures as directed by local emergency responders (fire departments, police, hazmat, etc.). Implement the following procedures if any school receives any kind of biohazard threat (including anthrax and chemical agents) or if your school has a biohazard emergency.

- Should you receive such a threat or have an actual biohazard emergency, immediately call 911 or report the threat; call the appropriate school district contact person.
- The persons immediately exposed to the potential agent *must* remain where they are. They should try to avoid inhaling or touching the substance.
- Try to contain the substance in the package in which it came. Do not attempt to clean any spilled contents. Cover the spilled contents and the package or letter with anything handy such as a trash can, cardboard box, paper, and so on.
- Proceed with lockdown procedures. Explain that information will be forthcoming. Try to dispel alarm and panic by keeping information basic. All staff members/students should remain in their respective areas until notified otherwise.
- Do not evacuate students outside or send them home until the emergency responders have done their investigation.
- If it is necessary to move or evacuate students and staff members to a different location, the hazmat team or other emergency responder will provide instructions to administrators as to how it will be done.

If students and staff members are moved/evacuated, remind staff members to take their grade books, purses, and seating charts.

- Administration must inform the custodial/maintenance staff to shut down the heating and air handling units in the affected area.
- Keep the faculty members, staff members, and students as informed as necessary. Work with emergency personnel who will provide the necessary and accurate information.
- Debrief students and staff members after the incident.

Appendixes

Note: The appendixes are intended as examples of an effective Crisis Management Plan. The Akron Public School System's plan has been used as a model. Actual offices, organizations, and circumstances may differ for each individual school system and region.

APPENDIX A

Prevention and Mitigation

The goal of the public school system (SS) is to protect and enhance the safety and well-being of its students, staff members, and others involved in SS operations. The SS promotes a number of varied programs aimed at reducing potential hazards and risks, reducing the likelihood of their occurrences, and/or the severity of their impact if experienced.

These proactive efforts fall broadly into the following principal areas:

- Physical Safety and Security
- Integrity of Facilities
- Drug/Violence Prevention
- Duty to Warn and Threat Assessment

An overview of programs, plans, and procedures follows. Specific and more detailed protocols and documentations are maintained by respective program stewards.

A.1. Physical Safety and Security

A.1.1. SAFETY COMMITTEE

The SS maintains a Safety Committee. See table A.1 for an example of individuals comprising a Safety Committee.

The objectives of the Safety Committee are to do as follows:

- Provide a safe and healthy educational environment for the student population.
- Provide a safe and healthy workplace for each employee.
- Provide a safe facility for the public.
- Reduce property, liability, and workers' compensation losses.
- Promote awareness and focus attention on safety issues.

The Safety Committee provides a mechanism for bringing the staff and management together in a non-adversarial, cooperative effort to promote safety and health in each district school and operating site.

The Safety Committee makes recommendations for change regarding facility and occupational safety and health issues.

Table A.1. Example of Safety Committee Members

• President	Akron Education Association
• Business agent	International Brotherhood of Firemen and Oilers Local 100
• President	OAPSE, Local 689
• Regional director	OAPSE
• President	OAPSE, Local 778
• Coordinator	Support Staff
• Executive director, Business Affairs	Akron Public Schools
• Coordinator	Business Support Services
• Coordinator	Transportation Department
• Coordinator	Classified and Certified Staff
• Executive director	Communications Department
• Foreman	Transportation Department
• Representative for Local 100	Buildings and Grounds
• Steward—Child Nutrition	C/O Garfield High School
• Coordinator	Buildings and Grounds
• President	Akron Association of Classified Personnel
• Labor Relations representative	Ohio Education Association; Summit/Portage Service Council
• Program manager	Energy, Environmental, Health, and Safety Office
• Manager	Fringe Benefits
• Coordinator	Facilities Services

Major activities of the Safety Committee include the following:

- Recommend health and safety policy.
- Review safety and health inspection reports to assist in correction of identified unsafe conditions or practices.
- Evaluate accident reports and investigations conducted to determine if the cause of the accident was properly identified and corrected, that is, unsafe act or unsafe condition.
- Evaluate effectiveness of accident and illness prevention programs, and make recommendations for improvement.
- Conduct inspections and investigations, when determined necessary by the committee.

Specific program details and records are maintained by the program manager for the Energy, Environmental, Health, and Safety Department.

A.1.2. SECURITY MEASURES

The SS has the following safety procedures in place at various schools and facilities and continues to seek additional security measures:

- All new employees are subject to security screening and background checks.
- All visitors at schools must check in at the main office. Students are encouraged to report strangers to the office. Security and staff members are instructed to stop anyone they do not know or a suspended/expelled student and escort/report them to the office.
- Uniformed school resource (police) officers are posted in all high schools and middle schools.
- All schools have lockdown procedures and drills.
- Training is provided to the school staff regarding the awareness and recognition of students who potentially may be violent.

- School administrators report incidents to the district office and the police department. Threats are dealt with individually, and each one is investigated thoroughly.
- Video surveillance cameras are in use at several facilities.
- School entrances and exit points are minimized and supervised on a regular basis by security officers and/or staff members.
- Infrequently used rooms and closets are locked.
- Access to utilities, roofs, janitorial rooms, and closets are kept locked.
- Delivery entrances used by vendors and/or school delivery vehicles are to be kept locked. Deliveries are monitored by the staff.
- VHF radios are distributed to school administrators and key staff members to ensure the ability to communicate during any potential or actual situation. The radios also enable direct communication with school resource officers.
- Outside classroom doors are to be kept locked during the school day.
- A strict policy regarding weapons on school property is enforced. Possession of any weapons of any kind results in immediate disciplinary action.
- Landscaping is routinely reviewed around buildings to ensure areas are not obscured by overgrowth of bushes or shrubs where contraband can be placed or persons can hide.
- Students are proactively encouraged to be observant and watchful of suspicious or out of the ordinary activity and report such to the staff.
- Clutter in hallways and classrooms is minimized to mitigate opportunities for hiding contraband, weapons, or other dangerous devices and to facilitate searching and inspection.
- Presence of instructional and maintenance-related hazardous, flammable, and potentially explosive materials is minimized.
- Fire extinguishers and pull stations are maintained throughout all facilities.
- Material Safety Data Sheets (MSDSs) are maintained on-site for all hazardous materials. MSDSs provide information regarding spill cleanup, first aid, and other emergency information.

Specific program details and records are maintained by the director of Student Services and security.

A.2. Integrity of Facilities

As noted below, the SS is involved in a number of major capital improvements and ongoing assessments to improve the vitality, effectiveness, and safety of its schools, facilities, and supporting infrastructure.

A.2.1. INSPECTIONS AND PREVENTIVE MAINTENANCE

Facility Services maintains a routine inspection and preventive maintenance program that address all schools and related facilities within the SS. The program includes routine and scheduled periodic inspections and general maintenance on all buildings, equipment, surrounding grounds and property, and supporting infrastructure. More substantial maintenance requirements are documented, and corrective action work orders are processed to undertake this work with either internal resources or external contractors. The overall goal of the program is to ensure to the maximum extent practicable that facilities are maintained in a safe and structurally sound manner.

The coordinator of Facility Services maintains specific program details and records.

A.2.2. SCHOOL REBUILDING PROJECT

Over the course of the next twelve to fifteen years, the Akron Public Schools will be rebuilding or renovating every school in the district. The State of Ohio–sponsored rebuilding program includes many mandated safety and security features that currently do not exist in Akron Public Schools or are present in only a few schools.

All buildings will have complete fire suppression systems, primarily by way of sprinkler systems. Fire alarm and burglar alarm systems will be current technology. Burglar alarm systems will be substantially expanded to include more motion sensors and more contact points. Closed-circuit television (CCTV) monitors will be a new addition to the buildings. Presently, most Akron Public Schools only have one camera at the entrance door. The new schools will have a minimum of six cameras, both inside and outside the building.

Entry into the schools will be improved by utilizing door access control technology such as magnetic key knobs for employees, reducing any need to leave doors unlocked. Vendor/delivery access will be at a specific door with CCTV and magnetic door lock access controlled by the Akron Public Schools staff.

A.2.3. HAZARD ANALYSIS

A Hazard Analysis was conducted at all public, private, and charter schools within the SS by representatives of the University of Akron Emergency Management Department. The Hazard Analysis focused on the identification of building-specific as well as surrounding area hazards that have an effect on site-specific facility emergency planning. The results of the Hazard Analysis are being utilized by Akron Public Schools to update individual school emergency response plans. A complete copy of the Hazard Analysis (conclusions, recommendations, and implementation strategy) is maintained in the Akron Public Schools Office of Energy, Environmental, Health, and Safety.

A.3. Drug/Violence Prevention

The SS maintains a very proactive program to facilitate and enable students and staff members to work, learn, and grow in a safe and drug-free environment. These efforts involve close interaction between students, staff members, families, and community-based organizations to collectively promote the safety and well-being of all involved. The SS maintains a Drug-Free Schools Advisory Board to provide region and site-specific program direction and guidance. The board comprises members of the city government, police, parents, school personnel, medical professionals, City Prosecutor's Office, University of Akron, community agency personnel, treatment agencies, and the Health Department.

These program efforts are coordinated by the SS Office of Drug/Violence Prevention. Details of the program are found on the following Akron Public Schools website: www.akron.k12.oh.us/dept/083.

The objectives of the program are fivefold:

1. All students will demonstrate positive character traits.
2. All students will exemplify a lifestyle that is drug and violence free.
3. Suspension and expulsion rates as related to Alcohol, Tobacco, and Other Drugs (ATOD) and violence code violations will reflect a positive trend.
4. All SS staff members will facilitate a safe and positive drug-free learning environment through a partnership with the Office of Drug/Violence Prevention.
5. All families/community will work collaboratively with the Office of Drug/Violence Prevention in the promotion of ATOD/violence-free lifestyle.

A.3.1. PUBLIC SCHOOLS OFFICE OF DRUG/VIOLENCE PREVENTION PROGRAMS

The SS Office of Drug/Violence Prevention coordinates the development and implementation of the educational and intervention programs as listed below that are aimed at fostering a more collegial, co-operative, accepting, and safer environment. Furthermore, school site annual action plans identifying specific objectives and end-of-year performance metrics are implemented to promote and enhance safety and continual improvement.

Educational Programs

- Bullying Prevention: Work with staff members and students to stop bullying and help students avoid becoming targets of bullying behavior.
- Character Education: Teach universal ethics through the six Pillars of Character: Trustworthiness, Respect, Responsibility, Fairness, Caring, and Citizenship.
- Conflict Resolution: Provide the staff with the training, curricula, and resources from the Peace Education Foundation to assist them in teaching students healthy, nonviolent ways to handle conflict.
- D.A.R.E.: Teach the Drug Abuse Resistance Education curricula to elementary and middle school students in a collaborative work effort with the police department.
- Peaceful Families: Provide parents with the training, curricula, and resources from the Peace Education Foundation to assist them in teaching their children healthy, nonviolent ways to handle conflict.
- Parent to Parent: Assist parents struggling with teen abuse issues to come together for support and guidance.
- Peer Mediation: Resolve minor conflicts via students working with students.

Intervention Programs

- Tobacco Education Group: Offered through the school to students who have a tobacco violation in lieu of suspensions; runs two consecutive Saturday mornings.
- Saturday Family Workshop: Offered through the school to students who have a drug/alcohol violation (or have been referred or volunteered to attend). Workshop runs two consecutive Saturday mornings, and a parent or guardian must attend with the student. It is also offered in lieu of required suspension time.

Outreach Efforts

Program information is distributed to students and parents via high school freshmen orientations, brochures available in school offices, distribution of parent resource guides at the fourth-grade level, and distribution of periodic flyers to students during classroom sessions.

Comprehensive Building Action Plans

Individual schools are required to prepare annual action plans that identify specific objectives and reduction targets in the areas of student harm/behavior code violations, student insubordination, staff assault violations, and ATOD violations. The program involves monthly activity reporting, statistical trending, and end-of-year survey and assessments. Performance metrics are used to tailor ongoing and future programs at various locations to suit the needs of schools on a site-specific basis. See attachments A.1 and A.2 for examples of a Comprehensive Building Action Plan and End-of-Year Survey/Assessment.

A.4. Duty to Warn and Threat Assessment

Duty to Warn and Threat Assessment programs are administered by staff psychologists through the SS Child Study Department. These emergency mental health services are provided to possible-at-risk youth who present potential risk or threat to self or another individual. Duty to Warn/Protect procedures involve student and parent/guardian interviews, record review, student stabilization evaluation, student stressor assessments, and general risk assessments. Threat assessment procedures are coordinated with SS Student Services.

Attachment A.1.   Akron Public Schools Safe and Drug-Free School Comprehensive Building Action Plan (Example) 2005/2006

SCHOOL _____

Building Safe and Drug-Free Schools Action Committee

1. _____ Administrator
2. _____ Faculty Member/SIP Chair
3. _____ Liaison(s)

District Goal Structure
Goal 1—Provide a safe, disciplined, and drug-free school environment for students, staff members, and community members that contributes to the continuing improvement of teaching and learning.

Performance Objectives:

1. Reduce Student Harm Student Behavior Code Violations by at least 15 percent.
   Tier #1 _____ Tier #2 _____

2. Reduce Student Insubordination Code Violations by at least 15 percent.
   Tier #1 _____ Tier #2 _____

3. Reduce Staff Assault Violations by at least 50 percent.
   Tier #1 _____ Tier #2 _____

4. Maintain an atmosphere that results in a low incidence of ATOD code violations.
   Tier #1 _____ Tier #2 _____

Based upon 2004/2005 Student Behavior Code Violation for this building (attached), the action plan emphasis for specific building-level performance objectives should be indicated as follows: for each performance objective, place a check (√) in either or both the tier 1/tier 2 boxes. One or both performance objectives for each goal need to be selected as a building target (tier 1).

A **tier 1 check** indicates this/these objective(s) is/are to be targeted for expanded/special building-level activity.

A **tier 2 check** indicates this/these objective(s) is/are to be targeted for routine preventive maintenance.

DATE DUE: Friday, October 7, 2005

Send to: Drug/Violence Prevention Programs
            Ott SDC, Room 110

District Program Structure

Please check (√) those activities in which staff, student, and/or parent participation is planned in your building.

GOAL 1: VIOLENCE/ALCOHOL, TOBACCO, AND OTHER DRUGS (ATOD)* PREVENTION

1. **Conduct/participate in an Awareness Program for students, staff members, and/or parents focusing on reducing violence and substance abuse by way of the following:**

   a. School Policy/Code of Behavior Reviews/publication _____
   b. Conflict Management/Peer Mediation _____
   c. Special Violence/Substance Abuse Prevention Activities
      (Safe and Drug-Free Schools Month) _____
   d. Character Development Activities _____
   e. Targeting Building-/District-Level Behavioral Concerns (crises/chronic) _____
   f. Program/Material Study, Acquisition, Distribution, and Outreach (parents, staff) _____

2. **Conduct/participate in Direct Instruction Program.**

   a. Conflict Resolution _____
   b. Peer Mediation _____
   c. Character Education _____
   d. Gun Safety _____
   e. D.A.R.E. _____
   f. Locally Adopted Curricula/Prevention Programs _____ (List: _____)
   g. Health Units—K–12 targeting ATOD _____
   h. Health Units—K–12 targeting Violence Prevention _____
   i. Bullying Prevention _____
   j. ESCAPE School _____

(continued)

3. **Conduct/participate in staff development program focusing on _staff_ roles in violence/ATOD prevention.**

   a. New Teacher Training
   b. Local/State/National Conferences
   c. Peer Mediation Training (Staff Attends)
   d. Character Development Training (Staff)
   e. Conflict Resolution Training
   f. Other Violence Prevention–related Training
   g. Other ATOD Prevention–related Training
   h. Bullying Prevention Program
   i. AHA (Understanding Poverty in Education)

* ATOD = Alcohol, Tobacco, and Other Drugs

4. **Conduct/participate in special ATOD/violence prevention programs.**

   a. Peer Programs
   b. Peaceful Families Initiative (Conflict Resolution for Parents)
   c. Student Assistance Services
   d. Metal Detection Screening
   e. Parent/Community Outreach Programs
   f. Safe Prom Program Season Activities
   g. Smoking Cessation Programs
   h. Saturday Family Workshop
   i. Peer Prevention Training Programs
   j. F.A.S.T. Program
   k. Peer-to-Peer Programs
   l. Say Yes to Tennis
   m. PSI Services
   n. Character Education
   o. Bullying Prevention
   p. Say YES to School
   q. ESCAPE School

5. **Conduct/participate in grant activity facilitation.**

   a. Write/implement ATOD/Violence Prevention Action Plan   ___

   b. Evaluate Action Plan (Year-end Report)   ___

   c. Select/act upon Behavior Code Violations Significant to Your Building (tier 1 selection)

Building-Level Program Structure

Please identify the specific violence/ATOD prevention objectives selected for your building as **tier 1 only** efforts for the coming year, and briefly describe the actions to be taken to reduce the Student Behavior Code Violations associated with the selected objectives. (Identify the action model selected, or describe the program effort you will activate.)

Violence Prevention Objective (Describe <u>how</u> your building will address your tier 1 objective.)

1. **<u>Reduce Student Harm Violations</u>** (cite [1] actions to be taken, [2] strategies, [3] time frames, [4] targets):

2. **<u>Reduce Student Insubordination Code Violations</u>** (cite [1] actions to be taken, [2] strategies, [3] time frames, [4] targets):

3. **<u>Reduce Staff Assault Violations</u>** (cite [1] actions to be taken, [2] strategies, [3] time frames, [4] targets):

ATOD Prevention Objective

1. **<u>Maintain ATOD code violations</u>** (if checked as a tier 1 objective), the building-level strategy will entail the activation of the strategy/ies (cite [1] actions to be taken, [2] time frames, [3] targets):

(continued)

PLAN OF ACTION
MONTHLY ACTIVITIES
TO BE TURNED IN WITH ACTION PLAN

SEPTEMBER   FEBRUARY

OCTOBER   MARCH

NOVEMBER   APRIL

DECEMBER   MAY

JANUARY   ALL YEAR LONG

END-OF-YEAR SURVEY/ASSESSMENT (Example)
SUBSTANCE ABUSE/VIOLENCE PREVENTION ACTIVITIES
2005/2006

SCHOOL _____

LIAISON _____

Please complete this survey in support of the end of the year report (2005/2006) required by the State Department of Education, and in support of a new proposal, which will incorporate the needs of your building to effect a substance abuse/violence prevention program.

1.   Which of the following substance abuse/violence support systems (Conflict Resolution, Peer Mediation Second Step, Quest, No Bullies No Victims, Clear Choices, Cooperative learning, D.A.R.E., or other) _____

_____

_____

_____ were utilized in your building this year? **(Circle the selected responses; write in any others.)**

Do you consider the materials used to have been helpful in your substance abuse/violence prevention program?

        Yes____   No_____

Please describe, in brief, how the program(s) was/were implemented (grade level or other grouping served/time frames, that is, all fifth graders—six weeks—two days per week— D.A.R.E. Program). If used in the health education class, specify what grade levels were affected.

_____

_____

_____

_____

2.   What percentage of your students came in contact with a **formal** substance abuse prevention curriculum (health class modules or special programs)? _____ %

3.   What percentage of your students came in contact with a **formal** violence prevention curriculum? (health class modules or special programs)? _____ %

4.   Did your students participate (actively/passively) in **substance abuse prevention** activities during Safe and Drug-Free Schools during the school year? _____ %

(continued)

5. Did your students participate (actively/passively) in **violence abuse prevention** activities during Safe and Drug-Free Schools during the school year? _____%.

6. Did your students participate in Spring substance abuse prevention activities such as prom-graduation activities (e.g., **elementary level**—letter writing, No Name-calling week, summer alternatives; **secondary level**—prom promise, prom/graduation, lock-ins, grim reaper, None under 21, letter writing, BYOB, other)

   _____.

   Yes_____   No___   **If *Yes*, circle the activities conducted.**

7. Were any of the following groups active in your building last year?

_____ Support Groups (general groups)	_____ Anger Management groups
_____ Concerned Others Group	_____ FAST
_____ PANDA/Teen Institute	_____ Say YES to School groups
_____ SADD	_____ Other

8. Was a substance abuse or a violence prevention in-service provided to your <u>entire staff</u> during any staff meetings this year?

   Yes_____   No_____   **If *Yes*, please list the topic/s and/or speaker on page**

9. Please list any substance abuse or violence prevention speakers/programs presented for your general <u>student body</u> on page 6.

10. Was there parent participation in your building drug/violence prevention program(s) this year? Yes _____ No_____

11. Did any activities in your building involve commitments from students to stay drug free? Yes_____ No_____

12. Do you need any additional resources to continue your substance abuse/violence prevention programs for the coming year? Yes_____ No_____

   Please list your needs and the approximate cost:

   _____

13. Does your building have a peer prevention program? Yes____ No____

   If *Yes.*__
   • What types of activities were included in your peer prevention program?

____ Student Prevention Clubs	____ Lock-ins
____ Peer Mediation/Conflict Resolution	____ Peer Tutoring
____ Peer Presentations	____ Peer Listening
____ Parent involvement	____ Other _____
____ Other _____	____ Other _____

14. How many office referrals were reported this school year? _____
Was this MORE or LESS referrals than last year? More_____   Less_____

15. Did your building have a Student Assistance Services Team (SAS) or a process/team with a similar mission but different name?

Yes _____ No _____   **(If *Yes*, please provide name of program, e.g., IAT, IBAT, SAS**
_____)

If *Yes*,
- How many people served on the team? _____
- What was the frequency of meetings? ___weekly ___monthly ___other
- Who was the person chairing the SAS team this year?

_____

- How many students were <u>referred</u> to the service? _____

NOTE: ATOD—Alcohol, Tobacco, and Other Drugs

16. How many ATOD-related student interventions occurred in your building as a result of referrals from your core team/student assistance team/intervention assistance team or other referral method? _____

_____
(family or student problem?)

17. How many students in your building were referred* to an outside agency for ATOD diagnostic assessment? _____
*How many referred to Saturday Family Workshop? _____
*How many referred to Tobacco Education Program? _____

18. *How many students in your building received out-of-school professional ATOD treatment services? _____ (This may include inpatient or outpatient treatment.)

19. *How many students in your school received ATOD in-school (individual or group) support services? _____ (e.g., Saturday Family Workshop, Tobacco Education Program)

20. Please review your building-level action plan as regards involvement in the district-provided violence prevention activities (page 2) and assess your follow-through on proposed activities.

(continued)

Attachment A.2. *(continued)*
Assessment of Building Involvement in District Violence/ATOD Prevention Programs

	Awareness Campaign Activities		Direct Instruction Staff Activities		Staff Development Activities		Special Program Activities	
PROCESS STATUS	Violence Prevention	ATOD Prevention	Violence Prevention	ATOD Prevention	Violence Prevention	ATOD Prevention	Violence Prevention	ATOD Prevention
Major Commitment								
Moderate Commitment								
Minimal Commitment								
OUTCOME ASSESSMENT								
Effort Very Productive								
Effort Productive								
Effort Marginally Productive								
Effort Not Productive								

21. Please explain the following:

a. The reason(s) you feel your building efforts were major, moderate, or minimal (i.e., your building focused on "bullying prevention" this year, and it was incorporated into all aspects of your building goals . . . that would be a major focus).

b. The reason for your outcome status choice (excellent, adequate, marginal, or poor) (i.e., although your number of referrals for bullying behavior increased, you feel the outcome was "excellent" because of the awareness it created in your building).

22. Please review your building-level action plan 2005/2006 and assess your follow-through on only your proposed (tier 1) building-initiated activities.

Assessment of Building Special/Expanded Efforts (Tier 1) Targeting Selected Code Violations
(RESPOND ONLY to those checked as tier 1 Objectives)

Goal 1	Violence Prevention			ATOD Prevention
Process Status	Building efforts to reduce harm violations	Building efforts to reduce weapons violations	Building efforts to reduce insubordination	Building efforts to reduce alcohol/drug violations
Major Program Effort				
Moderate Commitment				
Minimal Commitment				
Outcome Status—Program quality (design/conduct) judged to be:				
Excellent				
Adequate				
Marginal				
Poor				

23. Please explain the following:

   a. The reason(s) you feel your building efforts were major, moderate, or minimal.

   b. The reason for your outcome status choice (excellent, adequate, marginal, or poor).

(continued)

24. List the following (indicate Topic of Speaker/Program—ATOD: Alcohol, Tobacco, and Other Drugs; VP: Violence Prevention; CC: Character Education, Differentiated Instruction, Bullying Prevention/Intervention); include address/phone number:

Speakers/programs held for staff in-service:

Assemblies held for the building:

Speakers for classrooms (check with your building teachers to see if any of them had speakers in the listed topics):

Speakers for the building:

Special programs held for classrooms (check with your building teachers to see if any of them had programs in the listed topics):

Special programs held for the building:

25. What is/are your BUILDING SIP Goal(s)?

26. How does ATOD/Violence Prevention/Character education fit into and/or affect those goals?

27. In what ways has our office supported your goals in the 2005/2006 school year? (i.e., purchased materials, sent students to workshops, provided transportation for events, provided services, funded programs, etc., speakers, presentations)
List All

28. How do you know that what you are doing in prevention is effective? (the materials and programs used, the videos shown, etc.; how do you know that they are effective with students?)

Crisis Intervention and Recovery Programs

The school system (SS) provides mental health crisis intervention, emergency assistance, debriefing, and in-class postincident support to assist students and staff members in dealing with traumatic events in a manner that sensitively facilitates recovery of school operations back to effective learning environments.

These services are provided by staff psychologists through the SS Child Study Department in collaboration with SS counselors positioned at various school sites. The SS maintains interrelationships with a number of community-based crisis intervention agencies, as well as area professional and health service providers throughout the area. These resources provide intervention and postcrisis support in three key areas:

- Family social services
- Student social services
- Health social services

An example of a complete listing of agencies and support services can be found at www.akronschools.com/community/community_partnerships.html.

The SS Child Study Department also maintains copies of the county Directory of Adolescent Services that further identifies adolescent-based consulting and other service providers.

B.1. Suicide/Crisis Intervention Program

The SS Child Study Department administers a Suicide/Crisis Intervention Program that addresses preincident awareness, intervention, and postintervention actions and considerations. The Suicide/Crisis Intervention Procedures follow.

Public School
Child Study Department
Coordinator of Psychologists
Phone: xxx-xxx-xxxx
Fax: xxx-xxx-xxxx

January 2004

To: ALL BUILDING PRINCIPALS, UNIT PRINCIPALS, PROGRAM DIRECTORS, COUN-SELORS (& OTHER PUBLIC SCHOOL STAFF INVOLVED IN STUDENT SAFETY, CRISIS TEAMS, OR DIRECT STUDENT CONTACT)

From: Coordinator of Psychologists and Director of Student Services

Re: SUICIDE/CRISIS MEMO

Please distribute this memo to all building administrators and counselors.

The memo was recently updated. Please review carefully.

Please place the memo in a convenient place for further reference.

Thank you,
Child Study Department

Office of the Superintendent   January 1, 2004

TO: All Building Principals, Assistant Principals, Counselors, Psychologists

FROM: Superintendent of Schools

RE: SUICIDE/CRISIS INTERVENTION PROCEDURES

This memorandum is the eighth revision of the communication to your office since the spring of 1988. It has been updated in order to provide additional information. Please discard the February 1, 2002, memo and disseminate this new communication to all teachers, other school personnel—including office support staff, custodians, LRC personnel, etc.—regular volunteers, and any applicable guest speakers.

(If there are any questions regarding this bulletin, please contact the Coordinator of Psychologists or the Deputy Superintendent.)

SUICIDE

I. If any student states or implies, by word or action that suicide/self injury is being considered, **some action must be taken by school personnel**. Volunteers/visitors (particularly speakers in related areas) are to notify the building principal or other appropriate administrators.

II. DO NOT IGNORE, DISREGARD, OR MINIMIZE ANY SIGN, REGARDLESS OF THE SITUATION, EVEN IF THOUGHT TO BE AN ATTENTION-GETTING BEHAVIOR. (Refer to attached Crisis Interview Form.)

III. **IF THE SUICIDE THREAT IS DEEMED TO BE IMMEDIATELY LIFE-THREATENING, THE STUDENT SHOULD NOT BE LEFT ALONE BY SCHOOL PERSONNEL.**

IV. School personnel are asked to contact the student's parent(s) before the student leaves school if the crisis is not deemed to be life-threatening, or is thought to be an attention-getting or manipulative action. (Refer to II above). Parents must be notified and a conference scheduled with school personnel the same day, if the crisis is deemed to be life-threatening. The school should also complete the "Notification of Emergency" form and place it in the student's file.

V. If the suicide threat occurs near the end of the school day and does not appear of a nature that would warrant emergency attention, school personnel should document contact (or attempts to contact) the parent(s) immediately, or that evening, and suggest appropriate follow-up at the parent meeting.

WITHIN THREE DAYS OF THE PARENT MEETING, SCHOOL PERSONNEL WILL CONTACT THE PARENT(S) FOR A FOLLOW-UP REPORT. IF THE PARENT(S) HAVE NOT PROVIDED THE FOLLOW-UP DEEMED NECESSARY BY SCHOOL PERSONNEL, IT WILL BE NECESSARY FOR SCHOOL PERSONNEL TO CONTACT: **CHILDREN SERVICES BOARD**, xxx-xxx-xxxx.

(Please see attachments according to child's age.)

PROCEDURES FOR CHILDREN AGES 5-17 YEARS

The following steps **MUST BE TAKEN** when dealing with **ANY** public school student **ages 5 - 17**:

I.   Contact parent/guardian. Parental contact may be made by:
- phone
- home visit
- certified letter *(if situation is not life-threatening.)*

        If parent of a student under the age of 18 cannot be located, contact designated emergency card referent and ask that they locate the parent *(Do not break confidentiality by explaining the situation.)*

II.   Ask parent to come to school to discuss situation as soon as possible.

III.   Depending on the severity of the situation, once parents arrive at the school, the following options should be discussed and documented on the 'Notification of Emergency' form:

- Schedule an emergency evaluation meeting at **Child Guidance & Family Solutions (CGFS) (330-762-0591)**. **STATE TO THE RECEPTIONIST THAT THIS IS AN EMERGENCY**. *(This agency has been designated as the Emergency Mental Health Service contact for children in the Akron-Summit County area)*; or,
- Contact Blick Clinic (330-762-5425, ext 231) if student is MD, CD, or ED; or,
- Contact private counselor/psychologist/psychiatrist or other mental health specialist; or,
- Consult with family physician/pediatrician *(Medication may be needed if depression is present).*; or,
- **If the child is out of control, EMERGENCY SERVICES may be available at CHILDREN'S HOSPITAL MEDICAL CENTER OF AKRON**. *(Parents must be present for emergency treatment.)*

IV.   If the parent cannot be located, or if the parent refuses to come to school, and the child's condition is deemed an **EMERGENCY**, contact the **CHILD GUIDANCE AND FAMILY SOLUTIONS (330-762-0591)** and ask for assistance from the **MOBILE CRISIS UNIT. STATE TO THE RECEPTIONIST THAT THIS IS AN EMERGENCY.** The following will happen:

- A CGFS Telephone Intake Worker will ask for demographic information and crisis interview data;
- If the student is a client of CGFS, information will be shared with that student's Clinician; If the Clinician agrees to see the child at CGFS but no guardian can be located, school personnel should call CSB and then arrange for the child to be transported to CGFS for further assessment
- For non-clients, a member of CGFS Crisis Staff will be sent to the school to interview the student
- If the Crisis Assessment indicates a need for hospitalization and a guardian cannot be located, CGFS Crisis Staff will contact CSB. Transportation to the hospital may be provided by APS security, EMS, APDD, etc. depending on the situation
- If at ANY time abuse or neglect is suspected, CSB MUST be contacted (330-379-1880)

*(Any specific concern or question regarding the **CGFS CRISIS UNIT** can be directed to: **Dr. Tim Bartlett, Intervention Program Coordinator.**)*

PROCEDURES FOR CHILDREN AGE 18 YEARS AND ABOVE

I. Students who are **18 years old or above** are considered legally independent from their parent(s) in view of confidentiality issues. Efforts should be made to obtain the student's permission to contact parent(s) in case of an emergency. If the adult student refuses, and the situation is felt to be critical, school officials should contact parent(s) and elicit their assistance in obtaining necessary psychiatric/medical help.

II. Students who are 18 years old or above may be served by:

- the **Portage Path Emergency Unit, 434-1214, 10 Penfield Avenue** *(the ADM Crisis Center)*; or,
- the **Child Guidance and Family Solutions (CGFS), 330-762-0591, 312 Locust Street** *(if student is a current client at this agency)*; or,
- the **Blick Clinic, 330-762-5425 ext. 231, 640 W. Market Street** *(for developmentally delayed students, including CD, MD, and ED, ask for William Mizer, Intake Specialist)*; or,
- the **Suicide Prevention Hotline, 330-434-9144** *(24 hours)*

III. If the student is a current client of **CGFS,** and if the situation warrants assistance from the child's Clinician, the following procedures are to be used:

- contact the **CGFS (330-762-0591)** and **STATE THAT THIS IS AN EMERGENCY**
- provide CGFS Admissions Department with demographic information and crisis interview data;
- provide private office for CGFS Crisis Worker to interview student.

IV. The following procedures are to be used to access the **PORTAGE PATH EMERGENCY UNIT:**

- Call the **PORTAGE PATH EMERGENCY UNIT (330-762-6110)** and discuss situation with Crisis Worker;
- ***Transport** student to the **PORTAGE PATH EMERGENCY UNIT (10 Penfleld Avenue)** for psychiatric evaluation.

*Transportation may be by parent, guardian, APS security, school staff, EMS, APD, etc., depending on the situation. *(Students in crisis should not drive themselves to the crisis center. Transportation should NOT be provided by another student.)*

*(Any specific concern or question regarding **Portage Path crisis services** can be directed to the charge nurse, or **Dr. Montinola,** Director of Psychiatric Emergency Services)*

<u>Notification of Emergency Conference Form</u>

I/We _____, the parent(s)/guardian of _____, were involved in a conference with school personnel on _____.
We have been notified that our child has expressed thoughts or ideas related to suicide or suicide behaviors. We have been advised of the procedures outlined in the Akron Public School guidelines to address this concern. Recommendations for follow-up have been provided.

1. Actions planned: _____

_____

_____

_____

2. Referrals suggested: _____

_____

_____

_____

_____   _____
Parent/Legal Guardian   School Personnel/Title

_____   _____
Parent/Legal Guardian   School Personnel/Title

_____   _____
Student (optional)   Administrator (optional)

AKRON PUBLIC SCHOOLS—CRISIS INTERVIEW

<u>SUICIDE RISK SCALE</u>
(Experimental Edition)

This form is to be completed when the student is feeling suicidal, threatening suicide, or in the process of attempting suicide

Evaluator's Name & Title _____ Date _____ School _____

Student's Name _____ Age _____ Sex _____ Grade _____

PART I

Assessing Risk: Circle all of the following items relating to the client's situation.

1. Student has a plan?   YES   NO

    Method: Firearms   Car Exhaust   Hanging
                     Drowning   Suffocating   Jumping
                     Drugs/Poinson   Cutting   Other _____

2. Method on hand?   YES NO   7. Suicide Survivor?   YES NO
3. Making final plans?   YES NO   8. Drug/alcohol use?   YES NO
4. Prior attempts?   YES NO   9. Male 15+   YES NO
5. Suicide note?   YES NO   10. Dependent children at home? YES NO
6. Previous psychiatric history? YES NO

PART II

From your conversation with the student, rate your impression of the student's status on each of the following items. (A core of 1 indicates the item is not an issue.) Ratings should be based on *initial perceptions of the student's present status*, rather than on changes resulting from your intervention.

	<u>NONE</u>				EXTREME
11. Sense of hopelessness	1	2	3	4	5
12. Sense of worthlessness	1	2	3	4	5
13. Social isolation	1	2	3	4	5
14. Depression	1	2	3	4	5
15. Impulsivity	1	2	3	4	5
16. Hostility	1	2	3	4	5
17. Intent to die	1	2	3	4	5
18. Environmental stress*	1	2	3	4	5

The level of stress preciipitated by any actual or anticipated events in the student's life, such as loss of a loved one, change in lifestyle, illness, etc.

PART I SUBTOTAL: _____   PART II SUBTOTAL: _____   TOTAL: _____
    (1 point for each "yes")   *(Sum of circled numbers)*   *(Part I + Part II)*

SUICIDAL RISK: **LOW** *(score 0–9)*   **Moderate:** *(score of 10–19)*   **HIGH** *(score of 20–50)*

Regardless of the risk level, items within this scale are important aspects to consider when assessing overall status

---

Engaged student in a "NO SUICIDE" contract? YES   NO
Utilized student's personal support systems for referral?   YES   NO
Mobilized emergency mental health delivery system? YES   NO

B.2. Crisis Situation Follow-up Guidelines

The following information may be useful in the days and weeks following a crisis. Longer term follow-up procedures are also listed.

DAY 2

The first day back at school following a crisis is a very important benchmark in the healing process. Reentry into the school structure and routine represents progress toward a "new normal." However, because emotions are close to the surface and triggers that spark disturbing memories are often unpredictable, the thought of going back to school can be daunting. Careful preparation in paving the way to the first day back is critical.

Careful attention should be paid to the needs of all members of the school community. Immediate needs on the first day back often include the following:

- Managing the media
- Providing meaningful expressions to mark the occasion
- Ensuring safety and security
- Activating a responsive referral system for students and staff members who need additional support
- Allowing opportunity for classroom discussion of what has occurred before transitioning into the school routine and returning to established curriculum.

All staff should meet prior to school to review the day's schedule and procedures. "Safe rooms" should be made available for students and staff members who may need to seek quiet or guidance. High-risk students should not be released to empty homes during or after school. Students should be encouraged to be aware of one another and to walk a student to an adult if they need help.

- Gather faculty members and update them on any additional information/procedures. Allow staff members the opportunity to discuss feelings and reactions.
- In case of death, provide funeral/visitation information if the affected family has given permission.
- Identify students in need of follow-up support, and in accordance with the school's crisis response plan, assign staff members to monitor vulnerable students.
  —Coordinate any ongoing counseling support for students on campus
  —Announce ongoing support for students with place, time, and staff facilitator
  —Notify parents of affected students about community resources available to students and their families.

IMMEDIATELY FOLLOWING RESOLUTION OF THE CRISIS

- Convene Crisis Response Team for debriefing as soon as possible:
  —Discuss successes, problems, and things to do differently next time.
  —Amend crisis response procedures as necessary.

LONG-TERM FOLLOW-UP AND EVALUATION

- Provide list of suggested readings to teachers, parents, and students.
- Write thank-you notes to out-of-building district and community resource people who provided (or are still providing) support during the crisis.
- Be alert on crisis anniversaries and holidays. Often students will experience "anniversary" grief reaction the following month or year on the date of the crisis or when similar crises occur that remind them of the original crisis. Holidays, too, are often difficult for students who have experienced loss.

CRISIS RESPONSE TEAM POSTINCIDENT DEBRIEFING

Postincident debriefing is a process that reviews the operations at the incident and how they may be improved.

The Benefits

Benefits of postincident debriefing include the following:

- A complete systematic account of the incident and an evaluation of the effectiveness of school procedures
- Evaluation of response times
- Evaluation of overall school, school division, and community Crisis Management Plans
- Review of the effectiveness of practices and procedures

The Process

The systematic process of debriefing should include a review of each of the following.

Initial Understanding of Crisis

Was the information we had accurate? Complete? Were there misunderstandings? Confusion?

Initial Strategies and Tactics

Did we take the correct first steps? What else should we have done?
What would we do differently?

Results of Strategies and Tactics

Did we achieve the intended results? Were there any unintended consequences of our actions? Improvements?

Obstacles Encountered

What? Who? Why?

What Worked Well and Why

What went well? Do we know why?

Recommendations for Improvement

What lessons did we learn?
Policies and/or procedures that need to be amended?
Additional training needed? Areas?
Communications?

Postvention

Postvention is supportive activity for adults and youth following a crisis. Such activities include debriefing sessions for those involved in the crisis and educational and support groups. The following is important to consider or keep in mind:

- Plan appropriate follow-up activities as needed for students and for faculty members as well. Crises can trigger problems in children who have heretofore not been identified as at risk. Offering ongoing support may avert further tragedy.
- Group meetings for bereaved students have often evolved from initial sessions and may be necessary for some students to recover.

- Some mental health centers have sent professionals to schools for designated periods of time to conduct sessions with students identified as having particular difficulty. Such sessions are voluntary and require parent permission.
- School librarians have compiled a useful list of reading material for young children on the subject of death. The list has been helpful to teachers and to parents who wish to discuss the loss of someone in the school community.
- Arrange crisis debriefing for those persons involved in the management of the crisis. These can take the form of one or two group sessions where both crisis management and personal stress are discussed. Community mental health personnel can assist in this activity.
- The school needs to follow up specifically on faculty or school staff members directly involved in the crisis (these might be custodians, cafeteria personnel, secretaries, bus drivers, teachers, counselors, or administrators). All need to be involved in a relatively intense "debriefing session" if they were directly involved.

CLASSROOM GUIDELINES: CLASSROOM DISCUSSION

When a Student Dies

- Review the facts and dispel rumors.
- Share your own reactions with the class and encourage students to express their reactions in a way appropriate for them, noting that people react in many ways and that is okay.
  —Possible discussion: What was it like for you when you first heard the news?
- Inform students of locations for grief support; reassure students that any adult in the building is available for support.
  —Possible discussion: How can you students help each other through this?
- Listen to what students have to say. It is important not to shut off discussion.
- Talk with students about their concerns regarding "what to say" to other bereaved students and the family of the deceased. If applicable, share information about the deceased's culture (beliefs and ceremonies), which will help students understand and respond comfortably to the affected family.
  —Possible discussion question: If you were a member of (the student's) family, what do you think you would want at a time like this?
- If the student died of an illness, discuss the illness if it is appropriate to do so. This is especially useful for younger children who may need to differentiate between the illness of the child who died and any medical problems of others the child knows.
- If a suicide occurs, discuss facts and myths about suicide.
- Allow students to discuss other losses they have experienced. Help them understand this loss often brings up past losses; this is a normal occurrence.
- Encourage students to discuss their feelings with their parents/families. Keep in mind a "regular" day may be too hard for grieving students. Offer choices of activities.

CLASSROOM GUIDELINES: POSSIBLE CLASSROOM ACTIVITIES

Activities after a Loss

Supporting Others

- Discussing and preparing for funeral (what to expect, people's reactions, what to do, and what to say)
- Encouraging mutual support
- Discussing ways to cope with traumatic situations

- Discussing the stages of grief
- Encouraging students to keep a journal of events and of their reactions, especially in an ongoing situation

Honoring the Deceased

- Writing a eulogy
- Writing stories about the victim
- Placing a collection box in school for notes to the family
- Designing a yearbook page commemorating the deceased
- Supporting a cause the deceased supported
- Collecting and displaying memorabilia
- Planting a tree, building a sculpture, or painting a mural
- Starting a new school activity such as a SADD (Students against Destructive Decisions) unit if a child was killed by a drunk driver.

Note: These activities are not recommended in the case of suicide; see "Suicide": "Dos" and "Don'ts."

Learning Activities

- Writing a reaction paper
- Discussing historical precedents about issues related to crisis
- Writing a "where I was when it happened" report
- Investigating laws governing similar incidents
- Conducting a mock trial if laws were broken
- Debating controversial issues
- Reading books about loss

HANDOUTS FOR STUDENTS

Helping a Grieving Friend

First Steps

- If you learn of a grieving friend outside of school hours, telephone and go over as quickly as you can, if possible, or at least telephone.
- If you learn of a grieving friend during school, try to see the friend or send a note until you are able to talk.
- Your presence is all that is needed; if you wish to take a flower or anything meaningful, that's all right, too.
- Don't be afraid to cry with your friend.
- Do not try to take away the pain from your grieving friend.

Communication

- Talk about the deceased person (grieving people really like telling stories about the deceased, such as "do you remember the time . . .")
- No cliché statements (e.g., "He's better off now since he now has no pain.")
- Don't be afraid you will upset your friend by asking or talking about the deceased; they are already very upset and should be.
- Just sitting with your friend may be all that's needed at times: don't be afraid of silence; the griever will most likely fill it talking about the deceased.
- Offer suggestions only when advice is asked.

- Listen, no matter what the topic.
- Do not tell the griever to feel better since there are other loved ones still alive.
- Call to check on the griever.

Attending a Visitation at the Funeral Home or Attending a Funeral

- If you have not ever been to a funeral home or a funeral, expect to feel nervous.
- Go with a friend or ask a parent to accompany you, if you wish.
- If this is the first time you've seen the grieving friend, simply offer your condolences; just saying "I am so sorry about _____'s death" will open a conversation, or simply point out something special to you about the deceased.
- If the visitation or funeral is open casket, view the physical remains if you want; you do not have to.

Later Involvement

- Ask your grieving friend to go places and do activities together (it's all right if he/she initially resists).
- If invitations are turned down, keep inviting.
- Call to check on and talk to your friend.
- Continue to talk about the deceased from time to time.

When a Grieving Classmate Returns

First Words

- The classmate probably feels like he/she is from a different planet when returning to school.
- There is very little you can say wrong; so, talk to the classmate.
- At least say "hello," "welcome back," "I'm glad to see you," or something similar.
- The brave might even say "I missed you," "I'm so sorry to hear about your _____'s death."
- Even braver friends might even make statements like "it must be incredibly tough to have your _____ die."
- Another option is to write a brief note.
- If your classmate cries, that is okay; you did not cause the grief, and you can't make the person feel worse. Offer comfort and a tissue.

Helping the Classmate Adjust to the Class

- Offer to provide past notes.
- Offer to provide notes for comparison for the next week or so (your classmate's attention span will probably vary for several weeks).
- Give the classmate your phone number to call if they have problems with homework.
- Ask your classmate if you can call to check on how homework is going.
- Ask the teacher if you can be the student's helper for a week.
- Offer to study together in person or over the phone; this might help with both motivation (grieving students frequently do not feel like doing schoolwork) and with concentration.

Some Don'ts

- Don't shun. Speak to the student.
- No cliché statements (e.g., "I know how you feel" when nobody knows the unique relationship the classmate had with the deceased).
- Don't expect the person to snap back into the "old self."
- Don't be surprised if the classmate seems unaffected by the loss; everybody has his/her own way of grieving.

- Don't be afraid to ask appropriate questions about the deceased, like "what did you and your _____ enjoy together?" (People never tire of talking about the people they grieve.)
- Just because the classmate may seem to be adjusting to school again, don't assume the grieving has stopped, nor that the need for comfort and friendship has ended.

Developed by Ken Roach, school psychologist, Chesterfield County Public Schools, Virginia.

Helping Grieving Parents

This information should be helpful when interacting with the parents of a deceased friend.

Always respect the wishes of grieving parents. These suggestions must fit the parents' needs and requests.

First Steps

- In the vast majority of cases, the parents very much want to see the friends of their deceased child; they find it comforting.
- If you were a close friend of the deceased and you know the parents, then go visit them at their home.
- If you were a friend but had not met the parents (yet they know who you are), you might still visit the home.
- Other friends might wait until the visitation, such as held at a funeral home, or wait until the funeral.
- Regardless of the depth of your relationship with the parents, let them hear from you either by a call or a note.

Communication

- When you visit, do not worry about what to say; your presence is all that is needed. If you wish to take a flower or anything meaningful, that's all right, too.
- Don't be afraid you will upset the parents by asking or talking about the deceased; they are already upset.
- Don't be afraid to cry with the parents.
- Just sitting with the parents may be all that's needed at times: don't be afraid of silence; the parents will most likely fill the silence by talking about their deceased child.
- Listen, no matter what the topic.
- If you were a really close friend, the parents might be pleased for you to even visit the deceased friend's room.
- Ask what you can do for them; ask other relatives what you might do to help.
- Do not try to take away the pain from the grieving parents.
- No cliché statements (e.g., "He's better off now since he now has no pain").
- Talk about the deceased person (grieving people really like telling stories about the deceased, such as "do you remember the time . . .").
- Offer suggestions only when advice is asked.
- Do not tell the parents to feel better since there are other children and loved ones still alive.

Attending a Visitation at a Funeral Home or Attending a Funeral

- Expect to feel nervous when going to a funeral home or a funeral.
- Go with a friend or ask a parent to accompany you.
- If this is the first time you've seen the parents, simply offer your condolences; just saying "I am so sorry about _____'s death" will probably open a conversation; or maybe better, simply allow the parents to point out something special to you about the deceased.
- If the visitation or funeral is open casket, view the physical remains if you want; you do not have to.

Later Involvement

- After the funeral, continue to visit the parents; they probably will continue to want to see the friends of their deceased child.
- Call to check on and talk to the parents.
- Continue to talk about their deceased child from time to time.

When Your Teacher Has Someone Die

Feelings

- Expect you and your classmates to experience different feelings, ranging from shock, sadness, and vulnerability ("this could happen to me or someone I know") to detachment or saying nothing. All are okay.
- Some in your class may even laugh because they are nervous hearing or talking about grief and death. This may be their way of handling it, so don't become angry.
- Don't be surprised to catch yourself asking how this might affect you, your grades, or your relationship with your teacher.
- It's okay to think about other people who have died.

What to Do

- Talk with somebody (a friend or parent) about what has happened. This helps make the situation seem more real and keeps you from holding everything in.
- Try to get the courage to communicate with your teacher.

Communicating with Your Grieving Teacher

- Your teacher probably has a lot to do and cannot take calls from students.
- Send a card (buy or make).
- Write a note (and you don't have to have fancy stationery).
- Just write "I'm sorry," "I'm thinking about you," or "I hope you are okay."
- Others may write more, even share their own experiences with grief. One student even composed a poem!
- There is nothing you can say that could make your grieving teacher feel worse.
- You are not going to remind a grieving person that he/she has had somebody die.
- Your teacher may never throw your card/note away; that's how important your communication will be. Your parents probably still have notes they've received.

Flowers and Donations

- They are not necessary.
- If you really want to do something, maybe you and some friends could pitch in together. Or maybe the class wants to do something as a group. It just takes one person to organize this.

What If You See Your Teacher out in the Community

- If you see your teacher at the grocery store, a part of you will want to hide. How will that make your teacher feel?
- Speak to your teacher! You don't have to say much. "How are you doing?" or "we miss you at school" is enough.

What About Funerals and Memorial Services

- You have to respect the wishes of grieving people.
- Some teachers may welcome students. Others may not feel ready to cope with you yet. Some may feel uncomfortable with you around when they feel "out of control."
- We have to understand and respect their needs.

- Also, 120 students take up a lot of space.
- Sometimes, there is no chance to talk with the family. Other times you can't leave the building without doing so.
- If given the opportunity, speak. Again, just say "we're sorry" or something brief.
- Have your first several words chosen to lessen your fear.

Visitation at a Funeral Home

- If students are invited, go, but take someone with you.
- Unless you have lots of experiences with visitation, you are going to feel scared and weird.
- If you go, speak simply as described above.

When Your Grieving Teacher Returns

Getting Ready

Plan some type of simple welcome back signal from the class to your grieving teacher. Consider the following:

- A card signed by all the class
- A small banner from "second period"
- Some flowers from a parent's yard, if in season
- A small, inexpensive bouquet
- If you have not communicated with your teacher, it's not too late to have a note ready just from you. It could be waiting in the teacher's mailbox on his/her return to school.
- Realize that the same teacher who left will return. Your teacher may initially seem a little distant or preoccupied, but this should not last long.
- Your teacher may have very poor concentration for a while after returning to work. He/she might repeat things. You may have to repeat your questions.
- Do not expect tests and homework to be returned as quickly as before; poor concentration, low motivation, and fatigue are typical grief reactions.

On the Big Day

- Expect to feel nervous. Your teacher will feel the same way.
- Your teacher will also probably feel like he/she is from a different planet.
- When you first see your teacher, at least say something simple, like "welcome back."
- The class could also even let a very brave volunteer speak for the class to formally welcome your teacher back. Or the volunteer could present the card.
- Show your good behavior; use your best listening skills. Help your teacher out; it will be a tough day. Smile!
- Some teachers will return quickly to teaching; others will discuss their grief. There is no single right way.

What If Your Teacher Cries?

- You do not have to do anything but be patient.
- Your class could have a brave volunteer designated to offer comfort by saying something simple, such as "we're supporting you."
- The student closest to the tissue box should take the box to the teacher. This shows the class cares and says it's okay to cry.
- At the end of class, students might individually offer brief words of comfort or encouragement ("it's okay to get upset" or "I'm glad you are back").
- Your teacher may be embarrassed by crying, but crying can be very helpful.

SUICIDE

A school's general response to a suicide does not differ markedly from a response to any sudden death crisis, and the Procedures for General Crisis Intervention can appropriately be implemented. However, some issues exclusive to suicide require specific attention. School administrators must allow students to grieve the loss of a peer without glorifying the method of death. Overemphasis of a suicide may be interpreted by vulnerable students as a glamorization of the suicidal act, which can assign legendary or idolized status to taking one's own life. Those who desire recognition may be encouraged to emulate the victim's behaviors.

The following "dos" and "don'ts" will help the school staff limit glamorization of suicide:

Dos

- Do verify the facts, and treat the death as a suicide.
- Do acknowledge the suicide as a tragic loss of life.
- Do provide support for students profoundly affected by the death.
- Do emphasize that no one is to blame for the suicide.
- Do consider establishing a fund for contributions to a local suicide prevention hotline or crisis center or to a national suicide prevention organization.

Don'ts

- Do not organize school assemblies to honor the deceased student or dedicate the yearbook or yearbook pages, newspaper articles, proms, athletic events, or advertisements to the deceased individual.
- Do not pay tribute to a suicidal act by planting trees, hanging engraved plaques, or holding other memorial activities. A suicide in the school community can heighten the likelihood, in the subsequent weeks, of "copycat" suicide attempts and threats among those especially vulnerable to the effects of a suicide. To prevent further tragedies, students considered to be especially susceptible to depression/ suicide must be carefully monitored and appropriate action taken if they are identified as high risk. These efforts require a limited, rather than schoolwide, response.
- Do not dismiss school or encourage funeral attendance during school hours.

Myths and Facts About Suicide

Myth: People who talk about suicide don't commit suicide.

Fact: Most people who commit suicide have given clues of some type to one or more people. It is not safe to assume that someone talking about suicide will not attempt it; the majority of those who attempt suicide have stated their intent to someone.

Myth: Suicide happens without warning.

Fact: While explicit verbal warnings are not always given, there are clues ahead of time. The difficulty is that not everyone recognizes the signs and symptoms that would alert him/her to the possibility of suicide.

Myth: Suicidal people are fully intent on dying.

Fact: Rather than specifically wanting to die, students who attempt/commit suicide often do so simply because they have exhausted their coping skills and see no other options for relief from pain.

Myth: Once suicidal, a person is suicidal forever.

Fact: Preoccupation with suicidal thoughts is usually time limited. Most young people who work through a suicidal crisis can go on to lead healthy lives.

Myth: Once a person attempts suicide, the humiliation and pain will prevent future attempts.

Fact: 80 percent of persons who commit suicide have made at least one prior attempt (taken from Brent Q. Hafen and Kathryn J. Frandsen's *Youth Suicide: Depression and Loneliness*, 1986). It is critical that concerned adults and peers monitor a student who has attempted suicide for several months following the attempt. Those students who receive help for their suicidal risk before they made an attempt have a better prognosis than those who were intervened upon following an attempted suicide.

Myth: Suicide occurs more often among the wealthy.

Fact: Suicide knows no socioeconomic boundaries.

Myth: Suicidal behavior is inherited.

Fact: As with other patterns of behavior, suicide sometimes seems to run in families. However, suicide is not a genetic trait, so it is not inherited. What can appear to be a family trait of suicide may be a result of family members sharing a common emotional environment and often adopting similar methods of coping. In a family where someone has committed suicide, suicide may be viewed as acceptable in times of distress.

Myth: People who attempt or commit suicide are mentally ill/psychotic.

Fact: Many suicidal persons historically have had difficulty in working through problems. Other people who attempt or commit suicide choose it as an option when their previously successful means of coping are not effective, and they are unable to otherwise stop the pain they are experiencing. A history of mental illness does not increase the risk of suicide.

Myth: Talking about suicide can encourage a person to attempt it.

Fact: On the contrary, initiating a discussion of suicidal feelings may give a suicidal adolescent permission to talk about the pain she/he is experiencing and, by so doing, provide significant relief. It is highly unlikely that discussing suicide would influence a nonsuicidal person to become preoccupied with the idea.

Myth: People who attempt suicide just want attention.

Fact: Suicide should be considered a "cry for help." Persons overwhelmed by pain may be unable to let others know they need help, and suicide may seem the best way to relieve the pain. Suicidal behavior may be a desperate move to reach out for much-needed help.

Myth: Suicide is most likely to occur at night as well as over the holiday season.

Fact: Suicides can occur at any time, regardless of season, time of day or night, and weather or holidays. Childhood and adolescent suicides, however, are most likely to occur in the spring, and second most likely to occur in the fall. Most childhood and adolescent suicides occur at home on weekends or between the hours of 3 p.m. and midnight.

Myth: When depression lifts, there is no longer a danger of suicide.

Fact: Although the existence of any form of depression increases the probability of suicide, this is a dangerous misconception. The lifting of depression often accompanies the development of a suicide plan and the final decision to commit suicide. If the improvement in mood is sudden and circumstances have not changed, the risk of suicide remains high. It is most useful to see suicidal behavior as a symptom, not a disease. As such it may be caused by a variety of factors.

APPENDIX C

Training and Exercises

No Crisis Management or emergency operations plan can be properly implemented and executed during a crisis or emergency unless all the expected participants are aware that the plan exists, what emergencies are covered, and what is expected of each (administrators, faculty members, staff members, and students) during an actual emergency. All participants must be adequately trained on those portions of the plan that affect them, and they must know that other participants understand and are able to perform their respective tasks safely and effectively.

No emergency operations plan can be considered adequate and complete until it has been tested and exercised, and participants cannot be considered to understand the plan and feel comfortable in their respective roles and assignments until they have participated in drills and exercises. All participants must have a level of trust in the plans and their personal ability to accomplish their assigned tasks in a stressful environment; this is only achieved through training and exercising.

Further, all school system (SS) employees must have at least a minimal understanding of the Incident Command System (ICS) utilized by all public safety first responders in the country to any emergency, regardless of its size.

Administrators, teachers, and some staff members will have specific ICS positions based on the nature and scope of the emergency. Upper-level administrators will have more expanded roles as the emergency becomes greater or encompasses more than one school or facility. By law, all schools are required to utilize an ICS that is compliant with the National Incident Management System (NIMS).

Goals

The goal sought in testing the emergency operations plan is to prepare SS personnel members and students for a real emergency; the goal is to save lives and limit property damage. It is important to remember that testing is a part of the training process—we are testing the plan, not the personnel. We can discover weaknesses in the plan, identify resource needs, improve coordination, and improve individual performance and readiness for a real emergency.

Training

All SS personnel will be provided with basic awareness-level training on the plan upon implementation; this training will be presented as basic orientation and will include the general concepts of the plan, specific assignments, and general emergency procedures. Those individuals requiring hands-on training in specialized skills (e.g., CPR-AED) will be provided this training based on the needs of the SS during the initial training phase and yearly thereafter as required (new hires, policy changes, new buildings, etc.).

NIMS-compliant ICS training will be provided to all personnel members based on their anticipated assignments, duties, and responsibilities during an emergency. The ICS training will be provided on three levels, as follows:

- Level 1—Provided to all teachers and staff members and will consist of basic ICS understanding at the orientation level. Trainees will have an understanding of ICS, how it works, and why it is used. They will understand the relationship between the ICS used by the SS and its interface with the public safety first responders ICS. (two hours)
- Level 2—Provided to principals, assistant principals, secretaries, and custodial staff at each school (personnel members who would have a position on the Crisis Response Team at the school). Level 2 includes all level 1 training plus ICS at the operational level. Trainees will understand the ICS utilized by the SS, will be able to implement ICS and execute the Crisis Management Plan at their respective school, and will be able to staff those positions that would be required during the various emergencies addressed in the plan. (four hours)
- Level 3—Provided to district managers and administrators who would have a position on the Crisis Management Team and/or make policy-level decisions during a major emergency. Level 3 is similar to level 2 but will focus on the ICS at the policy level. Trainees will have the same ICS knowledge base as the level 2 group but will also be prepared to implement the ICS during a crisis at the district level, regardless of the nature and scope of the emergency. Trainees will understand the ICS and its ability to aid in the management of a crisis and will be able to interact with the public safety first responder ICS at the state and federal level, if warranted by the emergency. (four hours)

Drills and Exercises

Exercises are the preferred method of testing the Crisis Management Plan on both a school and district level. Exercises fall into two general categories, the tabletop and the functional; both are used to test the plan, and the SS will do at least one tabletop and one functional exercise during the school year.

A tabletop exercise is the simulation of an emergency during which a scenario is presented to all participants and each participant explains what they or their operational unit would do to respond to the scenario as presented. The timeline is artificial and is controlled by the facilitator. There is no physical deployment of assets, no operations are actually conducted, and the Crisis Management Plan and response procedures are tested in a safe, controlled environment. All four phases of emergency management are tested, and gaps in the Crisis Management Plan are identified. Outside agencies are generally invited to participate and provide a heightened sense of realism. Tabletop exercises are the preferred method of testing a new or revised Crisis Management Plan, due to their low cost and minimal resource requirements. They usually run for about three to four hours.

Drills are utilized to practice and perfect a single emergency response, such as fire drills, bomb threats, tornados, and so forth, and will continue on the current schedule used by the SS. Drills are not a good method of testing a Crisis Management Plan.

A functional exercise is the simulation of a real emergency under high-stress conditions involving multiple responders and multiple agencies. An actual emergency situation is physically created as a simulation, and all participants and responders deploy and perform the same functions using the same equipment as they would in a real incident. Communications equipment is used, Command Posts are physically set up and staffed, emergency operations centers are opened, and a real timeline is used, compromised only by the prestaging of equipment and responders to save time during the exercise. A functional exercise tests the Crisis Management Plan, the ICS, the response procedures, and the public safety responders in a stressful environment. Role players are used, victims are presented, and all equipment is deployed. Functional exercises are a superb test of the entire Crisis Management Plan but are time consuming and fairly expensive. They usually run about six to eight hours.

Forms

STAFF SKILLS SURVEY AND INVENTORY

Name and School _____ / _____ Room _____
　　　　　　　　　　　　　　　Name　　　　　　　　　　　　　　School

During any disaster situation, it is important to be able to draw from all available resources. The special skills, training, and capabilities of the staff will play a vital role in coping with the effects of any disaster incident, and they will be of paramount importance during and after a major or catastrophic disaster. The purpose of this survey/inventory is to pinpoint those staff members with equipment and the special skills that might be needed. Please indicate the areas that apply to you and return this survey to your administrator.

PLEASE CHECK ANY OF THE FOLLOWING IN WHICH YOU HAVE EXPERTISE and TRAINING. CIRCLE YES OR NO WHERE APPROPRIATE.

_____ First Aid (current card yes/no)　　_____ CPR (current yes/no)　　　　_____ Triage　　_____ Firefighting

_____ Construction (electrical, plumbing, carpentry, etc.)　　　　　　　　_____ Running/Jogging

_____ Emergency Planning　　　_____ Emergency Management　　_____ Search and Rescue

_____ Law Enforcement　　　_____ Bi/Multilingual (what language [s]) _____

_____ Mechanical Ability　　　_____ Structural Engineering　　_____ Bus/Truck Driver
　　　　　　　　　　　　　　　　　　　　　　　　　　　　　　　　(Class 1 or 2 license yes/no)

_____ Shelter Management　　　_____ Survival Training and Techniques　　_____ Food Preparation

_____ Ham Radio Operator　　　_____ CB Radio　　　　　_____ Journalism

_____ Camping　　　　　　_____ Waste Disposal　　　　_____ Recreational Leader

DO YOU KEEP A PERSONAL EMERGENCY KIT? _____ In your car? _____ In your room? _____

DO YOU HAVE MATERIALS IN YOUR ROOM THAT WOULD BE OF USE DURING AN EMERGENCY?
(i.e., athletic bibs, traffic cones, carpet squares, etc.) _____ Yes _____ No

DO YOU HAVE EQUIPMENT OR ACCESS TO EQUIPMENT OR MATERIALS AT YOUR SCHOOL SITE THAT COULD BE USED AN IN EMERGENCY? _____ YES _____ NO
PLEASE LIST EQUIPMENT AND MATERIALS.

_____

_____

COMMENTS _____

_____

WHAT WOULD MAKE YOU FEEL MORE PREPARED SHOULD A DISASTER STRIKE WHILE YOU WERE AT SCHOOL?

_____

_____

EMERGENCY INFORMATION SHEET

Room Number _____

Student's Name _____ Grade _____

Address _____ Home Phone _____

Parent/Guardian Names _____

Mother/Guardian Work Address _____

Father/Guardian Work Address _____

Mother/Guardian Work Phone _____ Father/Guardian Work Phone _____

In an emergency or major disaster during school hours, my child may be released to the following persons:
(THESE NAMES SHOULD BE THE SAME AS ON YOUR CHILD'S GREEN EMERGENCY CARD)

Name _____ Address _____ Phone _____

Name _____ Address _____ Phone _____

Name _____ Address _____ Phone _____

Name _____ Address _____ Phone _____

Name _____ Address _____ Phone _____

My child needs to take the following medication: _____

Medication _____ Dosage _____ Time_____

Have you provided the school office with a supply of this medicine? _____

My child may _____ or may not _____ have Tylenol if needed during an emergency.

List allergies to medicine or foods _____

Doctor_____ Address _____ Phone _____

Family out-of-state telephone contact to be used in an emergency:

Name _____Phone _____

   (outside of state)   (Area code and number)

Date _____ Parent/Guardian Signature _____

Student Released to: _____

Date: _____ Time: _____ Destination: _____

STUDENT ACCOUNTING FORM

Room No. _____   Date _____

Enrolled per Register _____   Reported by _____

Not in School Today _____   Received by _____

Present Now _____

1. Students or classroom volunteers elsewhere (off campus, left in room, other location, etc.)

Name   Location   Problem

_____

_____

_____

_____

_____

_____

_____

2. Students on playground needing more first aid than you can handle:

Name   Location   Problem

_____

_____

_____

_____

_____

_____

_____

Additional comments (report fire, gas/water leaks, blocked exits, structural damage, etc.):

NOTICE OF FIRST AID CARE

DATE: _____

SCHOOL: _____

Dear Parent:

_____ was injured at school and has been given first aid. If you feel further care is necessary please consult your family physician.

Destination (if not presently on-site): _____

Transporting Agency (if not presently on-site): _____

Time: _____

Remarks:

Please sign and return one copy to school. Retain a copy for your records.

_____   _____
PARENT'S SIGNATURE   SCHOOL REPRESENTATIVE'S SIGNATURE

Note: 1 copy goes home with student
     1 copy stays with teacher or medical treatment team records

[Date]

SITE STATUS REPORT

TO: _____ FROM (name): _____ LOCATION: _____

DATE: _____ TIME: _____ PERSON IN CHARGE AT SITE: _____

Message via: Two-way Radio _____   Telephone _____   Messenger _____

EMPLOYEE/STUDENT STATUS

	Absent	Injured	# Sent to hosp./med.	Dead	Missing	Unaccounted for (away from site)	# Released to parents	# Being supervised
Students								
Site Staff								
Others								

STRUCTURAL DAMAGE Check damage/problem and indicate location(s).

Check ✓	Damage/Problem	Location(s)
	Gas leak	
	Water leak	
	Fire	
	Electrical	
	Communications	
	Heating/cooling	
	Other (list):	

MESSAGE (include kind of immediate assistance required; can you hold out without assistance/how long? overall condition of campus, neighborhood, and street conditions; outside agencies on campus and actions; names of injured, dead, missing, and accounted for ASAP):

UPDATE REPORT

Name _____   Time _____

_____ # children remaining at school

_____ # staff members remaining to care for children

_____ Assistance required: _____ water _____ food _____ blankets _____ # people to help

UPDATE REPORT

Name _____   Time _____

_____ # children remaining at school

_____ # staff members remaining to care for children

_____ Assistance required: _____ water _____ food _____ blankets _____ # people to help

UPDATE REPORT

Name _____   Time _____

_____ # children remaining at school

_____ # staff members remaining to care for children

_____ Assistance required: _____ water _____ food _____ blankets _____ # people to help

UPDATE REPORT

Name _____   Time _____

_____ # children remaining at school

_____ # staff members remaining to care for children

_____ Assistance required: _____ water _____ food _____ blankets _____ # people to help

STUDENT RELEASE FORM
To be taken by runner

Please Print

Student's Name _____

Teacher _____ Grade _____

Requested By _____

****

To be filled in by Request Gate staff

Proof of ID _____ Name on Emergency Card _____
                                                    (yes) (no)

****

Student's Status
To be filled in by teacher

Sent with runner _____ Absent _____ First Aid _____ Missing _____ ____

****

To be filled in by Request Gate staff

Proof of ID _____ Name on Emergency Card _____
                                                    (yes) (no)

****

To be filled in by requester
at Release Gate

Requester Signature: _____

Destination: _____

Date: _____

Time: _____

****

SEARCH AND RESCUE TEAMS

SEARCH AND RESCUE TEAM LEADER _____

Note: Number of teams will vary
depending on size of campus.

	NAMES	Radio	Keys	Hard Hat	Goggles	Bucket	Vest	Clipboard	Backpack
SEARCH AND RESCUE TEAM 1 NOTES:	1. _____ 2. _____ _____								
SEARCH AND RESCUE TEAM 2 NOTES:	1. _____ 2. _____ _____								
SEARCH AND RESCUE TEAM 3 NOTES:	1. _____ 2. _____ _____								
SEARCH AND RESCUE TEAM 4 NOTES:	1. _____ 2. _____ _____								
SEARCH AND RESCUE TEAM 5 NOTES:	1. _____ 2. _____ _____								

S&R Team Leader
- Assign teams based on available manpower, minimum two persons. Attempt to place one experienced person on each team.
- Perform visual check of outfitted team leaving Command Post; include radio check. Advise teams of known injuries.
- Remain at Command Post table.
- Be attentive to all S&R-related communications.
- Utilize boxes above to record location of injured students. Example: report of two injured students in room 20 would be recorded as "S/2 = RM 20" in box under team 3.
- Utilize manpower pool to aid S&R (i.e., request for backboard and carryout or request for rescue equipment).

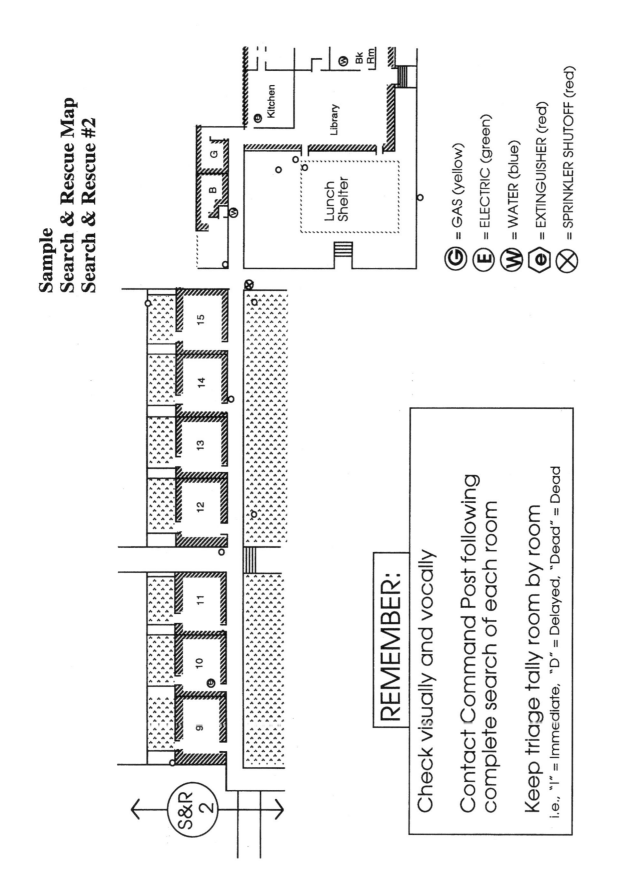

Sample
Search & Rescue Map
Search & Rescue #2

Kitchen

Bk Rm

Library

B G

Lunch Shelter

15 14 13 12 11 10 9

S&R 2

ⓖ = GAS (yellow)
Ⓔ = ELECTRIC (green)
Ⓦ = WATER (blue)
ⓔ = EXTINGUISHER (red)
⊗ = SPRINKLER SHUTOFF (red)

REMEMBER:

Check visually and vocally

Contact Command Post following complete search of each room

Keep triage tally room by room
i.e., "I" = Immediate, "D" = Delayed, "Dead" = Dead

PUBLIC INFORMATION RELEASE

Check (_) as appropriate: District/Districtwide _____ School _____

Date: _____   Time: _____

NOTE: If this is used as a script, read only those items checked. Make no other comments.

(Check off, fill in, and cross off as appropriate.)

_____ has just experienced a(n) _____

__ The (students/employees) [(are being) or (have been)] accounted for.

__ No further information is available at this time.

__ Emergency medical services [(are here) or (are on the way) or (are not available to us)].

__ Police [(are here) or (are on the way) or (are not available to us)].

__ Fire dept./paramedics [(are here) or (are on the way) or (are not available to us)].

_____ [(are here) or (are on the way) or (are not available to us)].

__ Communication Center(s) for parents (is/are) being set up at _____
     to answer questions about individual students.

__ Communication Center(s) for families (is/are) being set up at _____
     to answer questions about individual employees.

__ Injuries have been reported at _____ and are being treated at the site by
     (staff/professional medical responders).   (#) _____ reported injured.

__ Students have been taken to a safe area, _____ , and are with [(classroom
     teachers/staff members) or (_____)].

__ (#) Students have been taken to the local emergency room for treatment of serious injury.
     Parents of injured students should go to the emergency room at _____

__ (#) Confirmed deaths have been reported at _____
     Names cannot be released until families have been notified.

__ Structural damage has been reported at the following sites: _____

Release restrictions _____ No   _____ Yes
     If yes, what?

Released to the public as Public Information Release # _____
                              (Date/Time: _____)

EMERGENCY TIME/SITUATION/RESPONSE REPORT

TIME	SITUATION	RESPONSE	INITIAL

SAMPLE LOG

Date _____

Important: A permanent log may be typed or rewritten at a later time for clarity and better understanding. Keep all original notes and records. **They are legal documents!**

Time   **Recorded Action(s)**

WE ARE
SHELTERING IN PLACE

DO NOT ENTER

SHELTER-IN-PLACE DRILL CHECKLIST

Good   **Need to Improve How?**

_____   _____   1. Parents were informed about the drill.

_____   _____   2. Scenario reviewed with staff prior to event.

_____   _____   3. Students/staff members went inside, closed the doors, and closed and locked all windows.

_____   _____   4. Hang signs on doors and office to indicate "Sheltering in Place."

_____   _____   5. Roll call of students and staff members.

_____   _____   6. Place wet towels across the bottom of doors to the outside. (Simulate during drill.)

_____   _____   7. Tape up any vents that can't be closed. (Simulate during drill.)

_____   _____   8. Tape around window if air is leaking in. (Simulate during drill.)

_____   _____   9. Turn off air conditioning and exhaust fan in kitchen. (Simulate during drill.)

_____   _____   10. Close drapes and curtains.

_____   _____   11. Turn off pilot lights, but electricity should remain on. (Simulate during drill.)

_____   _____   12. Designate room for people who come to school during drill.

_____   _____   13. Post signs indicating location of visitor's room.

_____   _____   14. Alternate restroom facilities available in each room.

_____   _____   15. Alternate source of water for rooms without sinks.

_____   _____   16. Are there provisions for students needing medication during shelter-in-place?

_____   _____   17. Call 911 and the school district to tell them you are sheltering in place. (Simulate during drill.)

_____   _____   18. No one goes out during this time.

_____   _____   19. Do you have a method of communicating with the office during a drill?

Please use the reverse side of this checklist for your suggestions and candid comments. Please return this form within five days to the principal. This form should be completed by all adult participants and observers at school site.

Name: _____ Date: _____ Site: _____

Duck/Cover/Hold:

- The teacher led duck/cover/hold on by example.
- The students knew the proper procedure:

  The students ☐ ducked under cover ☐ covered their eyes ☐ held on
- The teacher gave instructions and reassurances.
- The teacher checked self and evaluated situation.
- The teacher asked the students to check themselves and others.
- The teacher evaluated the situation and waited for class composure before asking for an evacuation.
- The teacher checked with the buddy teacher.

Special situations: If there were special situations, either planned or unplanned, how were they handled?

Evacuation and Student Accounting:

- Evacuation was orderly.
- If there were no serious "injuries," the teacher evacuated with the buddy teacher, one at the front of the line, one at the rear. If a teacher was incapacitated, buddy teacher evacuated both classes. If a student was injured and could not be moved, one teacher remained with the injured, while the buddy teacher evacuated both classes to the assembly area.
- At the assembly area, the students sat down while the teacher took roll.
- A Student Accounting Form was sent to the Command Post.

Special situations: If there were special situations, either planned or unplanned, how were they handled?

Comments:

CHECKLIST TO CLOSE SCHOOL

☐ The school director is notified of a situation that might require the closing of a school or site, either by local authorities (police, fire, hazmat, civil defense, etc.), or by status report(s) to the district emergency operations center (EOC) from the sites.

☐ Gather information (weather forecasts, road conditions, damage assessment of facilities, injuries, staff available, utilities and sanitation capabilities, local authority recommendations/directives) in the EOC.

☐ Only the district superintendent is authorized to close schools. The recommendation to close schools will be made by the school director.

☐ All requests/recommendations by local civil authorities and/or agencies (police, fire, hazmat, Red Cross, etc.) shall be directed to the emergency manager.

☐ If school is to be closed the following day, this decision will be made, if possible, before sending children and staff home.

☐ Affected sites are notified.

☐ Civil authorities are notified.

☐ County is notified to begin the Emergency Alert System.

☐ The superintendent will put the message on the telephone information line. Updates will be made periodically.

☐ Transportation is notified when and where busses are needed.

☐ The superintendent notifies the school board.

☐ The district public information officer notifies (community relations director), who will furnish the media with up-to-date information. Updates will be made periodically.

For reopening:

☐ Decision to reopen site is made. Date/Time _____

☐ District public information officer _____ notifies the media as to the reopening.

☐ Information message is updated.

☐ Personnel is notified of site reopening.

CLOSING OF SCHOOL ACTION CHECKLIST

This checklist delineates the action to be taken if school, schools, or the entire district must be closed due to an emergency situation. It is imperative that all staff members be aware of these procedures and be prepared to carry them out if the principal is not available to make the determinations required. If specific persons are designated to perform these tasks, their names should be noted as appropriate.

A copy of this checklist must be forwarded to the school director and the district emergency manager following the incident.

Site:_____ Date: _____

Type of Incident:_____ Time: _____

Check off completed tasks as appropriate to the circumstances of the situation.

☐ The site requested/directed by civil authority to close school.

      Immediately _____ Next day _____

      Request made by (name and agency) _____

☐ School director advised of civil authority's directive to close school.

☐ Superintendent makes final decision. Decision: _____

      _____

☐ Decision announced to site. By _____ Time: _____

☐ Telephone calling trees began. By _____ Time: _____

Reopening of site:

☐ School is notified to reopen. By _____

      Date: _____ Time: _____

☐ Employees are notified. By _____

      Date: _____ Time: _____

☐ Students are notified. Calling trees began by _____

      Date: _____ Time: _____

UNSAFE BUILDING EVACUATION PLAN WORKSHEET

PERSON IN CHARGE OF SCHOOL:	ALTERNATE:	ALTERNATE:

STAFF ASSIGNMENTS

DUTY	STAFF NAME	ALTERNATE
All teachers are to stay with classroom groups or assigned neighborhood groups.		
Notify the following from an off-site location Emergency assistance: 911 or _____ Security: xxx-xxxx Superintendent: xxx-xxxx or xxx-xxxx Transportation: xxx-xxxx or xxx-xxxx		
Search halls, rest rooms, common areas, and kitchen.		
Replacements for missing or injured teachers.		
Provide medical assistance.		
Shut off power, gas, and water.		
Notify as appropriate PTA Evacuation Leader: Name_____ Phone _____ PTA Evacuation Alternate: Name_____ Phone _____ Emergency message: xxx-xxxx (general public) Emergency message: xxx-xxxx (employees) Activate CALLING TREE: Phone _____		
Post premade signs and direct the public.		
Lead students and teachers to alternate site (attach map and agreement). Site 1 _____ Site 2 _____		
Emergency Equipment ____ Air horn or bell ____ Radio (battery or ____ First aid kit solar) ____ Answering machine ____ Lights/lanterns ____ Generator ____ Unlisted phone line ____ Evacuation ____ Megaphone ____ plan/master lists ____ Paper and marker ____ Evacuation boxes pens ____ Stretcher		
Other		

SAFE BUILDING EVACUATION PLAN WORKSHEET

PERSON IN CHARGE OF SCHOOL:	ALTERNATE:	ALTERNATE:

STAFF ASSIGNMENTS

DUTY	STAFF NAME	ALTERNATE
Notify Superintendent: xxx-xxxx or xxx-xxxx		
Notify as appropriate PTA Evacuation Leader: Name_____ Phone_____ PTA Evacuation Alternate: Name_____ Phone_____ Emergency message: xxx-xxxx (general public) Emergency message: xxx-xxxx (employees) Activate CALLING TREE: Phone_____		
Call students and teachers to preassigned inside locations.		
Post premade signs and direct the public.		
Sign out students to responsible adults.		
Emergency Equipment		
____ Air horn or bell ____ Radio (battery/solar) ____ First aid kit ____ Lights/lanterns ____ Answering machine ____ Unlisted phone line ____ Generator ____ Megaphone ____ Evacuation ____ Paper and marker plan/master lists pens ____ Evacuation boxes ____ Stretcher		

IF A LONG DURATION STAY IS REQUIRED

Trauma, shock, and medical care		
Provide light and warmth		
Food arrangements		
Sleeping accommodations		
Internal communication/morale		
Other		

CRISIS RESPONSE TEAM REPORT FORMAT

Report to document crisis management activities, to be submitted to the executive director, Business Affairs, within five days of the incident:

Crises Response Team Report

Date of Report_____

School _____

Student's(s) Name(s):   Parent/Guardian:

_____   _____

_____   _____

_____   _____

Description of incident (include date, time, and place):

Immediate intervention by Crisis Response Team:

Follow-up procedures (with student, with student body [if appropriate], and with faculty members):

Follow-up with parent(s)/guardian(s) of student(s) involved:

Case manager: _____

Reviewed by principal: _____

Date: _____

EVALUATION OF CRISIS MANAGEMENT TEAM INTERVENTION

The _____ School System Crisis Management Team (CMT) seeks your input to help us assess the effectiveness of the intervention during the recent crisis at your school. We would appreciate you taking a few minutes of your time to complete this form as soon as possible and return it to the executive director, Business Affairs, within five days of the incident.

Please indicate with an X the response that most closely reflects your evaluation of the following:

1. Speed of CMT's response to the crisis:

_____ _____ _____ _____ _____
Very delayed   Adequate   Very timely

2. Comprehensiveness of CMT's response:

_____ _____ _____ _____ _____
Very limited   Adequate   Exceptional

3. Effectiveness of team's response in meeting students' needs:

_____ _____ _____ _____ _____
Not helpful   Adequate   Very helpful

4. Assistance to teachers in the classroom:

_____ _____ _____ _____ _____
Not supportive   Adequate   Very supportive

5. Quality of communication with the school faculty and staff:

_____ _____ _____ _____ _____
Not informative   Adequate   Very explanatory

6. Support and guidance to individual teachers and staff members:

_____ _____ _____ _____ _____
Ineffectual   Adequate   Very empathetic

7. Assistance to the administrative staff:

_____ _____ _____ _____ _____
Limited   Adequate   Very comprehensive

8. Amount of time allocated for intervention:

_____ _____ _____ _____ _____
Insufficient   Adequate   Very sufficient

9. Support to families in need:

_____ _____ _____ _____ _____
Lacking   Adequate   Outstanding

10. Communication of information to parents:

_____ _____ _____ _____ _____
Minimal   Adequate   Thorough

11. Please circle the adjectives that best describe the students' reactions to the CMT's intervention:

ambivalent	angry	apathetic	grateful	hostile
negative	positive	receptive	relieved	satisfied

12. Please describe any significant reactions the students had to the CMT intervention that should be considered in future interventions.

13. Please comment on any aspects of the intervention you found particularly helpful or areas that you think should be modified.

School:

_____

Signature (Optional):

_____
Please return to executive director, Business Affairs
(within five days of the incident)

AUTHORIZATION TO RELEASE CHILDREN IN AN EMERGENCY

Our school has developed an emergency plan in case of any disaster that might occur. The emergency plan is devoted to the welfare and safety of your child during school hours. The plan is available for inspection in the school office.

We are requesting your assistance at this time:

Should there be an emergency, such as a major fire, tornado, explosion, and so forth, your child may be required to remain in the care of the school until it is deemed safe by an emergency services authority that the child can be released. At that point, children may be released only to properly authorized parents and/or designees. Therefore, please list as many names (with local telephone numbers and addresses) as possible, of those persons to whom you would allow your child's release in the event of an emergency. Be sure to notify those persons listed that you have authorized their supervision in case of an emergency.

In the event that you should be unable to come to school, it is essential that others be designated to care for your child. No child will be released to the care of unauthorized persons.

We appreciate your cooperation in this important matter.

Child: _____   **Teacher:** _____   **School Year:**
_____

Please release my child to any of the persons listed below:

Name	Relationship	Address	Phone
			Home
			Work
			Cell
			Home
			Work
			Cell
			Home
			Work
			Cell
			Home
			Work
			Cell

Parent/Guardian: _____   **Date:** _____
                              Signature

Home Phone: _____   **Work Phone:** _____   **Cell Phone:** _____

SITE CRISIS RESPONSE TEAM ASSIGNMENT FORM

POSITION   **ORGANIZATION**   **NAME**

Command Section:
- **Incident Commander**
    - Safety Officer
    - Public Information Officer
    - Liaison Officer

Operations Section:
- **Operations Section Chief**
    - Site Facility Check/Security
    - Student Care
    - Student Release

Planning Section:
- **Planning Section Chief**
    - Documentation
    - Situation Analysis

Logistics Section:
- **Logistics Section Chief**
    - Supplies/Facilities
    - Staffing
    - Communications

Finance/Administration Section:
- **Finance/Administration Section Chief**
    - Timekeeping
    - Purchasing

General Message Form

Incident Name/Location: | **Date/Time of Message:**

To:

From:

Message:

Reply:

Signature (Person replying): | **Date/Time of Reply:**

Sample Communications and Letters

Tips for Communicating with Parents

In the event of an emergency, parents have very specific information needs. First, parents want to know their child is safe; then, parents want to know the details of the emergency situation, to know how it was handled, and to know that their children will be safe in the future.

The first reactions are likely to involve fear. Upon learning of an incident at the school, parents are likely to descend upon the school in search of their child or to telephone, frantically seeking information. Establishing a system for responding quickly to parent needs for information is an important part of preplanning.

Anger is another common reaction of parents, particularly in the case of senseless acts of violence. In the event of a crisis or disaster, do the following:

1. Tell parents exactly what is known to have happened. Do not embellish or speculate.
2. Implement the plan to manage phone calls and parents who arrive at school.
3. Schedule and attend an open question-and-answer meeting for parents as soon after the incident as possible. The meeting is an opportunity for school officials to listen and respond to parent concerns (which are helpful in combating rumors and other misinformation) and to work on restoring parental trust in the school.
4. In the event of an incident that involved damage or destruction, an open house for parents and other members of the community to see the school restored to its "normal" state helps everyone get beyond the crisis.

Sample Annual Letter to Parents/Guardians: Description of School District Emergency Program and Parent/Guardian Expectations

Dear Parents/Guardians,

We want you to be aware that this school has made many preparations to deal effectively with emergency situations that could occur in or around the school, both during the school day and during after-hours activities. While we hope that a natural disaster or other serious incident never occurs, our goal is to be prepared for any potential emergency. At all times, our first priority is to protect all students, staff members, and guests from harm.

In order for our emergency response plans to be effective, we depend on the cooperation and assistance of many people, such as the police and the fire department. We also depend on you, as parents and guardians, to support our disaster preparation and response efforts. Your cooperation is vital to helping us protect the safety and welfare of all children and school employees.

Therefore, we ask parents to observe the following procedures in the event of a school emergency:

1. Do not telephone the school. We understand and respect your concern, but it is essential that the telephone system is available for emergency communications.
2. Make sure that we have emergency contact information for each of your children at all times. We must be able to contact you or your designated representative in an emergency.
3. Tune your radio to [provide list of stations] for emergency announcements and status reports. You also will receive instructions on where you should go and how/when you may be able to pick up your children. Our school emergency plan includes evacuation procedures with several alternative destinations. When appropriate and safe, students may be released to their parents/guardians from these shelter locations. Under those circumstances, we will be prepared to implement procedures for confirming the identity of individuals who arrive to pick up each child. When arriving to pick up your children, please make sure that you have with you your driver's license or government-issued picture identification.
4. Do not come to the school or alternate destination until instructed to do so. It may be necessary to keep the streets and parking lot clear for emergency vehicles. If evacuation is required, students may be transported to a location away from school. You will be notified of this through the media bulletins.
5. Talk to your children and emphasize how important it is for them to follow instructions from their teachers and school officials during any emergency.
6. Parents and other adults must stay calm and focused in an emergency, mindful that their actions and comments will be the example that, to a great extent, determines the children's response.
7. Carefully read all information you receive from the school. You may receive updates about our safety procedures from time to time.
8. When your child is at home following an emergency, try to keep your child away from news being broadcast over the various media. Have an emergency plan at home. Decide on a telephone number to call outside our community or a place to rendezvous if separated. Keep a "disaster supplies kit" containing drinking water, nonperishable food, batteries, flashlight, radio, medication, toothbrushes, and so on.

We are proud that [school name] is a safe school, and we are doing everything possible to keep it that way. We appreciate your cooperation and support. If you have any questions about this letter or other aspects of our safety procedures, please contact me at _____.

Sincerely,

Principal

Sample Letter to Parents/Guardians: Notice of Bus Accident

Dear Parents/Guardians,

This morning, prior to school, there was an accident involving a school bus and an automobile. There were known injuries to the passengers of the car. The children on bus #__ witnessed the aftermath of the accident but were not involved in it.

The children from the bus involved in the accident were taken to the library by the guidance counselors and administration.

The children were asked if they were injured in any way, and their parents were then contacted. Your child, because of being on bus # __, may show a delayed reaction to the accident. Please be alert over the next several days to symptoms of delayed reaction, including the following:

- a desire to be alone, unusually quiet
- loss of appetite
- problems with sleeping, nightmares
- difficulty with concentration
- crying
- angry outburst, short temper
- headaches, upset stomach
- depressed, sad

Your child may also exhibit some physical complaints. Please contact (principal's name) to fill out an accident report.

The school will be offered support services for students needing help dealing with the accident. We will also provide counseling services to parents in helping their children to cope. Please don't hesitate to call if you have any questions or concerns.

Sincerely,

Principal

Sample Joint Akron Public Schools/Community Letter to Parents/Guardians About Crisis (i.e., Shooting or Other Violent Acts)

[School Letterhead]

Dear Parents,

The tragic event of [date] has hurt/affected the entire [school name] community. This unfortunate incident shows us that we must band together as parents and seek positive solutions to problems that victimize us.

It is for this reason I'm asking *all* parents to join me in a special meeting [day, date, and time] in the school auditorium.

We will learn the steps the administration is taking to ensure the welfare and safety of our children; we will discuss what we, as parents and community, can do to assist our children and school staff.

There will be representatives from the school staff, schools administration, school police department, guidance office, and the representatives of the school Mayor's Office to address *all* our concerns.

Bus transportation will be provided for the (area) families. [Here include the place and time of bus pickups.]

Child care will be provided at the school for your convenience.

Refreshments will be served at the end of the meeting.

If you would like further information about this meeting, contact [name/telephone].

Cordially,

Principal Mayor's Office

Sample Thank-You Letter to Faculty and Staff Members

[School Letterhead]

Dear Faculty and Staff Members,

We would like to thank you for your support during the recent crisis at our school. Your professionalism and dedication were evident as we all worked to quiet and soothe scared students and allay their fears while still tending to instructional responsibilities.

We know that this has been an extremely difficult time for you as well as the students.

Without your courage and concern, our school could not possibly have come through this crisis as well as we did.

Thank you once again. Your expertise and commitment have enabled all of us to work together as a team and overcome this tragic situation.

Sincerely,

Principal/Superintendent

Sample Letter to Students and Parents: Student Sudden Death

Dear Students and Parents,

On Friday, John Doe, a fifth-grade student at [insert name of school] was in a terrible accident. Apparently, John was hit by a car that was speeding and had crossed over the median strip to the wrong side of the road. John died instantly.

John's death is a tragic, emotional loss for the entire school family. I am sure all of us will make every effort to comfort and support John's family as they attempt to deal with this traumatic loss. There are no adequate words to express our sense of grief and sympathy for the family.

Because John's death is felt so deeply by so many, on Monday and thereafter as needed we will bring in our crisis team to discuss this accident and loss with students and faculty members.

We encourage each of you to discuss this loss with your child. In order to help you do so, we are holding a parent meeting on [date and time], in the school cafeteria. The topic will be ways to help children cope with loss and will be presented by a local mental health professional. John's family, friends, and the school are suffering deeply. Please join us in supporting John's family.

Sincerely,

Principal

Sample Letter to Families following an Assault/Sexual Assault

Dear Parents/Caregivers,

This letter is to inform you that a student assault has occurred. [Insert information here regarding whether the assault took place on or off campus and any other information that can be provided without violating a victim's confidentiality.]

All of us will be feeling a variety of emotions, including shock, sadness, and anger. I want you to know that we, the [school name] staff, care about the feelings our students may be experiencing.

The Crisis Management Team has made plans to respond to the emotional needs of the students. [Clarify what is being done: grief counseling, classroom debriefing, and referrals.]

Any time violence touches us, it is extremely stressful. Please inform your child's [teacher or counselor] if there is additional information the school should be aware of so we can provide the support your child needs.

Please feel free to call me at [school telephone number] if you have any questions or concerns.

Sincerely,

Principal

Sample Letter to Parents, Students, and Staff Members: Following a Bomb Threat

Dear Parents, Students, and Staff Members,

Somewhere between 7:30 a.m. and 7:45 a.m. [add day/date], a note was left in the drop box in the attendance office making reference to a bomb going off at school. There was no specific reference to a location, [school name], a date, or a time.

The attendance clerk contacted the school administration immediately. The police were notified along with District Office personnel. School police responded to the site within minutes. Law enforcement officers and site administrators evacuated classes at 9 a.m., and the faculty and deputies conducted an organized and thorough room-by-room search. At approximately 10:15 a.m. law enforcement officials determined that the school/facility was safe and gave us permission to reenter the building. After a short break, classes resumed as regularly scheduled.

The administration of [school name] and local law enforcement agencies are taking this event very seriously. If anyone has information regarding the person responsible for leaving the note, please contact the police immediately.

School will be open tomorrow; classes will be conducted as usual. Increased security will be in place. We will continue to communicate with you via the auto dialer and written messages. Counselors and administrative staff members are available to assist students who wish to talk about their concerns or fears regarding this or other issues that are going on nationally. Please feel free to contact us for further information and remember the anonymous tip line is available for your use as needed by dialing [phone number].

Sincerely,

Principal

Sample Letter to Families following a Death

Dear Parents /Guardians,

I am sorry to inform you that a [staff person/student/friend], [name] at [school name], died on [day/date]. [Insert what information can be shared about the cause and circumstances of the death.]

Death can be difficult for us to understand, especially when it is sudden. All of us will be feeling a variety of emotions: shock, sadness, and confusion. What is important is that we care for and support each other.

The Crisis Management Team has made plans to respond to the emotional needs of the students. [Spell out what is being done: grief counseling, classroom debriefing, and referrals.]

If your family has experienced a death or similar loss recently, the death of [name] may bring up feelings about that death. This is a normal experience. Please let your child's [teacher or counselor] know if there is any additional information the school should be aware of so we can provide the support your child needs.

Any time death touches us, it is extremely stressful. This sudden death may be disturbing to you as well as to your child.

It is for this reason we especially want you to know of our care and support.

Sincerely,

Principal

Sample Letter to Staff following a Death

Dear Staff,

There are times when it is necessary to communicate news that is painful for all of us. During those times we must be prepared to support each other as we deal with the many feelings that we begin to experience. It is with great sorrow that I inform you that [name of person] at [school name] has died.

Death can be difficult for us to understand, especially when it is sudden. We will all begin to feel different emotions: shock, sadness, confusion, and even some anger. What is most important is that we care for and support each other.

Although rare, sometimes students may be so overwhelmed by the death of someone important to them that they may express suicidal thoughts or actions. Please contact an appropriate staff person or counselor if you notice a student who appears to be having more difficulty with his/her feelings than might be expected. Information regarding youth suicide is included in this letter.

In memory of [name], [indicate here what activity or activities the school is planning]. Administration will keep you updated as more information is given to us at the school.

Sincerely,

Principal

Sample Letter to Students following a Death

Dear Students,

I have asked your teacher to read this letter to you because I want to make sure that all students received the same information about the recent tragedy at our school. It gives me a great sorrow to inform you that [name], a [teacher, student, or friend] at [school name], died on [day/date]. [Insert what information can be shared about the cause and circumstances of the death.]

Death can be difficult for us to understand, especially when it is sudden. Many of us may be confronted with a variety of emotions, which might include shock, sadness, and confusion. I want to assure you that we, the [school name] staff, care about you and the feelings you may be experiencing.

Please know that we want to support you during this time. The Crisis Management Team will be available to meet with you in [place] to assist you in dealing with any feeling you may be having. You might wish to share memories you have of [name]. Crisis Management Team members will also be available at any time during the day to help you if you feel a more urgent need to talk with someone. [Insert here specific information on how students can access team members for support.]

I want to encourage those students who may be particularly upset, perhaps even struggling with a death in the family or of a friend, to talk with Crisis Management Team members. They will be available all day to meet with you.

Anytime death touches us, it is extremely stressful. This sudden death may be quite shocking to you and confuse you.

For these reasons, we especially want you to know of our care and support.

Sincerely,

Principal

Sample Letter to Families following Tragedy

Dear Parents/Guardians,

I would like to share with you the response of our school district to today's tragedy. Although these events were sudden and unexpected, students acted appropriately and staff members responded professionally. Many teachers discussed the events with students. Students who were uncomfortable or worried were allowed to go to the office for assistance.

I would like to offer some guidelines for supporting your children through this challenging time, as follows:

- Take the lead from your child. If your child wants to talk about the events, do so. Focus on the facts. Listen to their thoughts and feelings. Listening is more important than talking, but do share your own feelings as a way to help them accept and understand their feelings.
- Students who were emotionally fragile prior to these events may have a bigger response than others. Some children's reactions may be delayed by several days.
- Children may need assurance that actions are being taken to keep them safe and secure.
- Especially for younger children, using art to express feelings may be helpful. Provide paper and drawing implements to give children an opportunity for this expression.
- An opportunity to write about the events of the day may also be a good release.
- Phone calls or visits with close friends and extended family members may create a sense of security and closeness.

We will continue to assess the needs of our students and respond to those needs. Please let your child's teacher or school administrator know if you have a particular concern, if you think your child needs some extra attention and support, or if your family has suffered a loss during these events.

Pending any action by state officials, all of our schools will remain in session. However, if you feel you want to keep your child at home, please do so. As usual, call the office to report the absence.

If you need further information, contact the Office of the Superintendent at [phone number], or the Office of Instruction at [phone number].

Sincerely,

Principal

Sample Letter to Media following a Trauma

TO: [community/media group]
RE: [specific event]

This letter is to inform you that a traumatic event has occurred on our campus. I am writing this letter because I feel it is important that the community receives the same information about the recent tragedy. (Insert what information can be shared about the cause and circumstance of the event without violating confidentiality.)

All of us will be feeling a variety of emotions, including shock, sadness, and anger. I want you to know that we, the [school name] staff care about the feelings our students and community may be experiencing.

The Crisis Management Team has made plans to respond to the emotional needs of the students and their families.

(Clarify what is being done: grief counseling, classroom debriefing, and referrals.)

Anytime violence touches us it is extremely stressful. This recent event may trigger feelings about personal trauma and loss. This is a normal experience. We hope all affected will receive the support needed.

Sincerely,

Principal

Sample Announcement: Student Suicide

[To be read to the students by the classroom teacher]

TO: School Faculty
FROM: Principal
SUBJECT: [crisis]

John Doe committed suicide early Saturday morning. As a faculty we extend our sympathy to John's family and friends.

We encourage all students to consider the tragic nature of this death and to realize that death is final. John's death is a reminder to us all that the act of taking one's life is not an appropriate solution to any of life's problems, nor is it an act of courage. Please let your teachers know if you would like to talk to a counselor or other staff member.

Funeral services for John will be held in [location], and there will/will not be a memorial service in this area.

Expressions of sympathy may be sent to [name and address].

Examples of Status Boards

Table F.1.   Incident Facts Update Status Board

Time	Event

Table F.2. CMT Sign-In Status Board

CURRENT SHIFT			NEXT SHIFT		
Date: _____ Shift: _____			Date: _____ Shift: _____		
POSITION	PERSON		POSITION	PERSON	

Table F.3. CMT Issues/Impacts Worksheet

• PEOPLE:
• ENVIRONMENT:
• PROPERTY:
• BUSINESS IMPACTS/RECOVERY:
• REPUTATION:

STAKEHOLDERS		REPUTATION	
			Accountability
			Credibility
			Goodwill
			Viability
		FINANCIAL	
			Loss
			Response Cost
			Replacement Cost
		OPERATIONAL	
			Facilities
			Infrastructure
LEGAL		**POLITICAL**	
	Fines		Local
	Lawsuits		State
	Compliance		Federal

Table F.4.　Help Requested Status Board

TIME/DATE OF REQUEST	NATURE OF REQUEST	NATURE OF HELP PROVIDED	RESPONSIBLE PERSON(S)

Table F.5. CMT Action Plan Status Board

ISSUES/IMPACTS	ACTIONS	RESPONSIBLE PERSON(S)

Table F.6.   Schedule of CMT Meetings Status Board

TIME/DATE	TYPE OF MEETING	LOCATION OF MEETING

Table F.7. Action Items from CMT Meetings Status Board

MEETINGS	ACTION ITEMS	RESPONSIBLE PERSON(S)

About the Editors

Don Philpott is an award-winning writer, journalist, and broadcaster, and founder and president of Mediawise Communications. He worked for twenty years as a senior correspondent and editor with Reuters-Press Association. He has published over five thousand articles in newspapers and magazines in the United States and the United Kingdom, and written more than ninety books on a wide range of subjects, including *Education Facility Security Handbook* (2007), *The Wounded Warrior Handbook* (2008), and *The Workplace Violence Prevention Handbook* (2009), all published by Government Institutes.

Paul Serluco is vice president of Mediawise Communications and a seasoned corporate money manager with twenty years of experience in the financial arena. Prior to joining Mediawise, he was the chief financial officer and general manager of a $15-million-a-year, award-winning financial publications firm where he managed all financial operations including SEC reporting, budgeting, forecasting, and investor relations, as well as administrative functions.